Reading Teachers

This engaging text offers primary school educators a principled way forward on their mission to nurture the life-changing habit of reading in childhood. Informed and inspiring, *Reading Teachers* accessibly demonstrates how teachers who are motivated, engaged and reflective readers themselves, can develop new understandings of reading for pleasure and make a difference to young learners.

Drawing on a range of research evidence, including studies on reading teachers, dis/engaged boy readers, student teachers as readers and work with over 150 schools developing communities of readers, this book provides an accessible overview of international research alongside a highly practical classroom focus. Combining the insights of academics with 24 reading teachers in co-authored chapters, the book includes:

- Case studies of how practitioners have used research to inform and improve their practice;
- 'In conversation' dialogues between educators about classroom practice that fosters positive reader identities;
- Reflections on the editors own reading habits, practices and histories;
- Recommended reading and suggestions of engaging children's books.

Reading Teachers: Nurturing Reading for Pleasure enables practitioners to develop principled practice, helping *all* children find pleasure and purpose in reading. This book is therefore essential reading for all primary teachers, head teachers, literacy coordinators and trainee teachers.

Teresa Cremin is Professor of Education (Literacy) at the Open University, UK, and Co-Director of the Literacy and Social Justice Centre.

Helen Hendry is a lecturer in education at the Open University, UK, where she recently co-chaired the MA/Ed in Educational Leadership and contributes to the Education Studies (Primary) programme and open access courses.

Lucy Rodriguez Leon is a lecturer in education (early childhood) at the Open University, UK, where she teaches on undergraduate distance learning modules and writes open access courses.

Natalia Kucirkova is Professor of Early Childhood Education and Development at the University of Stavanger, Norway, and Professor of Reading and Children's Development at the Open University, UK.

Underpinned by the editors' considerable research and enriched by experienced educators, this book makes a powerful argument that being a Reading Teacher does not just mean being a teacher who reads, but one who reflects on the relationships between their own reading and school reading, models what it's like to be a reader, and takes time to get to know the readers in their class. This accessible and persuasive book is a must for all beginning and experienced teachers. And of course, it is a great read.

—**Professor Cathy Burnett**, *Sheffield Hallam University, UK*

Reading Teachers is a brilliant book that will fan the flames of the 'reading fire' and help schools nurture passionate, engaged and motivated readers.

—**Jon Biddle**, *Teacher and English Leader*

This highly accessible book will further practitioners' understanding of effective approaches for encouraging reading for pleasure, including what it really means to be a Reading Teacher and why that is so important. The art of providing meaningful opportunities for children to become engaged, volitional readers is brought to life through real-world case studies that cannot fail to inspire teachers and librarians whatever their school, context or role.

—**Fiona Evans**, *Director of School Programmes, National Literacy Trust*

Reading Teachers

Nurturing Reading for Pleasure

Edited by Teresa Cremin, Helen Hendry,
Lucy Rodriguez Leon and
Natalia Kucirkova

LONDON AND NEW YORK

Cover image: © Getty Images

First published 2023
by Routledge
4 Park Square, Milton Park, Abingdon, Oxon OX14 4RN

and by Routledge
605 Third Avenue, New York, NY 10158

Routledge is an imprint of the Taylor & Francis Group, an informa business

© 2023 selection and editorial matter, Teresa Cremin, Helen Hendry, Lucy Rodriguez Leon and Natalia Kucirkova; individual chapters, the contributors

The right of Teresa Cremin, Helen Hendry, Lucy Rodriguez Leon and Natalia Kucirkova to be identified as the authors of the editorial material, and of the authors for their individual chapters, has been asserted in accordance with sections 77 and 78 of the Copyright, Designs and Patents Act 1988.

All rights reserved. No part of this book may be reprinted or reproduced or utilised in any form or by any electronic, mechanical, or other means, now known or hereafter invented, including photocopying and recording, or in any information storage or retrieval system, without permission in writing from the publishers.

Trademark notice: Product or corporate names may be trademarks or registered trademarks, and are used only for identification and explanation without intent to infringe.

British Library Cataloguing-in-Publication Data
A catalogue record for this book is available from the British Library

Library of Congress Cataloging-in-Publication Data
Names: Cremin, Teresa, 1959– editor. | Hendry, Helen, editor. | Rodriguez
  Leon, Lucy, editor. | Kucirkova, Natalia, editor.
Title: Reading teachers : nurturing reading for pleasure / edited by Teresa
  Cremin, Helen Hendry, Lucy Rodriguez Leon and Natalia Kucirkova.
Description: Abingdon, Oxon ; New York, NY : Routledge, 2023. | Includes
  bibliographical references and index. | Identifiers: LCCN 2022009972 |
  ISBN 9781032104928 (hardback) | ISBN 9781032105024 (paperback) |
  ISBN 9781003215615 (ebook)
Subjects: LCSH: Reading (Primary) | Reading promotion. | Children—Books
  and reading. | Teachers—Books and reading.
Classification: LCC LB1525 .R374 2023 | DDC 372.4—dc23/eng/20220421
  LC record available at https://lccn.loc.gov/2022009972

ISBN: 978-1-032-10492-8 (hbk)
ISBN: 978-1-032-10502-4 (pbk)
ISBN: 978-1-003-21561-5 (ebk)

DOI: 10.4324/9781003215615

Typeset in Bembo
by Apex CoVantage, LLC

For Product Safety Concerns and Information please contact our EU representative: GPSR@taylorandfrancis.com
Taylor & Francis
Verlag GmbH, Kaufingerstraße 24, 80331 München, Germany

Printed and bound in Great Britain by
TJ Books, Padstow, Cornwall

Contents

About the editors vii
List of contributors viii

Introduction: Reading Teachers 1
TERESA CREMIN

Reflecting on my reader identity 13
NATALIA KUCIRKOVA

SECTION I
Texts and readers 17

1 Children's literature and other texts 21
SARAH BROWNSWORD, SARAH MERCHANT AND RICHARD CHARLESWORTH

2 Digital books enriching children's literacy lives 35
NATALIA KUCIRKOVA, NIGEL LUNGENMUSS-WARD AND
NICOLA MANSFIELD-NEIMI

3 Exploring gender and reading for pleasure 45
AMELIA HEMPEL-JORGENSEN, TOM BRASSINGTON AND MEGAN DIXON

4 Supporting readers' social motivation 56
MARILYN MOTTRAM, KATHARINE YOUNG AND KIRAN SATTI

My reading practices 68
HELEN HENDRY

SECTION 2
Reading for pleasure pedagogy — 71

5 Reading aloud — 73
TERESA CREMIN, BEN HARRIS AND MATTHEW COURTNEY

6 Informal book talk and reader recommendations — 87
LUCY RODRIGUEZ LEON AND JON BIDDLE

7 Time to read — 101
JO TREGENZA, PHOEBE LAWTON AND SADIE PHILLIPS

8 Social reading environments — 114
ROGER MCDONALD, ERIN HAMILTON AND LISA HESMONDHALGH

Reflections on the rights of the reader — 127
LUCY RODRIGUEZ LEON

SECTION 3
Reading communities — 131

9 Reading Head Teachers — 135
HELEN HENDRY, SONIA THOMPSON AND ANDREW TRUBY

10 Reading Librarians and school libraries — 150
JEN AGGLETON, CAROL CARTER AND MARY ROSE GRIEVE

11 Parental and community involvement — 162
RACHAEL LEVY, JULIE DOYLE AND EVE CAIRNS VOLLANS

12 Celebrating reading — 176
SARAH JANE MUKHERJEE, CLARE MCGREEVY AND CLAIRE WILLIAMS

Reading places — 188
TERESA CREMIN

Conclusion: Reading Teachers of tomorrow — 193
TERESA CREMIN, HELEN HENDRY, LUCY RODRIGUEZ LEON
AND NATALIA KUCIRKOVA

Index — 198

About the editors

Teresa Cremin is Professor of Education (Literacy) at The Open University, UK, and Co-Director of the Literacy and Social Justice Centre. An ex-teacher and teacher educator, Teresa's socio-cultural research focuses on volitional reading and writing, teachers' literate identities and creative pedagogies. A Fellow of the English Association, the Academy of Social Sciences, and the Royal Society of the Arts, Teresa is a trustee of the UK Literacy Association and advises the DfE on reading for pleasure. She has written and edited over 30 books and is committed to exploring research and practice synergies to support young learners. Teresa leads the OU's professional user-community website and wider movement to support the development of children's and teachers' pleasure in reading, https://ourfp.org/.

Dr Helen Hendry is a lecturer in education at The Open University, UK, where she recently co-chaired the MA/Ed in Educational Leadership and currently contributes to the Education Studies (Primary) programme and online open access courses. Helen draws on over 25 years' experience as a teacher educator, advisory teacher and senior leader in primary education. Helen previously led initial teacher education for English, and the Education Studies Undergraduate Programme at Bishop Grosseteste University. Helen's research interests include teacher development for literacy teaching, particularly early reading and reading for pleasure. She is currently collaborating with OU colleagues to research approaches to children's volitional reading and writing and student teachers' identities as readers.

Dr Lucy Rodriguez Leon is a lecturer in education (early childhood) at The Open University, UK, where she teaches on undergraduate distance learning modules and writes open access online courses. Since 2016, Lucy's research has focused on young children's everyday literacies and the ways in which they make meaning, make relationships and make identities with multimodal texts. Her doctoral thesis was awarded the United Kingdom Literacy Association's Postgraduate Research Prize in 2020. She is a former early years practitioner, with over 15 years of experience working with children and families in a disadvantaged community in England.

Natalia Kucirkova is Professor of Early Childhood Education and Development at the University of Stavanger, Norway, and Professor of Reading and Children's Development at The Open University, UK. Natalia is Co-Director of the Literacy and Social Justice Centre and her work is concerned with social justice in children's literacy and use of technologies. She is the founder of the International Collective of Children's Digital Books, which connects research and design in children's e-books and literacy apps. Her research takes place collaboratively across academia, commercial and third sectors.

Contributors

Dr Jen Aggleton is a lecturer in education studies (primary) at The Open University. She is a qualified teacher and librarian and spent several years as a primary school teacher in Hampshire and Cambridgeshire and has worked in both school and academic libraries. She completed her PhD in education and children's literature at the University of Cambridge in 2019, and has previously taught education, children's literature and children's librarianship courses at City, University of London and the University of Cambridge. Her publications include articles on illustrated novels, comics, and children's participation in library collection development.

Jon Biddle is a teacher and English lead at Moorlands Primary Academy in Norfolk. He is the coordinator of the national Patron of Reading initiative, as well as an advisor for Empathy Lab. In 2018, he won the Egmont, OU/UKLA Reading for Pleasure Experienced Teacher of the Year award, and, in 2021, his school won the Farshore, OU/UKLA Reading for Pleasure School of the Year award. Jon regularly delivers training about the importance of reading for pleasure in schools and has been on the judging panel for several children's book awards. He is part of the editorial team for UKLA's *English 4–11* magazine and a member of UKLA National Council.

Tom Brassington is a primary school teacher at St Modwen's Catholic Primary School in the Midlands. As well as working alongside the UKLA and OU to lead and support reading for pleasure CPD opportunities for other primary practitioners, Tom has also recently co-written a children's picture book with his brother, Joe, named *Bottled*. A keen reader, Tom enjoys promoting a culture of reading for pleasure within his school.

Sarah Brownsword is a lecturer in education at the School of Education and Lifelong Learning at the University of East Anglia. She is a course co-director of the Primary PGCE and leads the English and Primary Languages programmes. Sarah's research interests include race and diversity in education, particularly in the context of children's literature and reading. She is currently researching primary teachers' knowledge and understanding of diverse representation in children's literature. Prior to joining the University of East Anglia, Sarah held teaching and leadership positions in Norfolk, Suffolk, Indonesia and France.

Eve Cairns Vollans is a teacher, reading/phonics lead, CPD lead and lower KS2 lead at Mayflower Community Academy in Plymouth. In 2020, Eve won the Egmont OU/UKLA Reading for Pleasure 'Experienced Teacher' award. Eve has led the Plymouth OU/UKLA Teacher Reading Group for the past three years and has recently branched out to involve CPD for Teaching Assistants and parent/community CPD. She regularly leads reading and phonics training across the Academy. Eve was featured in the book *Organising Ideas* by Caviglioli and Goodwin, as well as writing for *Teach Primary*. She has recently been videoed, discussing reading strategies and community involvement, for a leadership website.

Carol Carter is Library and Resources Co-ordinator at Headlands Primary School in Northampton, England. After a decade working as a secondary geography teacher, followed by a year travelling around the world with her family, she was looking for a role that enabled her to 'teach' and support children in a less target-driven way. Four years later, she has not looked back once.

Richard Charlesworth is an experienced KS2 teacher and Professional Teaching Enhancement Lead of English at Springwell School, Heston. He is an advisor for the OU Reading for Pleasure website and has spoken at various conferences exploring creative writing, picture fiction and RfP. Richard is the UKLA representative for London and part of the editorial team for the journal *Literacy*. Having studied the effect that graphic novels may have on their readers in his own MA research, he is interested in developing children's empathy through a wider range of texts and is an Empathy Lab judge.

Matthew Courtney is a teacher at Orchard Meadow Primary School in Oxford. He is also a training facilitator at the Teacher Development Trust and an evidence lead in education for Greenshaw Research School. Matthew co-authored the *Lit in Colour* research which was commissioned by Penguin and the Runnymede Trust and explored ethnic diversity in the texts taught in schools in England. He is an OU/UKLA Teacher Reading Group Leader. Matthew recently completed a master's degree in education research design and methodology at the University of Oxford.

Megan Dixon is a teacher, senior leader and part-time researcher. She divides her time between working as a senior leader for a multi-academy trust in the North West of England and studying for a doctorate at the University of Sussex School of Psychology exploring how teachers develop reading comprehension in the classroom. Megan is fascinated in how children learn to read and the pedagogies that support this. She is a monthly columnist for the *Times Educational Supplement* and Associate Lecturer at Sheffield Hallam University.

Julie Doyle is a reading recovery teacher, reading lead and KS1 lead at Sneinton C of E Primary School in Nottingham, which was reaccredited with world class status in 2021. In 2019, her school was joint winner of the Egmont OU/UKLA Reading for Pleasure Award. Her school has also been a Reading Recovery School of the Year, and Julie was awarded Reading Recovery Teacher of the Year in 2017. She has been leading the Nottingham OU/UKLA Teacher Reading Group for the past three years. Julie regularly delivers training nationally at English Hubs, schools, and conferences about the importance of reading for pleasure. She is also a member of the UKLA National Council.

Mary Rose Grieve has been the librarian at Hartland International School in Dubai since December 2013, during which time the libraries have doubled in size. She runs the primary, secondary and staff libraries at the school. Mary Rose was UAE Librarian of the Year in 2019 and is a national committee member of the CILIP School Libraries Group. She has run an OU/UKLA Teachers Reading Group in Dubai for four years and is currently working towards chartership with the Chartered Institute for Library and Information Professionals.

Erin Hamilton is Reading Lead for ASSET Education Trust, based in Suffolk. She is passionate about reading for pleasure, school libraries and graphic novels. Erin leads a TRG in Ipswich and has for the past couple of years. Erin writes reviews for *Just Imagine*, *Armadillo Magazine* and *The School Librarian*, as well as managing her own blog, 'My Shelves Are Full'. She is also an executive committee member of the Federation of Children's Book Groups, managing their blog, social media and National Share a Story month campaign.

Ben Harris is lead for English at Dunmow St. Mary's Primary in Essex. He has worked as an assistant head teacher there and also as an advanced skills teacher with a specialisation in English. In 2018, his example of practice exploring the value of talk during read-aloud times was Highly Commended in the Egmont OU/UKLA Reading for Pleasure Awards, and, in 2021, his class were awarded the UKLA 'Our Class Loves this Book' prize. The spoken and sung word are also important to Ben's other major interest: he is a trained composer and has written a children's opera with Kevin Crossley-Holland and narrated two works, *The Blackbird and the Snail* and *Moments of Vision*, by his teacher Robin Holloway. The latter was recorded by Sheva Contemporary.

Amelia Hempel-Jorgensen is Research Fellow/Lecturer at The Open University. Her research focuses on inequity, social justice and pedagogy mainly in the English education system and has more recently started researching wellbeing for children and young people. Recent research projects have focused on developing an intersectionality approach to understanding boys' engagement with reading; an evaluation of Hackney Learning Trusts reading programme; changes to practices within schools during the Covid-19 pandemic and their impact on children and young people's wellbeing; reading for pleasure and wellbeing for children.

Lisa Hesmondhalgh is a head teacher of a small mixed-age primary school in Cheshire. She has been teaching for over 25 years and worked with children in a variety of different settings. She is also the director of English for the Aspire Educational Trust, a large primary-led Multi-Academy Trust covering Cheshire East, Cheshire West and Manchester. Lisa works with schools to develop the quality of the teaching of English, especially curriculum development and disciplinary subject knowledge. A large part of this is introducing schools to the importance of RfP. She is passionate about reading and sees herself as a Reading Head Teacher and is an avid reader of children's literature.

Phoebe Lawton is a teacher and RfP, RE and SMSC lead at the Wilmslow Academy in Cheshire East. She graduated in Dance Practices at Liverpool John Moores University in 2017 before completing a PGCE in primary education at Manchester University. She predominately works within KS2 with a passion for all things English, in particular reading. In 2020, Phoebe was Highly Commended in the Egmont OU/UKLA Reading for Pleasure Early Career Teacher Awards, and, in 2021, she won the Farshore OU/UKLA Reading for Pleasure Early Career Teacher of the Year Award. Her research focused on integrating a love of reading. Phoebe regularly delivers training about the importance of RfP in schools and has been leading an OU/UKLA Teacher Reading Group for three years.

Dr Rachael Levy is Associate Professor at UCL Institute of Education, London, where her teaching is informed by her research in early childhood literacy. She has published widely in the field of young children's reading and is the author of *Young Children Reading at Home and at School*. More recently, Rachael led an ESRC-funded study into shared reading practices in young children's homes, the findings of which have been published in the book *Family Literacies: Reading with Young Children*. She has worked closely with the UKLA and was the editor for their Minibook series for eight years.

Nigel Lungenmuss-Ward is a teacher by training and worked in schools for four years before leaving the classroom to focus on his writing. His debut picture book *Freddie's Impossible Dream* was published in 2020. He also runs his own online tutoring business: That Book Guy – Tuition Services. He is a member of UKLA and was the proud winner of Early Career Teacher 2020 in the Egmont OU/UKLA Reading for Pleasure Awards for his research on using digital platforms for promoting reading for pleasure. Nigel continues to promote RfP at every opportunity.

Nicola Mansfield-Neimi is an assistant head teacher and reading lead in a two-form entry school in Milton Keynes, she also runs an OU/UKLA Teacher Reading Group and is passionate about making reading a lifelong activity for all the children within her school. She was a runner up of the Egmont OU/UKLA Whole School Reading for Pleasure Award in 2020.

Dr Roger McDonald is an associate professor in the School of Education at the University of Greenwich, London. Roger initially worked as a primary school teacher for 17 years before moving into academia in 2012. Roger has a passion for literacy, particularly drama and the use of picture books to enhance possibility thinking. In 2021, Roger was proud to have been appointed President of the United Kingdom Literacy Association (UKLA). Roger's research interests centre around reading for pleasure and the importance of creating opportunities for imagining within the primary curriculum.

Clare McGreevy is a teacher, phase leader and reading for pleasure lead at Sandbrook Community School in Rochdale, Greater Manchester. Clare has led the OU/UKLA Teacher Reading Group since 2018 and regularly delivers training on the importance of RfP. She is the founder and coordinator of the annual Rochdale Spelling Bee and Rochdale Children's Literature Festival. In 2019, she was shortlisted for the Egmont OU/UKLA Reading for Pleasure Teacher of the Year Award for her work on developing an innovative and community-based school library space.

Sarah Merchant is a specialist leader of education for English, and her areas of interest are traditional storytelling and writing for purpose and pleasure. Since training in Hertfordshire and London, Sarah has been teaching in Suffolk for 23 years, working in primary and middle schools across the county as a leading literacy teacher and mentor to trainee teachers. Having come from a disadvantaged background, she is passionate about equity and improving pupils' life chances. Out of the classroom, Sarah likes reading, theatre, watching football with her son and writing poetry.

Marilyn Mottram was a primary teacher for many years and taught in a variety of contexts including initial teacher education. She has extensive experience of leadership and improvement work across a number of local authorities. Between 2011 and 2019, Marilyn was one of Her Majesty's Inspectors (HMI). In her role as HMI, she led national surveys, contributed to the chief inspector's annual report and was Ofsted's deputy national lead for English. Between 2012 and 2015, Marilyn was part of The Open University's Teachers as Readers research team. She is currently working with the OU's Reading Schools Programme: Building a Culture of Reading.

Dr Sarah Jane Mukherjee is a lecturer in applied linguistics and English language at The Open University. She teaches on undergraduate distance learning modules and writes open access online courses with a focus on reading for pleasure, linguistics and children's literature. Sarah has also worked as a researcher on the OU RfP Programme and has contributed to evaluations of different reading for pleasure initiatives. Her research draws on linguistics and has included children's meaning making in classroom role-play, young children's conceptions of play and learning in different cultural contexts and the multimodal meanings in children's picture fiction.

Sadie Phillips is a primary English specialist and Head of English at Blackheath Preparatory School in London. In 2019, she won the Egmont OU/UKLA Reading for Pleasure Experienced Teacher of the Year Award. She is passionate about promoting the importance of reading and leads CPD workshops focused on reading and writing for pleasure across the UK. Sadie is currently a UK Literacy Association regional representative for London and part of the editorial team for the journal *Literacy*. She also studies on the MA in children's literature at Goldsmith's University, London.

Kiran Satti is a primary teacher, with just over ten years' experience. She has taught across the primary phases and is a KS1 Phase Leader, Reading Lead and Primary Trust Literacy Lead Practitioner at Shireland Collegiate Academy Trust. Kiran is passionate about advocating alternative fairy tales, diversifying representation of gender and ethnicities and empowering fiction for girls alongside her work with @WomenEd, where she is a regional leader and runs the @WomenEdBookClub. She has a master's in teaching studies; her research focused on dialogic talk and diversity in texts, characters and themes. She was a shortlisted rising star for 2020 and 2021.

Sonia Thompson is a head teacher at St. Matthew's C.E. Primary School and the director of St. Matthew's Research School in Nechells, Birmingham. She has had a number of educational articles published and regularly reviews blogs for SchoolsWeek. She has a chapter in *The ResearchED Guide to the Curriculum* and a case study in *Closing the Reading Gap*. Sonia has run an OU/UKLA Teacher Reading Group and currently mentors several such leaders. She regularly delivers training to schools and MATs about reading for pleasure and progress and is a judge for Empathy Lab, UKLA Book Awards and Branford Boase Awards. Sonia is a member of the UKLA National Council, representing the Teacher Reading Groups and is a trustee for LoveMYBooks.

Jo Tregenza is a reader in primary education at the University of Sussex where she has been Director of Initial Teacher Education for six years. She teaches on undergraduate and postgraduate courses. Her research into reading comprehension with Dr Maureen Lewis led her to write teaching notes for the Oxford University Press Project X series. She is undertaking doctoral research on the best approaches to teaching reading and focusing on how schools with high percentages of disadvantaged pupils are positively impacting on pupils' attitudes to reading. She is currently the vice president of the UKLA and has over 30 years of experience as a primary teacher, advisor and consultant.

Andrew Truby was executive head teacher of three primary schools in South Yorkshire, a National Leader of Education and the strategic lead for an English Hub. Andrew played a key role in founding the South Yorkshire Reading Guarantee. In 2022, Andrew took up the role of CEO of St. Joseph CMAT, a new Catholic turnaround Trust in the North West of England.

Claire Williams is a Year 6 teacher at St. Andrew's C of E Primary School and Reading Lead for the All Saints Academy Trust, to which St. Andrew's belongs. She completed an MEd in children's literature, which explored the potential of meta-fictive picture books to support children's growth as writers, at the University of Cambridge and has been a member of the Teacher Advisory Group for The Open University reading for pleasure development work. Claire is a member of the UKLA National Council as Regional Representative for the East of England and coordinates the UKLA Student and Early Career Teacher network.

Katharine Young is a teacher, assistant head and English Hub lead at Elmhurst Primary School in Newham, London. In 2019, her school won the Egmont, OU/UKLA Reading for Pleasure Whole School Award. She has run an OU/UKLA Teachers' Reading Group for a number of years and supports other group leaders as a mentor for The Open University. She regularly delivers training on RfP both locally and nationally, working with schools to develop their practice. Katharine co-wrote a Reading for Pleasure Leadership Development Programme for the DfE English Hubs network to deliver across England.

Introduction
Reading Teachers

Teresa Cremin

Introduction: reading for pleasure

Reading matters. Every teacher knows that. But being able to read and being a keen reader are not the same thing. While both are fundamental, as the OECD and countless research studies show, it is choosing to read – reading for pleasure – that makes the difference. Being a frequent reader impacts on children's academic outcomes, which in turn leads to better employment and economic prospects (OECD, 2010). In addition, being a reader has the potential to enhance children's social and emotional well-being, broaden their understanding of the world and enrich their imaginations. Reading changes lives and is therefore an issue of equality and social justice, so as the OECD state:

> Finding ways to engage students in reading may be one of the most effective ways to leverage social change.
>
> (OECD, 2021)

Internationally however there is a worrying decline in young people choosing to read (OECD, 2018). Two large-scale ongoing surveys – the Progress in International Reading

DOI: 10.4324/9781003215615-1

Literacy study (PIRLS) for 10-year-olds and the Programme for Student Assessment (PISA) for 15-year-olds, track this trend, although it is not evident in every country. In the last PISA survey, England was ranked tenth in the world for reading attainment, but received the lowest ranking for pupil enjoyment and engagement in reading (in English speaking countries), bar Australia (McGrane, Stiff, Baird, Lenkeit and Hopfenbeck, 2017). In 2019, a UK survey underscored this concern, reporting the lowest level of daily reading in 5- to 18-year-olds since 2005 (Clark and Teravainen-Goff, 2020). Gender differences also remain, with boys frequently underachieving in terms of reading outcomes compared to girls, nationally (Clark and Picton, 2020) and internationally (OECD, 2018).

In England, reading for pleasure is mandated in the National Curriculum (DfE, 2014). In other countries such self-initiated reading is described as 'recreational reading' or 'free voluntary independent reading' (Krashen, 2004). Whatever the title, this is purposeful choice-led reading undertaken for each individual's personal satisfaction, often in their own time. Nurturing children's independent choice-led reading therefore means nurturing 'readers with agency'. Synonyms for pleasure include desire, preference, wish, choice and liking – all of which connect to reading *for* pleasure – to individual agency. Whilst some texts create less than positive emotions, for example evoking memories of loss or causing us to respond with anger at a fictional character's behaviour or a politician's plan, nonetheless if we chose to read it (or chose to step away aggrieved) we are exercising our rights as readers – our individual agency.

As adults, we also exercise our rights over *what* we read, our choice-led reading for pleasure can involve any kind of text – novels, magazines, poetry, comics or non-fiction for example, in electronic as well as in printed form. We read *where* we like too – at home, at school, in a café, a park, on a bus, a beach, – literally anywhere. We can *choose to talk* to others about what we read too, voicing our views in casual conversations or through book clubs, online or in person. Historically, reading has been characterised as a solitary and silent activity, yet research reveals the profoundly social, relational and emotional nature of reading, of being a reader and of choosing to read (e.g., Cremin et al., 2014; Billington et al., 2013).

The rights of the reader, both adults and children, are important, as Pennac (2006), Mangan (2018), Mackey (2016) and many others have shown. Reading Teachers not only exert their own rights they also reflect upon them in order to consider how to enrich children's experience of reading and nurture engaged readers. In this introductory chapter, to contextualise the book and its focus, the multiple advantages which accrue to keen young readers are explored, the challenges of motivating children to read are considered, and our central concept of being a Reading Teacher (capital R, capital T) is examined. We are adamant that such teachers are not simply school based teachers of reading. Nor are they simply teachers who read. Reading Teachers are enhanced professionals and reading role models who reflect upon the relationship between being a reader in their personal lives and being a teacher of reading in their professional lives, and then they consider adjusting their work with children to make the experience of reading more authentic and more relevant. This, our previous research has shown, alongside knowledge of texts and readers and a high-quality RfP pedagogy, effectively motivates children to read for pleasure and helps to build reading communities (Cremin et al., 2014; Cremin, 2019).

The benefits of being a keen reader

It is widely recognised that there is a strong reciprocal relationship between being a reader and reading attainment. The **will** to read influences the **skill** and vice versa. The international research evidence indicating this is both substantial and growing, year on year. Studies from the USA (Schugar and Dreher, 2017), Ireland (Gilleece and Eivers, 2018), the Netherlands, (Rogiers, van Keer and Merchie, 2020), Turkey (Tavsancil, Yildrim and Demir, 2019), the UK (McGrane et al., 2017) and Finland (Torppa et al., 2020) all indicate, albeit with slightly different emphases, that there is a clear relationship between reading enjoyment, reading amount and reading attainment. Intriguingly too, research indicates the particular power of fiction in this association between reading and young people's academic attainment (Jerrim and Moss, 2018). This may be because reading fiction requires sustained time and persistence, deep engagement and is often cognitively demanding.

Keen young readers spend more time reading than weak, unmotivated readers and in the process these readers regularly give themselves 'untaught lessons'. Through reading frequently at home and in school, keen readers enrich their comprehension (Schugar and Dreher, 2017) and widen their knowledge of the world. Reading also impacts positively on their writing skills (Senechal, Hill and Malette, 2018). Children who have read texts (fact or fiction) about refugees, the Romans or recycling, for example, will bring much wider background knowledge to their cross curricular studies in school. In addition, those who read frequently will be able to draw on a far richer range of vocabulary, both in conversation and in their own writing (Sullivan and Brown, 2015). 'Free reading' is seen to be far more efficient in terms of time and vocabulary acquisition than direct vocabulary instruction (McQuillan, 2019). The incidental gains in vocabulary which 'just reading' enables, provides a bridge to more challenging subject specific vocabulary and complex concepts, thus supporting children's learning.

Furthermore, keen readers experience social, emotional and relational benefits. Adults recognise that reading can offer a place of refuge and relaxation, and that literature in particular triggers emotions which are sensed as real and that this may give rise to being 'lost in a book' – a sense of living through the narrative (Mar and Rain, 2015). In one UK survey, those young people who reported high levels of enjoyment and pleasure in reading, on average, had higher mental well-being scores than their peers who didn't view reading in the same way and who held more negative attitudes towards reading (Clark and Teravainen-Goff, 2018). In addition, when enjoyment of reading is placed at the centre of classroom practice and teachers participate as fellow-readers, then research reveals that new reader-reader relationships between adults and children and amongst children develop (Cremin et al., 2014). These relationships offer social connections, a sense of belonging and gradually help to build reading communities.

Equally as importantly, motivated readers develop a strong sense of their own self-competence and confidence, this not only increases their willingness and ability to discuss texts (Ho and Lau, 2018; Moses and Kelly, 2018), but also supports their learning right across the curriculum. Those children who not only can, but do choose to read regularly and widely, benefit from the built-in advantages of being a keen reader and will be well positioned to access the secondary curriculum (Sullivan and Brown, 2015).

However, even motivated readers need support. Regardless of age, as readers we are shaped by the texts we read and the company we keep. Maybe you too have experienced periods when you have read less, not found the time or the 'right' text that tempted you enough at that moment in your life. All readers need sustained support. For young 'becoming readers' who are newer on this journey, help is particularly critical. This will come from their teachers, families, friends and the wider community of readers in school and beyond. In addition, they will be supported (or otherwise) by the hearts and minds of the authors and illustrators who journey with them. So, the texts offered matter, although each child's right to choose what they wish to read remains.

'RfP disadvantaged' readers

Young people who initially find reading a challenge, who struggle from the outset for a range of complex reasons, and who have 'yet to find what reading is good for' (Meek, 1991) need additional opportunities to enrich their skills *and* to nurture their desire – the will to read. However, in school, more attention tends to be paid to their skills. Those with the lowest literacy levels are more likely to be placed in 'low-ability' groups, and there is a danger that they experience a more limited reading diet with simplified texts. They may also be obliged to spend more time practising phonics or discrete reading skills (Hempel-Jorgensen, Cremin, Harris and Chamberlain, 2018). Hence, the problems faced by less able readers are exacerbated. This has been described as 'the Matthew effect' in which 'the rich get rich and the poor get poorer' (Stanovich, 1986). If children are held back by a combination of limited early success, reduced access to quality texts that bear relevance to their lives and an impoverished pedagogy (Hempel-Jorgensen, 2015), they can become caught up in a cycle of disadvantage from which it is difficult to break free.

These are clearly 'RfP disadvantaged' readers, but they are not the only ones. Other children who are capable readers but rarely choose to read, are also disadvantaged as they will not benefit from the enhanced attainment and social and emotional well-being that accrues to those who read frequently. These 'can but don't readers' (Moss, 2000) may have decided that reading is not for them, and may seek to avoid it, perhaps repositioning themselves as 'cool' amongst friends who are equally disinterested. Regardless of the reason for a child's lack of engagement in recreational reading, RfP disadvantaged readers do not indicate that they are engaged or interested, they are unlikely to be sharing texts with others beyond school and may not often be read to at home. Their experience of reading is far more contained and constrained than their peers who are motivated to read. However, in the classroom of a thoughtful Reading Teacher, who seeks to find out more about children's reading identities and offers enriched opportunities to nurture their engagement, these learners are likely, over time, to adopt a more positive disposition towards reading and become readers who can *and do* choose to read. Nonetheless, for all teachers' challenges remain.

The challenges

Despite the weight of evidence revealing the benefits of being a frequent reader, tensions and difficulties persist. Research findings don't create time in classroom timetables, teachers and schools do, and time is a scarce and precious resource in education. National or local policy documents may endorse RfP, but in countries where high stakes testing holds sway, there is pressure on teachers to prioritise the assessed skills and focus on phonics and comprehension, side-lining choice-led reading. Additionally, senior leaders do not always endorse or retain a focus on developing readers with agency as core to education, seeing it rather as an additional extra, or a project to be done and dusted. Furthermore, fostering a love of reading is viewed by some teachers and parents as an 'orphaned responsibility' (Merga and Ledger, 2018); once children can read, it is seen to be their choice if they choose to do so or not.

Schools are full of children and young people who have learned to read, but who do not choose to do so in their own time. Many of these young people don't associate reading with pleasure and actively disengage from it. These are not readers; they are simply children who can read. Additionally, other young people, who are still struggling as proficient readers and may have struggled from the outset, are unlikely ever to make the time to read unless they are offered enriched support. Another difficulty is that teachers are accustomed to considering young readers' abilities, their scores on reading tests of phonics, vocabulary or comprehension, but less attention is paid to children's attitudes to reading, their behaviours and motivation. Moreover, deficit discourses about some children and families persist and research suggests teachers may inadvertently position some groups of children as less likely to become keen readers due to assumptions made about their gender, ethnicity and/or social class (Hempel-Jorgensen and Cremin, 2022).

Additionally, financial constraints influence the texts available, especially in areas which are already under-resourced, further impoverishing children's chances to find texts that connect to their lives. As Sims Bishop (1990) argued over 30 years ago, children deserve to see themselves in the mirror of fiction and to view others' lives through reading books that metaphorically operate as windows and sliding glass doors on the world. Yet studies indicate that there is a long way to go before children's publishing reflects the ethnicity of the UK population (CLPE, 2021) and ensures that children can access narratives that positively represent their diversities.

In response to these myriad tensions and difficulties, and the highly influential nature of PISA and PIRLS, more policymakers, schools and practitioners are turning their attention to RfP. Many are recognising the game-changing nature of volitional reading and its potential as a tool to respond to inequalities. In England, the Early Years Foundation Stage Framework (DfE, 2021a) states 'It is crucial for children to develop a life-long love of reading', The Reading Framework (DfE, 2021b) highlights the potency of independent reading and the Education Endowment Foundation recognise that 'motivation and engagement are important for pupils' progress in literacy' (EEF, 2021: 15); this helps children develop enjoyment, satisfaction and resilience as readers. Furthermore, Ofsted (2019) inspections involve a 'deep dive' methodology which seeks to understand the extent to which children are engaged as readers, not simply whether they are being effectively taught to read. Ofsted appreciate there is a vast difference between being able to read and being a reader. Reading Teachers also realise that reading instruction and reading for pleasure are neither diametrically opposed nor incompatible, and can be planned in a rigorous and responsible manner in order to create a rich reading curriculum that engages every child and motivates free reading.

Reading Teachers: capital R, capital T

The concept of reading teachers – teachers who read and readers who teach – was first coined by Commeyras, Bisplinghoff and Olson (2003) while working with students on a masters course in the USA. These educators reflected on their reading lives and discussed possible consequences for their classrooms. The academics thought there may be a link between teachers reader identities and their pedagogy and listened to their teachers' views on this. In a later study, it was found that US teachers who ascribed the most value to reading in their own lives, gave more time in school for children to read and discuss their free-choice texts, recommended texts and shared reflections from their own reading far more frequently than their peers who ascribed less personal value to reading (McKool and Gespass, 2009). Both these studies drew on self-reporting not observation, so the UK *Teachers as Readers* (TaRs) research examined this idea in action in classrooms, documenting teachers' reader identities and the impact of these on young readers over time. The findings showed that some of the teachers more actively adopted this dual identity position and came to develop more fully into what the team called Reading Teachers: capital R, capital T. The research showed that those who also found out about the children as readers, and who explored possible classroom actions related to their own and the children's lives as readers, made a more marked and a more positive impact on children's engagement – on their volitional reading – than their fellow teachers who simply shared their love of reading with children (Cremin, 2010; Cremin et al., 2014). Through reflection, these enhanced professionals and fully fledged Reading Teachers became more conscious of their own identities, histories and strategies as readers and developed more engaged classroom reading communities (Cremin, 2021).

How teachers both see themselves and are seen by others as readers is important since their engagement enables them to model the value, pleasure and satisfaction they find in reading, and to induct children into such pleasures (Gennrich and Janks, 2013). Primary children are aware of their teachers' attitudes to reading, as an Australian study has shown (Merga, 2016). The children in this research, noticed that some teachers talked about books and shared recommendations, they also registered that some teachers read aloud to the class with enjoyment, affective engagement and expression. The young people additionally noticed that some teachers always had reading materials to hand. All these practices were associated with the children's desire to read in the classroom too. In recent years working alongside members of the profession, the concept of being a Reading Teacher has been explored further, with action research projects indicating close and nuanced synergies between teachers and children as readers (Cremin, Thomson, Williams and Davies, 2018; Cremin, Williams and Denby, 2019; Cremin, Harris and Birchall, 2020).

Reading Teachers work hard to understand children's identities as readers and recognise the role that self-efficacy and a sense of self as a reader plays in shaping their reading journeys. When teachers are more aware of their own and the children's reader identities and diverse practices and preferences beyond the classroom, they may consider the kinds of opportunities and reader identity positions they make available to individual children. Whether for example, through grouping or intervention activities, labels are internalised and children adopt the classroom-constructed roles of readers deemed 'good' or 'reluctant' for instance (Hall, 2012). This has consequences for their engagement as readers. Looking across the studies, a continuum of additive practices has been found to characterise Reading Teachers – capital R, capital T (see Figure 0.1).

While all teachers read, only some develop fully as Reading Teachers. Such professionals may initially share their pleasure in reading with children, deliberately offering positive reading role models. Others will seek to go one step further and investigate their reading lives and practices, reflecting on the nature of reading and being a reader. Additionally, some will also seek to find out about children's reading identities and consider what counts as reading in their classroom, recognising they are partly responsible for this. The final step to becoming a more fully-fledged Reading Teacher involves building on one's own and the children's knowledge and understanding of reading and being a reader, and adapting classroom practice in newly aligned ways that seek to nurture reading for pleasure.

As noted earlier, those teachers who developed most fully as Reading Teachers positively influenced children's attitudes towards reading and the frequency of their reading at home and school. In addition, these teachers developed stronger teacher-child reader relationships which impacted upon the children's knowledge and perception of

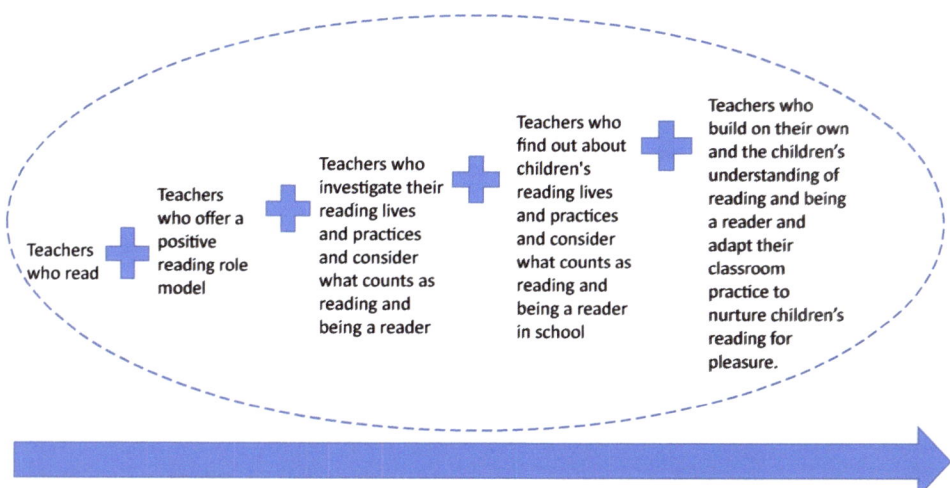

Figure 0.1 A continuum of additive practices to represent Reading Teachers

their teachers as readers (Cremin, 2010; Cremin et al., 2014). Reading became a more sociable, relaxed experience in their classrooms and the teachers, as fellow readers, participated in a less hierarchical manner in informal book talk and reader recommendations with children. To what extent do you participate in school as a reader? Perhaps pause a moment and ponder on your own position in relation to this notion of being a Reading Teacher. You might ask yourself:

- Do the children see you as a reader?
- Are you a reading model for the young learners?
- Do they know anything about your habits, interests, likes and dislikes as a reader?
- Do you explicitly share your reading life with them?
- Do they know where, when and what you like to read for pleasure? Would they care? Does it matter?
- Do you ever stop to reflect on your reading history or life as a reader within and beyond school?

Considering your identity as a reader and your practices, past and present, is important in order to develop as a Reading Teacher.

Becoming more conscious as a reader

In becoming more aware of your own reading identity, rights and practices, you will enhance your knowledge and understanding about the nature of reading. In TaRs, when the teachers shared their reading practices with one another, this led to stronger understandings of the uniqueness of readers and highlighted difference and diversity (Cremin et al., 2014). Some teachers for example reported they had several books on the go, others were aghast at this, their practices differed. The influence of the texts themselves was discussed at length, and teachers came to appreciate the salience of different readers' preferences for particular genres, authors or styles of writing. Reading practices and habits attached to various text types were also shared, such as reading the end of a novel first, turning pages down to revisit favourite phrases or passages, skipping descriptive parts or giving up on books.

Additionally, reading contexts were debated long and hard: what difference does the environment make, the presence of others, the opportunity to talk about the issues in the text? What motivates and engages some readers and turns others off? It became clear that readers' identities, our sense of self as readers is not fixed, much depends on what we are reading, why, where, with whom and the wider context. Alongside difference and diversity, what was common was the degree of agency which the adult readers exercised. Making this agency visible through reflection and discussion was invaluable.

However, teachers do not always extend the same rights or agency to children. Schooled versions of 'reading' are often dominated by the standards agenda and reading for pleasure practices can become routinised. Too often the lived experience of reading and being a reader in the 21st century is overlooked. Through reflection and action, Reading Teachers seek to enable children to engage more authentically and affectively as readers. This does not involve a 'do as I do' mindset with children imitating their teachers, rather it involves offering more informed support for each young reader's journey, enabled by a rich understanding of the personal, affective, social, situated and relational nature of reading.

Notice, document, reflect and act

There are multiple ways you can develop as a Reading Teacher, and through reading this book you will encounter many which you may wish to try. Essentially the process of self-reflection on being a reader can be described as *Notice – Document – Reflect* and *Act*. In coming to notice your own practices and preferences anew, through documenting them and reflecting on what they reveal about reading or you as a reader, you will be able to act upon your insights in order to support young readers. You will also be able to explore the younger readers' practices and identities.

For instance, by becoming more aware of your desire to read novels that touch an emotional nerve, or your pleasure in losing yourself in a story during times of stress, you may begin to ponder on the children's purposes for reading. Are they aware of these? Might an exploration of why and what you all read help children recognise how different we are as readers and enable you to fine-tune your provision for individuals? Children, like adults, choose to read for diverse personal purposes, consciously and unconsciously. They seek and find different kinds of satisfaction through different texts at different times, for example to relax, to escape, to laugh, to find out, to feel involved, to connect with friends and so on (McGeown et al., 2020). Understanding more about the children's perspectives on this issue and sharing your own, opens up a space for discussion and will support you in discerning possible next steps for your readers.

The purpose of a Reading Teacher's thoughtful movement from private self-noticing to wider professional action is to support children more effectively – to nurture choice-led reading. The process of noticing, documenting, reflecting and acting is also powerful when considering younger readers. Reading Teachers pay close attention to children's reading attitudes, behaviours and practices as Chapter 4 highlights. By engaging in professional noticing, particularly of the RfP disadvantaged, documenting what they observe and reflecting upon this, Reading Teachers are better positioned to help these children find pleasure in reading.

Conclusion

Readers' identities matter. Reading Teachers recognise this and hold a mirror up to their own identities as readers, past and present, becoming more aware of how these are influenced by text and context and are typified by difference and diversity. As they do so, they may, as our previous research has shown, transform their understanding of reading and reshape their classroom practice in ways that support children's desire to read (Cremin et al., 2014). This book builds on the core findings from the *Teachers of Readers* research project which identified:

- A coherent strategy to develop children's reading for pleasure by enhancing teachers' subject knowledge and pedagogic practice;
- The value of developing 'Reading Teachers' as actively engaged role models;
- The significance of creating reciprocal reading communities that nurture children's pleasure in reading;
- A need to build different professional relationships based on new conceptions of reading and increased reciprocity between children, families and teachers.

(Cremin et al., 2014: 158)

Reflecting back on this research and the recent work of the Open University team in sharing the original project findings, via the website (ourfp.org), through over 450 OU/UKLA Teacher Reading Groups since 2018, 35 Higher Education partners and the yearlong Reading Schools programmes (with over 150 schools), we felt that the concept of being a Reading Teacher deserved more attention. We wanted to offer student teachers and more experienced practitioners a window on the original research and more recent studies and share the thoughtful practice of current Reading Teachers in order to enrich opportunities for tomorrow's young readers. So, we turned to esteemed colleagues with whom we have had the privilege of working and invited them to join us as co-authors. While there were so many more we might have embroiled, we are deeply grateful to the 23 Reading Teachers, Reading Librarians and Reading Head Teachers who joined us on this journey.

This book has created opportunities for these highly reflective professionals and the academics involved to share their reading lives, to discuss synergies between research and practice, and to learn together. Many meetings were held, new relationships formed and new insights established. The trios who authored each chapter seized the chance in different ways to advance their understanding. Some set themselves the challenge of developing new practices based on agreed research reading, while others drew on existing RfP pedagogy and theorised this. All of the 35 educators involved shaped their emerging arguments through reflection, discussion and action.

As co-authors, we have all become more aware of our adult reading identities and practices, which are shared in the chapters, and as vignettes between the book's main sections. In the latter cases, through reflecting on a chosen aspect of our reading lives, we have as editors made more visible our own understandings about the nature of reading. We hope these reflections on reading and being a reader will offer you tools for thinking about the uniqueness of readers – of whatever age. Our Reading Teachers co-authors, without exception, have not only looked inwards (at themselves as readers), but in a parallel manner, have also looked outwards, to re-view their schools, classrooms and the children through a reader's lens. They have engaged in enhanced professional noticing of young readers' behaviours, attitudes and engagement, and have listened to and acted upon the children's multiple perspectives.

The result we hope you will agree is worth reading. We consider that the reflective stance, positioning and pedagogic actions of Reading Teachers offers an authentic and reader-relevant way forward to motivate and support young readers.

References

Billington, J., et al. (2013) Literature-based interventions for older people living with dementia. *Perspectives in Public Health*, 133(3): 165–173.

Bishop, R. S. (1990) Mirrors, windows and sliding glass doors. *Perspectives: Choosing and Using Books for the Classroom*, 6(3).

Centre for Literacy in Primary Education (2021) *Reflecting Realities: Survey of Ethnic Representation in UK Children's Literature 2021*. Available at: https://clpe.org.uk/system/files/2021-11/CLPE%20Reflecting%20Realities%20Report%202021.pdf

Clark, C. and Picton, I. (2020) *Children and Young People's Reading in 2020 before and During the COVID-19 Lockdown*. London: National Literacy Trust.

Clark, C. and Teravainen-Goff, A. (2018) *Mental Wellbeing, Reading and Writing: How Children and Young People's Mental Wellbeing is Related to Their Reading and Writing Experiences*. Available at: https://cdn.literacytrust.org.uk/media/documents/Mental_wellbeing_reading_and_writing_2017-18_-_FINAL2_qTxyxvg.pdf (Accessed 7 November 2021).

Clark, C. and Teravainen-Goff, A. (2020) *Children and Young People's Reading in 2019: Findings from Our Annual Literacy Survey*. Available at: https://cdn.literacytrust.org.uk/media/documents/Reading_trends_in_2019_-_Final.pdf

Commeyras, M., Bisplinghoff, B. S. and Olson, J. (2003) *Teachers as Readers*. New York: International Literacy Association.

Cremin, T. (2010) Poetry teachers: teachers who read and readers who teach poetry. In M. Styles, L. Joy and D. Whitley (Eds.), *Poetry and Childhood*, pp. 219–226. London: Trentham

Cremin, T. (2019) Teachers as readers and writers. In V. Bowers (Ed.), *Debates in Primary Education*. London: Routledge.

Cremin, T. (2021) Building reading communities. In A. Gill, J. Stephenson and D. Waugh (Eds.), *Developing a Love of Reading and Books*. London: Learning Matters, Sage.

Cremin, T., Harris, B. and Birchall, L. (2020) Reading for pleasure pedagogy for non-fiction. *English 4–11, No 69*, Spring 2020.

Cremin, T., Mottram, M., Powell, S., Collins, R. and Safford, K. (2014) *Building Communities of Engaged Readers: Reading for Pleasure*. London and New York: Routledge.

Cremin, T., Thomson, B., Williams, C. and Davies, S. (2018) Reading teachers. *English 4–11, No 62*, Spring 2018.

Cremin, T., Williams, C. and Denby, R. (2019) Reading teachers: Exploring non-fiction. *English 4–11, No 68*, Autumn 2019.

Department for Education (2014) *The National Curriculum in England: Key Stages 1 and 2*. Crown Copyright, Reference: DFE-00178-2013. Available at: https://assets.publishing.service.gov.uk/government/uploads/system/uploads/attachment_data/file/425601/PRIMARY_national_curriculum.pdf

Department for Education (2021a) *The Early Years Foundation Stage Framework 2021*. London: Department for Education. Available at: https://assets.publishing.service.gov.uk/government/uploads/system/uploads/attachment_data/file/974907/EYFS_framework_-_March_2021.pdf

Department for Education (2021b) *The Reading Framework: Teaching the Foundations of Literacy*, July 2021. London: Department for Education. Available at: www.gov.uk/government/publications/the-reading-framework-teaching-the-foundations-of-literacy

Education Endowment Foundation (2021) *Improving Literacy in Key Stage 1: Guidance Report*, London, 2nd ed., Education Endowment Foundation. Available at: Literacy_KS1_Guidance_Report_2020.pdf (d2tic4wvo1iusb.cloudfront.net)

Education Endowment Foundation (2021) *Improving Literacy at Key Stage 2*, London, EEF.

Gennrich, T. and Janks, H. (2013) Teachers' literate identities. In K. Hall, T. Cremin, B. Comber and L. Moll (Eds.), *The Wiley Blackwell International Research Handbook of Children's Literacy, Learning and Culture*, pp. 456–468. Oxford: Wiley Blackwell.

Gilleece, L. and Eivers, E. (2018) Characteristics associated with paper-based and online reading in Ireland: Findings from PIRLS and ePIRLS 2016. *International Journal of Educational Research*, 91: 16–27.

Hall, L. A. (2012) Rewriting identities: Creating spaces for students and teachers to challenge the norms of what it means to be a reader in school. *Journal of Adolescent & Adult Literacy*, 55(5): 68–373.

Hempel-Jorgensen, A. and Cremin, T. (forthcoming, 2022) An intersectionality approach to understanding 'boys' (dis)engagement with reading. *International Journal of Qualitative Studies in Education*.

Hempel-Jorgensen, A., Cremin, T., Harris, D. and Chamberlain, L. (2018) Pedagogy for reading for pleasure in low socio-economic primary schools: Beyond 'pedagogy of poverty'? *Literacy*, 52(2): 86–94.

Ho, E. S. C. and Lau, K. (2018) Reading engagement and reading literacy performance: Effective policy and practices at home and in school. *Journal of Research in Reading*, 41(4): 657–679.

Jerrim, J. and Moss, G. (2018) The link between fiction and teenagers' reading skills: International evidence from the OECD PISA study. *British Educational Research Journal*, 45(1): 161–181.

Krashen, S. (2004) *The Power of Reading: Insights from Research*. Portsmouth, NH: Heinemann.

Mackey, M. (2016) *One Child Reading: My Auto-bibliography*. Edmonton: The University of Alberta Press.

Mangan, L. (2018) *BookWorm: A Memoir of Childhood Reading*. London: Square Peg.

Mar, R. A. and Rain, M. (2015) Narrative fiction and expository nonfiction differentially predict verbal ability. *Scientific Studies of Reading*, 19: 419–433.

McGeown, S., Bonsall, J., Andries, V., Howarth, D., Wilkinson, K. and Sabeti, S. (2020) Growing up a reader: Exploring children's and adolescents' perceptions of 'a reader'. *Educational Research*, 62(2): 216–228.

McGrane, J., Stiff, J., Baird, J., Lenkeit, J. and Hopfenbeck, T. (2017) *Progress in International Reading Literacy Study (PIRLS): National Report for England*. London: Department for Education.

McKool, S. and Gespass, S. (2009) Does Johnny's Reading Teacher love to read? How teachers personal reading habits affect instructional practices. *Literacy Research and Instruction*, 48: 264–276.

McQuillan, J. (2019) The inefficiency of vocabulary instruction. *International Electronic Journal of Elementary Education*, 11(4): 309–318.

Meek, M. (1991) *On Being Literate*. London: Bodley Head.

Merga, M. K. (2016) 'I don't know if she likes reading': Are teachers perceived to be keen readers, and how is this determined? *English in Education*, 50(3): 255–269.

Merga, M. K. and Ledger, S. (2018) Parents' views on reading aloud to their children: Beyond the early years. *Australian Journal of Language and Literacy*, 41(3): 177–189.

Moses, L. and Kelly, L. (2018) 'We're a little loud. That's because we like to read!': Developing positive views of reading in a diverse, urban first grade'. *Journal of Early Childhood Literacy*, 18(3): 307–337.

Moss, G. (2000) Raising boys' attainment in reading: Some principles for intervention. *Reading*, 34(3): 101–106.

OECD (2010) *PISA 2009 Results: Learning to Learn – Student Engagement, Strategies and Practices (Volume III)*. Organization for Economic Cooperation and Development, Online library. Available at: http://doi.org/10.1787/9789264083943-en

OECD (2018) *Reading Performance (PISA) (Indicator)*. Organization for Economic Cooperation and Development, Online library. Available at: https://doi.org/10.1787/79913c69-en

OECD (2021) *21st-century Readers: Developing Literacy Skills in a Digital World*. Paris: OECD Publishing.

Ofsted (2019) *Education Inspection Framework*, updated 2021. Available at: www.gov.uk/government/publications/education-inspection-framework

Pennac, D. (2006) *The Rights of the Reader*. London: Walker.

Rogiers, A., Van Keer, H. and Merchie, E. (2020) The profile of the skilled reader: An investigation into the role of reading enjoyment and student characteristics. *International Journal of Educational Research*, 99.

Schugar, H. and Dreher, M. (2017) U. S. fourth graders' informational text comprehension: Indicators from NAEP. *International Electronic Journal of Elementary Education*, 9(3): 523–552.

Sénéchal, M., Hill, S. and Malette, M. (2018) Individual differences in grade 4 children's written compositions: The role of online planning and revising, oral storytelling, and reading for pleasure. *Cognitive Development*, 45: 92–104.

Stanovich, K. E. (1986) Matthew effects in reading: Some consequences of individual differences in the acquisition of literacy. *Reading Research Quarterly*, 21: 360–407.

Sullivan, A. and Brown, M. (2015) Reading for pleasure and progress in vocabulary and mathematics. *British Educational Research Journal*, 41(6): 971–991.

Tavsancil, E., Yildirim, O. and Bilican Demir, S. (2019) Direct and indirect effects of learning strategies and reading enjoyment on PISA 2009 reading performance. *Eurasian Journal of Educational Research*, 82: 169–189.

Torppa, M., et al. (2020) Leisure reading (but not any kind) and reading comprehension support each other – A longitudinal study across grades 1 and 9. *Child Development*, 91(3): 876–900.

Reflecting on my reader identity

Natalia Kucirkova

It was only when Teresa encouraged me to hold up the mirror to my own reading practice that I began thinking seriously about my reader identity. My first thought went back to my childhood and the fond memory of reading together with my grandfather. He and I used to read storybooks together. I remember sitting on my grandfather's lap and flicking through the colourful pages full of happy stories. I was very young and did not question why all stories featured someone from the family as the main protagonist – most often the main story hero was me.

Once I caught my grandfather telling a long story without turning the book pages. I challenged him about it, and he laughed and told me he did not read the text. He said he liked to make up his own stories based on the story illustrations. He told me I could do that too – I could be a storyteller just like he was. I remember how he smiled and said I didn't need to know what the letters meant to tell a good story. It was such a freeing moment when he said that. Suddenly there was no hierarchy between us, between the adult and the child, the reader and the non-reader – we were both storytellers. To this day I remember the curved wrinkles around my grandfather's lips as he smiled when I told him my first story. I see the freshly ironed shirt he wore and smell the mint candies we chewed on. I don't remember what the story was about, but I remember he was the main story hero in it.

I strongly believe that the story-sharing experience with my grandfather is the reason why I became so interested in stories later in my work as a researcher. I am passionate about my research and that passion is driven by a deep desire for ensuring that all children can experience the empowerment, enjoyment and reciprocity that shared stories can bring about. In addition to my grandfather, there were other family members who shaped my reader identity. My sister taught me read when I was about 5 years old. As soon as I understood that the quibbles next to an illustration tell a story, I became an avid reader. I devoured many, many books as a teen. I had a reading diary and sometimes wrote a short summary of what I had read. Sometimes I shared it with my sister and once I showed it to my literature teacher whom I really liked. But most often I was not sharing my reading experiences with anyone. Reading was a solitary affair for me; it was an encounter between me and the author and the story he or she conjured up.

I read rather randomly and in short bursts back then, often dipping in and out of texts. I would typically borrow 10 or 15 books from a library and read several of them in parallel. I could hold multiple narratives in mind at the same time. Perhaps reading several novels in parallel helped me draw a clearer line between fiction and real world. I identified strongly with Pollyanna or Anne of Green Gables. My parents

DOI: 10.4324/9781003215615-2

tell me that I was obsessed with Anne. Apparently I wanted them to call me Anne, and I learnt several passages of the book by heart. My parents remember that when they asked me something, I would recite the book text back to them, imitating Anna's voice. Perhaps reading multiple narratives simultaneously was part of a coping strategy to keep the fantasy and real world apart. Perhaps I found it overwhelming to become deeply immersed in one story at a time.

As an older teenager, I must have been around 15 or 16, I began reading fewer books and more in depth. I read all the Russian classics – Dostoevsky, Tolstoy, Pushkin, Gogol, Nabokov. The vastness of thought in the novels resonated with me, I identified with the passion of the main story protagonists and let my mind wander in the rugged and infinite Russian landscapes. I can't quite put my finger on what impressed me so much about the writing of these classic Russian authors; it could be my cultural heritage of growing up in post-communist Slovakia, it could be the proximity of Slovakian and Russian languages or it could simply be a personal preference. But the books exercised a unique power over me; I could not read them without being captivated. I could completely immerse myself in the narrative and would often delay reading the last chapter to savour a story as long as possible. I remember that when I finished reading *Anna Karenina* I was so upset that the story is over that I started reading it straight away again!

My reader identity evolved further when I started studying at the university. Reading fiction got subsided by reading psychology textbooks. Getting lost in a narrative became a luxury I could rarely afford. I read very little for pleasure during my undergraduate and postgraduate studies. When there was time to read, it would be spent on reading a research paper. That habit has continued into my academic jobs, with one big exception – reading poetry. While the busyness of my current work and the demands of everyday life make it difficult for me to prioritise sitting down with a novel, I do take the time to read poetry. Sometimes I read just one poem a day, sometimes I read a pamphlet per day. Reading poetry sustains my creativity and curiosity. I don't have a strong preference for a poetic style, I like both traditional and contemporary poetry; free verse or classic Shakespearean sonnets. I sometimes read poems on the screen, sometimes in a book format. But I always read them on my own, in a quiet room. I rarely sit by a desk or on an ordinary chair by the table, I am more likely to read poems on a sofa or sit on a cushion on the floor. I don't like strong light; I prefer dim light and light a candle or two when I read.

When reading poems at home, I switch on my beloved diffuser that emits various scents, from lavender to eucalyptus. When I read poems, it is a feast for all senses! Scents can activate memories, bring forward intense experiences and allow readers to make connections between the text and environment in new ways.

My poetry reading moments are my moments of joy, my moments of daydreaming. Last time when I was in such a blissed state of mind was when reading Daljit Nagra's collection. I am reading Clare Pollard's at the moment.

During the pandemic, my personal circumstances meant that I yearned for escaping the reality and craved narratives to immerse myself in. During lockdown, I read four books by Haruki Murakami and two by Rachel Cusk. I loved them all. It was as if Murakami and Cusk brought together my affection for poetry with the depth of realistic story plots of Russian authors. I found the writing lyrical, intriguing and inspiring. It is the kind of writing that creates fantasy worlds in my mind and inspires me

Reflecting on my reader identity 15

Figure 0.2 My reading environment: with a candle and portable scent diffuser

to write poetry. I have been writing poems since my early teenage years. As a published poet, I cannot see my reader identity separate from my writing identity. The two feed off each other and both give rise to an indescribable feeling of fulfilment.

I don't know whether any of these glimpses into my reader identities spark ideas in the readers of this book. If I were to articulate one request for all Reading Teachers raising the future generation of readers and writers, I would ask them to be generous. It was the generosity of my grandfather that shaped my reader identity and love for writing. It was his generous act of allowing me to find my own way into stories that freed me to explore diverse genres, various reading styles, and set up different priorities for fiction, non-fiction and poetry at different points in my life. I believe that freedom also encouraged me to be an active reader who follows her reading with writing. Nurturing future readers needs to be a generous act that liberates young children to tell, read and write their own stories.

Summary of recommendations:

- Encourage children to tell stories, especially if they cannot or struggle to read.
- Let children explore various genres.
- Support children's various styles of reading.
- Follow up children's interest in reading with writing.

Section 1

Texts and readers

Introduction

Reading for Pleasure (RfP) may be incorrectly perceived by some as an added extra in school, partly because of its limited place in the curriculum. For example, whilst the National Curriculum in England (Department for Education, 2014) highlights that children should learn to read and read frequently and widely, the curriculum guidance focuses on the technical skills of literacy. Teachers and the wider school community could be forgiven for assuming that the subject knowledge required to teach reading begins and ends with understanding phonics and comprehension. However, research shows that teachers' knowledge of children's texts, and of the reading preferences and practices of the children they work with is crucial in supporting children's volitional reading (Cremin, Mottram, Collins, Powell and Safford, 2014). For this reason, developing these aspects of teacher knowledge is a professional responsibility, as important as demonstrating sound mathematical or scientific understanding to underpin the teaching of other core subjects.

The following chapters offer some significant insights into the types of teacher knowledge needed to support RfP and how these can be developed and applied in the classroom.

DOI: 10.4324/9781003215615-3

Reading Teachers first need to reflect on and evaluate their knowledge of children's literature, of other texts and of the children themselves. Once they understand any gaps or weaknesses in their reading repertoire and have found out more about the interests of children in their class, they can develop strategies to enrich their subject knowledge. These strategies are ideally supported by a like-minded community of readers so that teachers can develop their understanding through social RfP opportunities to share texts in the staff team. This is not a short-term endeavour, but a professional commitment throughout each teacher's career.

Teacher knowledge for RfP is complex and nuanced and also involves Reading Teachers understanding how children identify with and are motivated by different types of texts and their identities as readers. This requires careful time and attention. For example, in an American study, Wilhelm (2016) interviewed 14-year-olds about their reading practices, favourite books and choice of genres, and found that students reading was quite different from their teachers' assumptions. Also, that during the reading process children engaged in powerful individual reflections. Wilhelm thus notes that teachers:

> need to trust kids' choices and remember that it's important to learn from kids how to best nurture and teach them. This means that we should ask students directly why they love the books they do love so much and engage them in conversation about the books . . . they love.
>
> (Wilhelm, 2016: 37)

The examples shared by the Reading Teachers in these chapters show how reading and reflection on texts, coupled with observation of children's reading practices and responses to reading, shape their RfP practices. This can include consideration of text representation and diversity, children's digital reading and even the hidden influences of gender stereotyping that might limit children's reading choices. The Reading Teachers use their knowledge to offer children a range of engaging reading materials and understand the different opportunities which specific text types (e.g. digital texts and graphic novels) offer (Hacking, 2021; Kucirkova, 2016). In this way, teacher knowledge and RfP pedagogy are inextricably linked.

At the centre of Reading Teachers' knowledge lies a layered understanding of reading and being a reader, an awareness of their own and children's identities as readers, and their motivations for reading (Hebbecker, Förster and Souvignier, 2019). Children's reading choices are also influenced by their social sphere, in particular their peers, teachers and families (OECD, 2021). To gather fundamental knowledge of children as readers, Reading Teachers must change the relationships around reading, opening up a space where children can share authentically with one another and their teacher. A space where texts and readers meet.

References

Cremin, T., Mottram, M., Collins, F. M., Powell, S. and Safford, K. (2014) *Building Communities of Engaged Readers: Reading for Pleasure*. London and New York: Routledge.

Department for Education (2014) *The National Curriculum in England: Complete Framework for Key Stages 1 to 4*. Available at: https://www.gov.uk/government/publications/national-curriculum-in-england-framework-for-key-stages-1-to-4 (Accessed 4 December 2021).

Hacking, C. (2021) Raising readers, changing lives: Supporting progress and pleasure in reading. *School Librarian*, 69(2): 6–7.

Hebbecker, K., Förster, N. and Souvignier, E. (2019) Reciprocal effects between reading achievement and intrinsic and extrinsic reading motivation. *Scientific Studies of Reading*, 23(5): 419–436.

Kucirkova, N. (2016) Personalisation: A theoretical possibility to reinvigorate children's interest in storybook reading and facilitate greater book diversity. *Contemporary Issues in Early Childhood*, 17(3): 304–316.

OECD (2021) *21st-Century Readers: Developing Literacy Skills in a Digital World*, PISA. Paris: OECD Publishing. Available at: https://doi.org/10.1787/a83d84cb-en (Accessed 4 December 2021).

Wilhelm, J. D. (2016) Recognising the power of pleasure: What engaged adolescent readers get from their free-choice reading, and how teachers can leverage this for all. *The Australian Journal of Language and Literacy*, 39(1): 30–41.

Chapter 1

Children's literature and other texts

Sarah Brownsword, Sarah Merchant and Richard Charlesworth

Introduction

Most of us can think of a book which we connected with at a young age; the first book that made us feel like a reader and made us want to keep on reading perhaps. Finding a book for each child to connect with in the same way sounds simple, but as every teacher knows, children have unique personalities, backgrounds, interests and needs which constantly change and develop. To be able to motivate children to choose to read and to offer personal recommendations, teachers need a breadth of knowledge of high-quality children's literature and other texts. This chapter focuses on why professional knowledge of children's literature is important; what kind of knowledge teachers need and how to develop this. It includes attention to other texts, including graphic novels and discusses the importance of having knowledge of a diverse range of texts which represent and reflect many different realities.

Research on teachers' knowledge of children's literature, suggests that many teachers do not have the breadth of knowledge needed to positively impact on children's RfP. Data from the Teachers as Readers (TaRs) research found teachers relied on their childhood reading and 'celebrity' authors, they did not keep up to date with contemporary texts, had narrow repertoires and in particular lacked knowledge of world literature and poetry (Cremin, Bearne, Mottram and Goodwin, 2008; Cremin, Mottram, Bearne and Goodwin, 2009). Despite taking place seven years later, Clark and Teravainen's (2015) research had similar findings; Roald Dahl, Michael Morpurgo and JK Rowling dominated these mainly secondary teachers' repertoires. When asked to name a new author, the majority noted David Walliams. Although there is nothing wrong with books by these authors, teachers limited literary repertoires constrain children's knowledge and potentially their pleasure in reading. Children need informed reading role models who voice their passion in reading and who can recommend and discuss a range of texts as fellow readers.

Research during the pandemic found that some teachers engaged with authors' and illustrators' online content (CLPE, 2021). When asked to name books which were particularly important to their classes during this time, *Here We Are* by Oliver Jeffers, *The Boy at the Back of the Class* by Onjali Q Rauf and *The Book of Hopes* by Katherine Rundell were highly noted. This could be indicative of a shift away from childhood reading and acknowledgement of the importance of books which focus on unity, diversity and comfort. However, their responses will also have been influenced but what was available online at that time.

Whilst picture books and novels are invaluable, a range of texts need to be recognised as supporting children's RfP, including non-fiction, poetry, magazines, comics, graphic novels, digital texts and film for instance. Some children are more personally invested in these texts. Although they might not consider themselves as readers, we have all observed children pouring over well-worn copies of *The Guinness Book of World Records* or sharing comics and graphic novels together – clearly engaged and RfP. When children 'read' a film, they understand the way the story unfolds and also pay attention to characters and plot. If teachers can widen their idea of what they consider to be good reading material, they are far more likely to be able to engage children in reading they actually find interesting and want to choose to read for pleasure.

However, it is not that easy for classroom teachers to find the time to expand their reading repertoires, especially as reading in school is often conceived as a skill to be taught and tested. Moreover, despite the inclusion of RfP in the National Curriculum in England, there is no requirement for teachers to develop this essential aspect of their subject knowledge, either in teacher training or through professional development. Nonetheless it is a professional responsibility to develop appropriate knowledge of children's texts, of representation and ways to widen repertoires and support a love of reading (see Figure 1.1).

This chapter explores these areas by looking at how two Reading Teachers – Sarah Merchant and Richard Charlesworth – develop and use their knowledge of children's texts and how their children respond. Both teach in large multicultural schools with high numbers of young people who are learning English as an Additional Language (EAL). We also offer ways that you can develop your subject knowledge of children's texts.

Auditing and documenting your reading

Richard's journey to becoming a Reading Teacher began when he started to critically reflect on the texts that he was using in class; the texts available to the children; and the texts he read in his own time. He used the Open University's Reading for Pleasure website audit of subject knowledge which invites teachers to reflect on their childhood

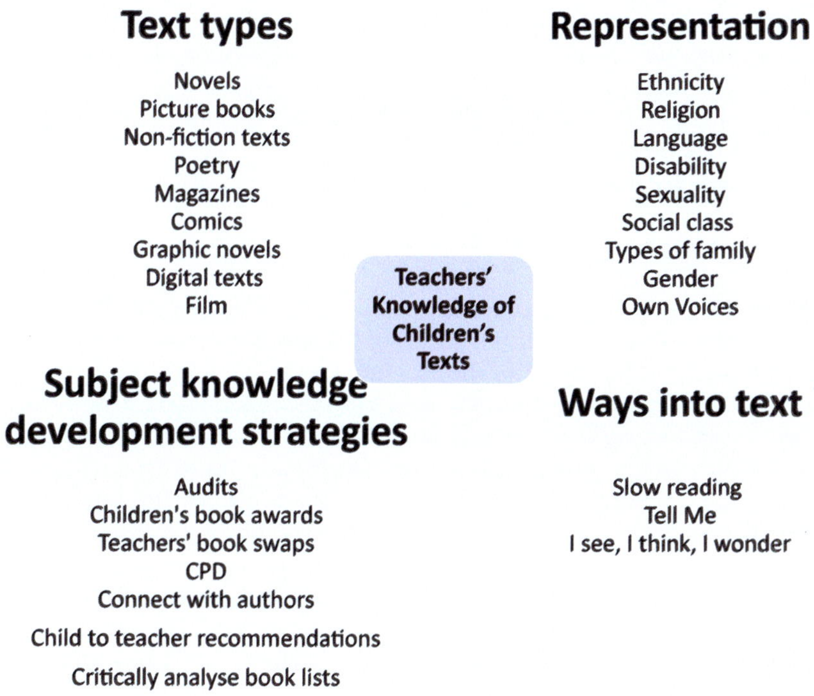

Text types

Novels
Picture books
Non-fiction texts
Poetry
Magazines
Comics
Graphic novels
Digital texts
Film

Representation

Ethnicity
Religion
Language
Disability
Sexuality
Social class
Types of family
Gender
Own Voices

Teachers' Knowledge of Children's Texts

Subject knowledge development strategies

Audits
Children's book awards
Teachers' book swaps
CPD
Connect with authors
Child to teacher recommendations
Critically analyse book lists

Ways into text

Slow reading
Tell Me
I see, I think, I wonder

Figure 1.1 Diagram of professional knowledge of children's texts to support RfP

favourites, recent books they have enjoyed, their access to books, their knowledge of texts and how they decide what children's books to use in their classrooms. For Richard, auditing is a continual process: one that he hopes will continue to deepen his understanding and develop awareness of the wide range of text types, creators and texts available to classroom practitioners.

To monitor his development, Richard uses a useful visual reminder in school every year. He papers pictures of the covers of the books which he shares onto his classroom door. This simple technique allows him to identify areas that are not represented or yet-to-be-read. Sometimes this is through a particular text type (e.g. poetry, graphic novel) or authorship (e.g. overdependence/reliance on a small number of author/illustrators). Through regular self-reflection, Richard continues to strive to develop a broader, deeper and up-to-date understanding of children's literature. In turn, recommendations he makes to pupils are more tailored, conversations richer and rewarding, and reading is something that you can 'feel' when you enter his classroom. Research reveals that children may not have access to the kinds of texts they want, and teachers may not appreciate their preferences (Merga, 2017) so Reading Teachers like Richard work hard to develop his understanding of the children's interests and the kinds of texts they may enjoy.

Joining social reading communities

When teachers have the opportunity to read and talk about children's books informally, they begin to respond to texts more as readers and not just as teachers (Collins, 2014). This community approach to developing subject knowledge helps to develop teachers' love of children's literature and different kinds of texts through recommendations. Social communities that can help you to develop your subject knowledge include:

- Teachers Reading Groups (e.g. OU/ UKLA Groups)
- Group communication platforms (e.g. WhatsApp)
- Social cataloguing websites (e.g. GoodReads)
- Social media platforms (e.g. Twitter)

After lockdown, the head teacher in Sarah's school created an additional 30-minute 'reconnect' time in the timetable and as a Reading Teacher, she devoted this to reading for purpose and pleasure. Seventeen of the 22 children (10–11 years old) in her classroom, reported that they did not choose to read outside school, citing reasons such as their difficulties with reading and a lack of books at home. Many also referred to their preferred use of time: video games, Zoom calls with friends and television streaming. It was clear that they were selecting highly visual and/or social activities over reading books. Reflecting on Kucirkova and Cremin's (2020: 2) observation that 'What texts children read matters. But do all texts incite their desire to read equally?', Sarah kept her class' preference for the 'visual' and 'social' in mind and joined a Twitter group Let's Talk Graphic Novels. There are benefits in teachers forming their own peer-based professional networks to collaborate and communicate (Tour, 2017) and Sarah found this online group invaluable.

As a result of the network's monthly meetings and a class survey to find out what kind of books her class would like to read, Sarah worked to expand her knowledge, and selected texts to read to them and promote their independent reading of other texts by the same authors. These included *Can Bears Ski?* by Raymond Antrobus and Polly Dunbar, *When Stars Are Scattered* by Victoria Jamieson and Omar Mohamed and *Rhythm and Poetry* by Karl Nova.

Diverse children's books

One of the key reasons for children choosing and enjoying texts, is the characters they meet, enjoy, relate to and, in many cases, form relationships with. When characters are similar to us, or we relate to them personally in some way, we are far more engaged in our reading. Yet research reveals that children's literature published in the UK featuring children from ethnically diverse backgrounds as main characters is very limited; and where there is representation it is sometimes problematic (CLPE, 2020, 2021).

Books can act as mirrors which reflect our own world and experiences back to us (Sims Bishop, 1990), as well as windows which offer us insight into others' worlds. In this way, reading can become both a form of self-affirmation and a source of new understanding. However the National Literacy Trust's annual survey found that 33% of children did not feel represented in the books they read; this rose to 40% of children from minority ethnic backgrounds (Best, Clark and Picton, 2020). The number of primary aged children who did not feel represented in books was double that of secondary age children, suggesting this is particularly a primary school problem. The issue of representation was also of significance for children who receive free school meals, and those who identify as a gender other than boy or girl (Best et al., 2020). If children grow up without finding themselves in books or only finding problematic representations, this may put them off reading and reduce the likelihood they will read for pleasure and gain all that benefits that accrue to frequent readers. Multicultural picture books in particular can enable children to have 'their personal and collective experiences, histories, and knowledge bases related to race affirmed and celebrated' (Husband, 2019: 1069). Graphic novels too, which are more diverse than many other forms of children's literature offer opportunities to increase the number of 'mirroring' characters to children from minority ethnic backgrounds (Boerman-Cornell and Kim, 2020). Fantasy genre texts by contrast tend to offer problematic representation of characters; white heroes and dark 'others' are commonplace (Thomas, 2019).

Children's literature which is diverse in its representation of characters is not just important for children from minority ethnic backgrounds but for all children. Despite increasing diversity in many areas, a number of children grow up in predominantly white and monocultural communities. For these young people, books are crucial to help them develop an understanding of different cultures, communities and individuals. Furthermore, Reading Teachers like Sarah and Richard will want to ensure that children can access narratives and non-fiction that positively represent and reflect the full range of diversities, such as characters from a variety of backgrounds, with disabilities and that are inclusive of the LGBTQ community.

Own voice and authentic texts

The term 'Own Voices' gained popularity after being used as a hashtag on Twitter by author Corinne Duyvis in 2015. It refers to children's texts featuring characters who share an ethnic, cultural or racial background with their author. It is important because worlds and voices which historically have been less represented in children's books should be as authentic and accurate as possible. When Reading Teachers recommend 'Own Voice' texts, they can be more confident that representations will not be perpetuating stereotypes. The term has now moved beyond ethnicity to refer to books in which the characters share a marginalised identity with their author. In Sarah's class 'Own Voices' texts are strongly favoured:

> I have read a few books by Muslims but never with Muslim main characters. To see another Muslim leading a story would be incredible. I would like a story with a Yusuf' in it!'
>
> (Yusuf)

As Sarah began to display and share more texts that reflect the lives of the children, including graphic novels and picture books, she noticed the atmosphere in the classroom gradually begin to shift. Children were quicker at coming in to read each morning, quiet conversations of 'Can I have that one after you?' or 'Look at this bit 'cos it's like anime. I finished it in one night!' were heard. Seemingly, the children were pairing up and grouping together to discuss their latest reads. Sarah heard lots of laughter and hoped this was the beginnings of a reading community.

As a Reading Teacher, Sarah also brought her personal experience to the text when sharing *Can Bears Ski?* (Antrobus and Dunbar) about Bear, who is deaf. As the parent of a deaf child, Sarah modelled her own response and voiced her experiences also using selected poems from *The Perseverance* (Antrobus). She described how this text 'hit her' on an emotional level. Richard also chose *Can Bears Ski?* as a way of exploring deafness with a Year 2 class. Several children commented on the titular question as he was reading the text, pondering what it might mean. As the text unfolded, the children began to understand that Bear could not hear his father well, and was asking 'Can you hear me?' In a later conversation his dad supports Bear making sure his face is visible and that he speaks clearly (see Figure 1.2). The class discussed how difficult this might be when people's mouths are covered – which led to questions about sign language and the difference between being born Deaf (capitalised – deaf from birth) or deaf (not capitalised – someone who has a severe hearing problem or extremely hard of hearing). As both Antrobus and Dunbar have personal experience of hearing loss, they were able to bring their own lived experiences to the text and offer their readers insight into the world of audiologists, hearing aids and strategies to support hearing.

Building on this, Richard decided to focus on the area of disability in books. He selected this for several reasons:

- To foster empathy and understanding for those who have a physical or mental disability;
- To open dialogic spaces for talking about disabilities; and
- To explore the literature available for classroom use.

Being a topic that might be personal to young children and their families, Richard as a Reading Teacher was thorough in his research. He made sure texts were current (published within the last five to ten years), as society's views and attitudes towards disability have changed significantly and he wanted to avoid any outdated views. It was important to him that when sharing these texts there was no prescribed lesson objective or pre-planned ulterior motive or outcome, beyond discussion to open up the texts' themes. Richard

Figure 1.2 An extract from Antrobus and Dunbar's *Can Bears Ski?*

again prioritised Own Voice texts. Although authors and illustrators can research and write about people from a range of backgrounds and contexts, he felt that when reading about disability, children should hear from those who had experienced the disability (be it physical or mental) themselves. Where first-hand experience was not possible, Richard investigated instances of when the author/illustrator had talked about the creation of the text and the processes involved. His search brought a wide range of texts, usually recommended as part of a list, so in order to critically examine these, he used Kleekamp and Zapata's (2018) four guiding questions.

1. Does the author/illustrator present the character with a disability label as multidimensional?
2. Whose story is this and who gets to tell it?
3. As a reader, how have you been positioned to think about feel about the character with a disability label in this book?
4. What opportunities does the character with a disability label have in the book to engage in authentic relationships?

These questions made Richard consider the language, lens and positioning of the author/illustrator, as well as the depiction of the character with a disability.

Diverse texts triggering empathy

Finding books that resonate with children personally is important in engaging children in RfP (Kucirkova and Cremin, 2020). When children respond to texts with empathy by focusing on characters and feelings, their enjoyment of reading can increase (Empathy Lab, 2020). The graphic novel *When Stars Are Scattered* was chosen by both Richard and by the children in Sarah's class. It tells the story of Omar and his brother Hassan, who fled Somalia and lived in a Kenyan refugee camp for several years. Sarah's class chose this book for its 'big ideas', its format and its content.

> I am really interested in this book because the main characters leave their homeland. I see refugees on the news, but I don't know much about their lives. What's it like to leave your home behind? Why would you do that?
>
> (Sayem)

In order to ensure that the children were active agents in their reading of this text, Sarah decided that she would not ask any questions herself, unless it was to clarify a child's point. The children chose the agenda for discussion, the questions, and added to each other's responses, while her role was as a facilitator. The class enjoyed this sense of empowerment and Sarah strongly believed that the depth of discussion would not have been achieved if she had prescribed particular questions and tasks. It became clear that some children felt, to a certain degree, represented by this text. For example:

> I understand how much Fatuma is devoted to Allah and that her religion is important to her. The stars show the gap between the boys and their mum. Omar might be folding his bed to find space to pray. Miss, I can read that bit – it is Arabic!
>
> (Ahmed)

Victoria Jamieson shows rage well with flying water containers, scribbles and dust clouds. We know how Omar is feeling right now and not just because of the illustration, as the words tell us more. Piecing everything together, we have been in similar states but for different reasons.

(Louise and Miremba)

It was also interesting tracking one child, Renas, who was relatively new to English. With the help of an online tool, Sarah documented his responses, which showed a growing confidence and understanding:

> He's sad. Mum. He his brother.
> Boy Hassan he like it the goat.
> Hassan can be calm. It might be Hassan was born with a disability. The person who made this book is smart because I can understand everything. Omar's anger goes far. I guess he looks hungry all day. The stars (are) showing what is happening in the book like (a) mirror.
>
> (Renas, using an online translation tool a month later)

Slow reading of graphic novels

As well as children who find reading challenging, there are several extremely proficient readers in Sarah's class who she thought would benefit from reading more slowly and deeply. Picture books, graphic novels and other highly visual texts are a complex ensemble of pictures, text and layout which are rewarded by slow looking/reading which can help to develop children's appreciation interpretation and understanding (Pantaleo, 2020). The traditional teaching of reading can lead children to value written text over illustrations or pictures; however this does not work in the reading of graphic novels where readers must infer what is happening from one panel to the next and if children don't spend enough time on the illustrations this can cause comprehension problems (Smith and Pole, 2018). In order to support the children to read graphic novels for pleasure, Sarah taught them to slow down and look, moving a viewfinder over the text. This enabled them to zoom in on the tiniest detail and spot connections between panels. Compare these two comments from the same week by Ellie and Sophie, where they used a viewfinder and slowed down in the second instance:

> One boy has a red t-shirt and the other has blue. They have left their home in Somalia and feel lost.
>
> The dust cloud in the first frame shows that Omar is dragging his feet and worries. He does not have enough energy to lift his feet up. We notice there is repetition and it shows they wait a LONG TIME to queue as there is just one word in each panel. Omar sees his mother in the shadows and this is wishful thinking. We wonder why the phrase 'I am sorry, baby!' has been repeated from earlier in the book. Perhaps Fatuma is constantly needing to apologise and is powerless. Her eyebrows show this as well as the repeated words. The same old days repeat along with the same old words.
>
> (Ellie and Sophie)

In choosing to read this novel together, and in being supported, the two girls considered each other's responses and negotiated possible meanings between them

(Smith and Pole, 2018). This encouraged them to notice more, engage more deeply and fostered a positive view of the text and potentially Victoria Jamieson's other graphic novels.

Such slow reading approaches work well with reading strategies such as the See-Think-Wonder routines from Project Zero's Visible Thinking approach and Chambers' (2011) Tell Me approach. In Richard's class, he encourages children to respond using Chambers' structure of 'Likes, Dislikes, Puzzles and Connections' from the Tell Me approach. This means that discussion follows the children's interests, as opposed to a set question from the adult. Sometimes points raised are built upon by other pupils, or by the adult, allowing for better understanding or facilitation of additional questions. Through the discussion Richard noticed there were usually questions that were not able to be answered during the session. These were explored afterwards. With potentially complex themes, such as disability and refugees, it is important to move beyond the text, developing greater awareness and talking about the reputability of the sources.

There are many benefits of reading graphic novels for disengaged readers or dyslexic readers including pages which contain less text and therefore appear less stressful to children who worry about reading. Because the plot and characters are presented visually on the page, children who struggle to follow or remember details of a plot can more easily move backwards and forwards between the panels and pages to remind them of what has come before. What is perhaps less appreciated, is that graphic novels can also benefit the most fluent and confident readers. The need to shuttle between illustrations and text in order to find meaning can result in deeper critical engagement, as in these examples from 10-year-olds:

> Being hungry causes outbursts of anger. Refugees' eyes have wrinkles underneath them to show tiredness. I think Omar cannot stop thinking about his mother and this is an obsession. While Omar continues to stress, Hassan is more playful and inventive. The food lines are divided into men and women – why?
>
> (Emma)

> There are more women than men, perhaps because the men are fighting in a war. Fatuma is very understanding of the boys' situations. Nobody looks out for her. I am thinking of my Auntie, who is similar.
>
> (Imran)

> Depression reigns here. Days are empty. Omar's face is full of tension. There is a long wait and an illustration before the words 'Wouldn't she?' to suggest the boys are uncertain. I have never seen an illustration as a buffer before.
>
> (Joseph)

> I think that when illustrations break the frame, it represents force. The same pot is thrown in one frame and lands in another. I notice that Omar does not complain much as there is no point and he understands the poverty and hunger. I cannot imagine never having a cold drink in such a hot place. The younger children tend to lash out. I can see how Omar sometimes gets embarrassed by his mistakes and dwells on things because I do this too.
>
> (Louise)

Accessible texts

In a similar way to graphic novels, picture books offer an opportunity to explore complex themes, with an accessibility that includes all children, regardless of academic ability or language fluency. When books are accessible to children, they engage more deeply with them and this depth of engagement is key to children finding pleasure in reading.

As a widely read Reading Teacher, Richard is acutely aware of the value of picture books and that these are not just for younger children. Within his disability focus, he shared *What Happened to You?* (Catchpole and George, 2021) and *Emmanuel's Dream: The True Story of Emmanuel Ofosu Yeboah* (Thompson and Qualls, 2015) with 10- to 11-year-olds. Both texts have central characters with amelia (the congenital absence of a leg) and include afterwords which give advice and/or biographical information on a character. In the former, James Catchpole offers suggestions to younger readers and adults about how to discuss disability, and how to avoid potentially awkward interactions with individuals with a disability. Richard noticed this not only raised personal connections for a child, but that it also helped nondisabled children understand what it is like to be singled out for being different. He considered it encouraged the young readers to see the person first, fostering empathy in the process.

When reading with her class, Sarah was particularly interested in the responses of her children with dyslexia or dyslexic tendencies. Normally some of these young people did not choose to read because it was too difficult for them to be enjoyable. However when they read *When Stars Are Scattered*, they appeared to be rather more assured:

> Dust and bandages show depression. The houses have extended and we see that there are more tents and the grass has grown to show time passing. Maryam's husband treats her like a bit of a slave and his words are sharp. He stands above her. She should go to school because she is smart.
>
> (Liam and Leanne)

> I like sentences to be separated so I can read them. I like illustrations to help me. I was worried that graphic novels would be babyish but you read them so they can't be.
>
> (Noah)

By being able to focus on the visual narrative as well as the text, which is broken 'into bits', these children were able to respond to the tale in more depth and enjoyed the success of being able to read it to the end. As Leanne noted 'It feels more comfortable to read graphic novels' and Liam said 'I don't do reading – except them graphic novels'. As Sarah replied 'Then you are a reader'.

Developing a community of engaged readers

By expanding the type of texts that these Reading Teachers shared with their classes, and discussing them in a relaxed and open manner, Sarah and Richard began to build connections between readers. Sarah felt that through exploring Own Voices texts, slow reading and thinking about accessibility a community of readers gradually began to form. On one occasion, a child wrote on the makeshift agenda board, 'Why is the book called

When Stars Are Scattered?' In responding to this question, small groups formed. One group's collective response, captured on a series of post-it notes, is noted here.

> What the writers mean by stars are scattering could be that everything is moving away from the boys and they feel they are dying a little every day. The stars are scattered might be a sign of everyone growing apart in ideas. Or maybe each star in the sky represents a refugee. Families are scattered from each other and this is shown above. We see that some stars are still shining brightly so there is hope. Or you could see each star as someone who has died – we must remember them. We notice that Omar often thinks of his parents when he sees the stars – it is his only connection to them in the refugee camp. Maybe the stars are a vision of Omar's perfect world.
>
> (James, Ahmed, Ellie, Noah, Adam, Hannah and Miremba)

Their thoughtful voices ring out, demonstrating the impact of well-chosen texts, mediated with an openness to their views and perspectives and guided by their teacher. By the end of the term, 17 of Sarah's class said that they chose to read out of school and more than half of these chose graphic novels as their preferred format. They reported new kinds of enjoyment experienced by reading which echo the forms of successful engagement outlined earlier: an appreciation of being represented; the enjoyment of critical and empathetic thought, achieved by slowing down; and the pleasure of fully accessing a text right to the end. Their more positive dispositions towards reading were strengthened by and contributed to their social connection to one another in the emerging reading community. Partly as a result of this work, graphic novels and more Own Voices texts were added to the whole school reading diet. Yusuf has now discovered two texts with his name in them: *October, October* by Katya Balen and Angela Harding and *Mayhem Mission* by Burhana Islam and Farrah Khandaker. For the children who have not yet found their name in a book, personalised digital texts are an option (Kucirkova, 2021).

Improving subject knowledge of children's texts

In addition to the strategies used by Sarah and Richard, we offer some additional suggestions. You could:

- Shadow children's book awards – the UKLA children's book award (Judged by teachers), and Carnegie and Kate Greenaway medals all give teachers (and children) the opportunity to shadow the judging process. This involves reading, discussing and reviewing the shortlisted books.
- Join an OU/UKLA Teachers' Reading Group – free, evidence-based CPD focused on the understanding and supporting of Reading for Pleasure in schools. There are over 100 groups across the UK annually.
- Read to your height in books – challenge yourself over the year or take the 52-book challenge with your class.
- Create an Alphabet of Authors – and read them all. This idea can be expanded by adding different genres or types of books.
- Organise teachers' book swaps – within one school or across a group of schools.

- Share children's texts as an agenda item in staff meetings – this demonstrates the value placed on this and gives teachers an opportunity to share their knowledge, recommend briefly or red an extract to tempt others.
- Audit your own practice and knowledge – use surveys and questionnaires like Richard uses.

It is not just teachers but also librarians who are key in supporting children to choose appropriate and engaging texts and any of these suggestions could be used by librarians also. Teachers' knowledge of children's texts can additionally be developed through their relationship with authors and illustrators. You could seek out online resources of authors reading their books aloud, through exploring Book Trusts lists, school visits, or engaging with the Patron of Reading initiative.

Conclusion

In order to support children to be confident and engaged readers who choose to read in their own time, Reading Teachers, like Sarah and Richard work hard to develop a good knowledge of children's literature and other texts. As Cremin (2021: 7) has argued

> Teachers have a professional, social and moral responsibility to keep up to date with contemporary children's books and need a strong working knowledge of the 'old and gold' from yesteryear as well.

These classics can sit alongside contemporary texts, enriched by your knowledge of many different types of children's texts including non-fiction, poetry, comics, magazines and digital texts. The ability to critically analyse existing book lists for texts which may be accessible and engaging to your particular class each year is key. By auditing your subject knowledge, you will be able to identify where gaps lie and can work to set yourself reading challenges to help you become a more effective educator. Your knowledge can be developed further through becoming a part of a community of readers, whether that is within your own school, with teachers locally, online or in person.

Teachers' subject knowledge needs to go beyond this however, to developing as Reading Teachers. Many researchers have found that there is a relationship between teachers' identification of themselves as readers (or not) and their use of successful social RfP pedagogy (Commeyras, Bisplinghoff and Olson, 2003; Cremin, Mottram, Collins, Powell and Safford, 2014; Garces-Bacsal, Tupas, Kaur, Paculdar and Baja, 2018). The more teachers read themselves, and share something of themselves as readers, and the wider and deeper their knowledge of children's literature and other texts (as well as their knowledge of the children as readers) the better they are positioned to develop a love of reading in the young. So, Reading Teachers need to be committed to continually improving their repertoires of children's texts and to developing their pedagogy and skills. This will enable them to open up relevant and engaging texts that help children connect and entice them to want to keep on reading.

Recommended reading

CLPE (2021) *Reflecting Realities Research*. Available at: https://clpe.org.uk/research/reflecting-realities

Kucirkova, N. and Cremin, T. (2020) *Children Reading for Pleasure in the Digital Age: Mapping Reader Engagement*. London: Sage.

Meyer, C. K. and Jiménez, L. M. (2017) Using every word and image: Framing graphic novel instruction in the expanded four resources model. *Journal of Adolescent & Adult Literacy*, 61(2): 153–161.

Open University. *Reading for Pleasure: Teachers' Knowledge of Children's Literature and Other Texts*. Available at: https://ourfp.org/finding/teachers-knowledge-of-childrens-literature-and-other-texts/

Children's books

Antrobus, R. (2018) Dear hearing world. In *The Perseverance*. London: Penned in the Margins.
Antrobus, R. and Dunbar, P. (2021) *Can Bears Ski?* London: Walker Books.
Balen, K. and Harding, A. (2020) *October, October*. London: Knights of.
Catchpole, J. and George, K. (2021) *What Happened to You?* London: Faber & Faber.
Islam, B. and Khandaker, F. (2021) *Mayhem Mission*. London: Knights of.
Jamieson, V. and Mohamed, O. (2020) *When Stars are Scattered*. New York: Dial Books.
Jeffers, O. (2017) *Here We Are: Notes for Living on Planet Earth*. London: HarperCollins Children's Books.
Nova, K. (2017) *Rhythm and Poetry*. Silsden: Caboodle Books Ltd.
Rauf, O. Q. (2018) *The Boy at the Back of the Class*. London: Orion Children's Books.
Rundell, K. (2020) *The Book of Hopes*. London: Bloomsbury Children's Books.
Thompson, L. and Qualls, S. (2015) *Emmanuel's Dream: The True Story of Emmanuel Ofosu Yeboah*. New York: Schwarts & Wade.

References

Best, E., Clark, C. and Picton, I. (2020) *Seeing Yourself in What You Read: Diversity and Children and Young People's Reading in 2020*. London: National Literacy Trust.
Bishop, R. S. (1990) Mirrors, windows, and sliding glass doors. *Perspectives: Choosing and Using Books for the Classroom*, 6: 3.
Boerman-Cornell, W. and Kim, J. (2020) *Using Graphic Novels in the English Language Arts Classroom*. London: Bloomsbury.
Chambers, A. (2011) *Tell Me: Children, Reading and Talk*. Stroud: Thimble Press.
Clark, C. and Teravainen, A. (2015) *Teachers and Literacy: Their Perceptions, Understanding, Confidence and Awareness*. London: National Literacy Trust.
CLPE (2020) *Reflecting Realities: Survey of Ethnic Representation within UK Children's Literature 2019*. Available at: https://clpe.org.uk/RR
CLPE (2021) *Reflecting Realities: Survey of Ethnic Representation within UK Children's Literature 2020*. Available at: https://clpe.org.uk/research/reflecting-realities
Collins, F. (2014) Teachers' knowledge and use of children's literature. In T. Cremin, M. Mottram, F. Collins, S. Powell and K. Safford (Eds.), *Building Communities of Engaged Readers: Reading for Pleasure*, pp. 35–51. London: Routledge.
Commeyras, M., Bisplinghoff, B. S. and Olson, J. (2003) *Teachers as Readers*. New York: International Literacy Association.
Cremin, T. (2021) Building reading communities. In A. Gill, J. Stephenson and D. Waugh (Eds.), *Developing a Love of Reading and Books*, pp. 5–18. London: Learning Matters, Sage.
Cremin, T., Bearne, E., Mottram, M. and Goodwin, P. (2008) Primary teachers as readers. *English in Education*, 42(1): 1–16. ISSN: 0425 0494.
Cremin, T., Mottram, M., Bearne, E. and Goodwin, P. (2009) Exploring teachers' knowledge of children's literature. *Cambridge Journal of Education*, 38(4): 449–464.
Cremin, T., Mottram, M., Collins, F., Powell, S. and Safford, K. (2014) *Building Communities of Engaged Readers*. London: Routledge.
Empathy Lab (2020) *Report on Empathy Lab's Education Programme in Wales 2019–2020*. Available at: www.empathylab.uk/blog/empathy-education-our-latest-report
Garces-Bacsal, R. M., Tupas, R., Kaur, S., Paculdar, A. M. and Baja, E. S. (2018) Reading for pleasure: Whose job is it to build lifelong readers in the classroom? *Literacy*, 52(2): 95–102.

Husband, T. (2019) Using multicultural picture books to promote racial justice in urban early childhood literacy classrooms. *Urban Education*, 54(8): 1058–1084. https://doi.org/10.1177/00420 85918805145

Kleekamp, M. and Zapata, A. (2018) Interrogating Depictions of Disability in Children's Picturebooks. *The Reading Teacher*, 72(5): 589–597. https://ila.onlinelibrary.wiley.com/journal/19362714

Kucirkova, N. (2021) The educational power – and the limits – of personalized children's books. *Scientific American*. Available at: www.scientificamerican.com/article/the-educational-power-mdash-and-the-limits-mdash-of-personalized-children-rsquo-s-books/

Kucirkova, N. and Cremin, T. (2020) *Children Reading for Pleasure in the Digital Age: Mapping Reader Engagement*. London: Sage.

Merga, M. K. (2017) What would make children read for pleasure more frequently? *English in Education*, 51(2): 207–223.

Pantaleo, S. (2020) Slow looking: 'Reading picturebooks takes time'. *Literacy*, 54(1): 40–48.

Smith, J. M. and Pole, K. (2018) What's going on in a graphic novel? *The Reading Teacher*, 72(2): 169–177.

Thomas, E. (2019) *The Dark Fantastic*. New York: New York University Press.

Tour, E. (2017) Teachers' personal learning networks (PLNs): Exploring the nature of self-initiated professional learning online. *Literacy*, 51(1): 11–18.

Chapter 2

Digital books enriching children's literacy lives

Natalia Kucirkova, Nigel Lungenmuss-Ward and Nicola Mansfield-Neimi

Introduction

Stories frame our lives and stories captured in a book form are the frames holding our own and others' stories. Since Gutenberg's invention of the printing press in the 1440s, authors and publishers have been perfecting the quality of story frames. Fast forward to 2021 and there is a wide array of print books, digital books, hybrid and virtual books to choose from, offering a diverse collection of formats. With children's stories in particular, there has been a great progress to the forms and formats over the years. Some e-books do not contain only images and texts but they also engage children with sounds and interactive elements. Such digital books (sometimes called e-books or electronic books) can be shared, copied, edited, remade into different stories within the matter of seconds and enjoyed anytime, anywhere. Without a doubt, the advent of portable, internet-equipped technologies, has changed the nature of stories and the traditional definition of their frames. This change has been rarely considered from teachers' perspectives.

In this chapter, Nigel and Nicola share their experiences, reflections and struggles with digital books, with the intention to inspire fellow practitioners to develop their own practices for e-book use. There is currently no national professional development

DOI: 10.4324/9781003215615-5

training on e-book use. During the Covid-19 pandemic and the almost overnight switch to digital teaching, teachers had no choice but to learn 'on the go' how to read children's stories on and with screens. Digital books became the substitute for physical books that many children didn't have at home. The experience exposed the large gap in professional training concerning digital Reading for Pleasure (RfP). While any teacher can easily download free e-books on their device, the key consideration concerns the ways in which they can be used in a pedagogically sound manner that expands children's learning. These Reading Teachers' vignettes provide examples for how e-books can be incorporated into everyday practice and how they can benefit individual children's RfP and the classroom reading culture. However, before we move to 'how' teachers might use digital books, we need to answer the question of 'why' this might matter for the children in their classrooms. A short review of literature on the benefits of e-books is particularly important given that many parents, as well as teachers, worry that digital books will replace children's print-based reading and that this substitution will decrease the value of RfP. There tends to be a polarising debate between reading on screen and reading on paper, with the two formats perceived as standing in competition with each other. This, however, is not how what our work shows. As we outline next, digital and paper books have distinct benefits for different types of readers and reading purposes.

The benefits of digital books

There are concerns in some quarters that children will lose interest in print books if they are exposed to digital books from a young age or that they will apply skim reading strategies that are often associated with online reading when they read print materials (Wolf, 2018). We do not have longitudinal data to corroborate these concerns, but there are some studies that experimentally compared the value gained and the value lost of children's reading on paper versus reading digitally. A meta-analysis (Furenes, Kucirkova and Bus, 2021) that summarised these experiments offered two important insights.

First, the design of digital books is a crucial factor in establishing their benefits and limitations. E-books that are badly designed with many interactive features and distracting mini-games take children's attention away from the story, thus impeding their story comprehension. With such e-books, print books are a much better alternative. On the other hand, when the e-book enhancements are of good quality, such as e-books with dictionaries that explain unknown words to children during reading, they outperform print books. Children's vocabulary learning can be thus enhanced with such e-books better than with print books but these need to contain embedded dictionaries without any other, potentially distracting, features.

The meta-analysis also found that the advantage of e-books over print books is greater for children from lower socio-economic backgrounds, who typically have fewer print books at home and less history of reading in their families. For these children, digital books provide significant added value both for children's story comprehension and vocabulary learning (Furenes et al., 2021). Although studies with children with special educational needs are not as many, those that have examined the impact of e-books show significant benefits for children at risk of learning disability (Shamir, Korat and Fellah, 2012), children with Special Language Impairment (Korat, Graister and Altman, 2019) and children with poor letter knowledge (Rvachew, Rees, Carolan and Nadig, 2017). In light of these findings, researchers recommend focusing on the quality of digital books and a careful assessment of how the e-books' specific features expand the reading experiences for individual children. Researchers refer to this as the 3Cs framework and encourage the focus on the:

- Context of reading (for example is it happening in the home or classroom);
- Content of reading (for example are children reading fiction or non-fiction);
- Child (for example is the individual child an avid or reluctant reader).

Given that digital books are of specific benefit to children from disadvantaged backgrounds and children with special needs, supporting digital reading is often about supporting children who need teachers' support most. Furthermore, as many children and teachers experienced during the Covid-19 pandemic, digital books can be easily accessed on families' smartphone devices and they often facilitate reading in homes where print books are not available. As such, digital books can motivate learning environments that are inclusive and supportive for all readers.

Using digital books to motivate reluctant readers

Aware of this potential, Nicola was keen to develop creative literacy practices that would engage reluctant readers in e-reading. She worked with a group of reluctant readers across a year, in various stages. She began by probing gently and carefully, what types of texts the children did enjoy reading. She observed that while the children understood the language and comprehended the story plot, they struggle immersing themselves into the story. The feeling of getting lost in a book was foreign to these children and Nicola thought of several strategies to support children to find the 'escape feeling' of storybooks. Proficient readers often experience the feeling of flow when they are deeply immersed in a story and Nicola was keen to facilitate this experience with her group of reluctant readers. She came up with the idea of using graphic novels to spark children's interest in a story with images as well as words. Accessing graphic novels on iPads could open up even more doors for meaning-making, Nicola thought, as these could add the layer of engagement through direct interactivity and touch. In pursuing these ideas, Nicola structured some special reading sessions with her group of reluctant readers. She scheduled regular weekly meetings with them where they discussed books and reading, and these conversations enabled her to provide the group with books that matched their interests.

Graphic novels proved to be successful with the group: once the children received their print copies, the buzz about books started. They began swapping the books among them and discussing what they had thought and found funny. It was clear that it was the content of the story, and its specific layout in short texts and images, that sparked children's interest. Interestingly, when Nicola asked the group whether they enjoyed reading their books, they needed to pause as they did not immediately associate the enjoyable experience with reading. When questioned further, it transpired that they simply didn't view it as reading, it was far less taxing then the traditional read and more enjoyable than they had previously found it. Nicola decided to capitalise on the momentum and take it further with digital graphic novels. She expected that the children would be even more engaged when accessing such content on devices they were familiar with and that this would offer them additional engagement options. Nicola's anticipations proved to be correct: the children were enthralled with their novels. Whilst all children enjoyed the graphic novels in their print version, the group was more enthusiastic about reading them in the digital format.

The pedagogical implications

There are two important pedagogical points that can be derived from this example. First, identifying a group of children and their specific needs and interests helps with the identification of the right reading content. Nicola's strategic focus on a group of reluctant readers was central to setting in motion some helpful peer dynamics. The children could talk about their favourite graphic novels, exchange ideas and 'infect' each other with their enthusiasm. This added to the experience and created a sense of a mini-community of shared reading enjoyment. Second, the introduction to graphic novels first in print followed by the digital format allowed for scaffolding children's experience with gradual intensity of content representation. The possibility to first experience their favourite stories on paper, in images and texts, was further expanded with a digital version of the stories, in a higher resolution of images that could be enlarged as children wished, with voice-overs reading the texts aloud. This gradual engagement of individual senses ensured that the children were not overwhelmed by the experience, but rather were further stimulated and engaged in the reading. They thus achieved the unique feeling of reading immersion that Nicola had originally envisaged.

With her classroom experiment, Nicola found out what researchers have documented in their studies: namely, that when digital books are well-chosen and well-used, they can positively amplify a child's reading experience (see for example Schugar, Smith and Schugar, 2013). Children need both print and digital books and the two formats complement each other in offering a rich repertoire to young readers. It is not the book format but rather the combination of the quality of content and the purpose of reading for individual children that determine how children engage with the books and how they benefit from them (Courage, 2019). Furthermore, the group aspect was important to the positive reading experience. The more reading for pleasure happens as a collective and shared experience, the more children experience the power of reading communities and begin to perceive themselves as readers. Nigel capitalised on this understanding and approached the use of digital books in his classroom with the community idea in mind.

Using digital books to expand reading communities

Nigel's idea for an online reading community arose from two observations: first, he was aware of the impact the pandemic had had, with children feeling isolated and missing the daily blether about books he would normally have with them in the classroom. He was also aware, from discussions with the children's parents and caregivers, that the children would benefit from an online book club that would be safe for them to participate in and that would be managed by a knowledgeable teacher they could trust.

The structure for Nigel's online book club was simple: he contacted all the 7- to 11-year-olds with the invitation to meet for a book blether online, for an hour each week. What was more challenging was the choice of books that children would discuss at these weekly gatherings. On one hand, Nigel wanted to engage children by giving them a choice of texts they read. As Cambria and Guthrie (2010) point out, text choices are important factors in motivating children to initiate and sustain reading and Nigel wanted to honour children's choices. On the other hand, with a large array of children's books and e-books available on the market, Nigel wanted to prevent children going down the rabbit hole and getting overwhelmed with the choices available to them. He decided to offer children a controlled, or constrained, choice of texts. To ensure that his collection of texts is age appropriate and of high quality, he purchased the books shortlisted by that year's UKLA Book Awards in the 7–10+ category.

He sourced the digital versions of the books from his local Online Library (through the free Libby App that is used by many local and national libraries) and he purchased those that were not freely available through the Amazon Kindle app. Once the reading resources were in place, Nigel thought of ways of engaging children in a book-focused dialogue that would expand their literate identities. Drawing on research that shows how children's direct involvement and control in technology use enhance motivation (Scardamalia and Bereiter, 1991), he decided to position the children as the co-creators of the book club. Therefore, rather than presenting the children with a ready-made plan for the sessions, Nigel asked the children how they would like to run *their* book club. The children began chatting and enthusiastically share ideas. A simple online meeting turned into a focused discussion, in small groups and in a large group, with a lot of buzz and occasional laughter, more in alignment with the definition of a 'club' than an online meeting. Nigel and the children quickly realised that such brainstorming is a great way to involve everyone in the running of the club, and they decided to have room for a chat at the start of each book club session. They also came up with the idea of book-related quizzes, which could expand their chat to authors and stories that they were not all familiar with.

During the weekly sessions, after the children had each checked in, Nigel set about reading the text. He made himself available during the readings in that he encouraged children to comment on what they read and offered his own views. He introduced these micro-chats after the children had read a few chapters and made sure they were not too intrusive for the reading flow. Sometimes the micro-chats would last for five minutes and at other times the children had nothing to say at all, and Nigel emphasised that both were fine. However, making sure that all children contributed to the session and felt equally confident to read aloud, was initially a challenge. Jasmine in the group was very shy and told Nigel that she didn't feel confident enough to read in front of the other children. Over time, however, this girl became more comfortable with the group and in the final session, she overcame her fears and read a page for the group.

There were seven sessions in total and the children showed up every week for all seven, eager to talk with their fellow readers. They participated enthusiastically in the book discussions, often with predictions about what would happen to the story characters of their chosen text. The children also enjoyed the quizzes at the end of the sessions: Erica remarked the book quizzes were her favourite part of the session. The possibility to read the digital texts at their own pace and on their own devices at home, seemed to make a difference to children's reading confidence. In addition, the fact that all children could see the text on the screen and follow along with the narration, facilitated their reading comprehension. Although one book was only available as a PDF version of the print copy, the children were engaged in reading it on the screen, fully focused on the story plot. Such is the power of a good story – even if the format is not ideal, readers are gripped by the story plot and the story characters.

Upon reflection, Nigel realised that it was the combination of the technology, the story affordances and the power of the book club community that made a difference to children's engagement in the sessions. Certainly, the supportive community enabled all readers to feel confident to read the text by the end of the seven sessions. Nigel wrote into his reflective diary:

I felt the text captured the children, but it was also the environment and interactions that the children had, which enabled everyone to feel comfortable, valued and part of our reading community.

Nigel's reflections mirror those of other teachers and researchers who engaged in establishing or evaluating online book clubs. The common pedagogical principles that have emerged from these efforts centre on two main aspects: first, for a sustained reading engagement, children need to position as co-creators of the online community, and, second, teachers' support in creating and curating an online book club is essential for its success.

The pedagogical implications

Positioning children as agents of their learning is important for all activities, including that of reading, whether this happens on screen or off screen, as an individual or collective activity. As research has shown children's perceptions of control facilitate their reading engagement in stories (Vieira and Grantham, 2011) children's sense of control and ownership of a digital book club adds to their interest in participating in it and shaping it with their own reading choices.

While most research on children's agency in technology use has been focused on individual digital books or literacy apps rather than online communities (Kucirkova, 2018), parallel engagement patterns can be observed with online platforms too. In particular, children's sense of direct contribution to how the sessions are structured is comparable to their direct involvement in discussing a digital book. The more the conversation messages are synchronous, empathic and multimodal (for example enhanced with emojis), the more a conversation is perceived of higher social presence, and this is associated with higher social support (Petrocchi, Marciano, Annoni and Camerini, 2020). The dialogue possibilities in an online book club are expanded with multimedia language options, such as emojis, chats and a combination of text, audio and video, which might further stimulate conversation. There is no need for teachers to master diverse modalities for communication (such as texting or emoji language) – the teachers' role is to facilitate, not dominate, the conversation. Indeed, as shown by Nigel, a teacher's role in a successful book club is best described as that of a supporting reading buddy and conversational partner. As a Reading Teacher, Nigel had read the book, listened to others' views and shared his own. A member of the group, he was journeying through the book club as a co-reader, not as a hierarchically positioned teacher. Similarly to Nicola, Nigel reflected on his reading practice and modelled his reading behaviour by being congruent in the moment and allowing the children to see his reactions as the action unfolded. He also deliberately asked open ended questions to make it seem like there was no right or wrong answers, only predictions.

We all have adapted to the mobile reading culture, in that we access texts in print and digital, depending on where and what we read. We took this experience with us to the teaching and research practice, in which we do not draw strong boundaries between digital and print but rather between high-quality and low-quality reading, or reading that expands our thinking and reading that does not. This, we believe, is a more salient distinction than that linked to the reading format only.

Teachers' role with digital books

Teachers do not only introduce but also socialise children into the world of fiction and non-fiction and this process involves teaching the importance of print and digital reading formats. Reading Teachers' positive attitudes towards digital reading and online book conversations influence the extent to which young readers perceive them as positive. A cycle of positive mutual influence develops when teachers, together with other children, discuss the books they read, both in terms of content, context of their reading and the books' resonance with their individual lives. A lot can be achieved in a supportive community, as we saw in Nigel's example, the confidence of a shy reader can be boosted. In addition, crowdsourcing feedback on a specific digital book, whether positive or negative, can lead to engagement with the e-book's author or developer. At times it can even lead to the e-book's actual improvement. This possibility is a unique potential of digital books in that they can be more dynamically adapted and revised than their print equivalents. Designers and developers can be brought into the conversation and build on the readers' feedback to improve the design, something colleagues and I experienced when developing the Our Story app and designing the What Is That iBook for children. Alternatively, teachers and children can amend the design of digital books as their co-authors, co-illustrators or co-designers. When researchers are brought into such a partnership, Research, Practice and Development of e-books become part of one process focused on enriching children's digital reading (Kucirkova, 2016). I saw in my own work that when these different stakeholders come together as one community, they can significantly advance the quality of digital books available to young children. The International Collective of Children's Digital Books aims to enable the connections between researchers, teachers and e-book designers; it welcomes anyone interested in children's e-books and currently has members from more than 20 countries. With its inclusive approach to digital reading, the Collective is a good example of how children's digital books can bring together diverse communities of children and adults. It was established to support the community's interests but also to respond to a pressing need: the low educational quality of e-books currently available to young children.

Improving the educational quality of children's digital books

Both Nigel's and Nicola's examples made it clear that teachers need to make discerned choices about the digital books they offer young children. Positive reading effects can be reached only if the digital books are of high quality and unfortunately, the current most popular digital books offered to young children are of low educational quality (Sari, Takacs and Bus, 2019). Researchers have been lobbying for more interest in improving the quality of children's e-books since their appearance on the book market in early 2010 and, unfortunately, the situation has not improved much over the last decade (Korat and Falk, 2019). The reasons are multiple and include the lack of support of national government organisations into e-book development in local languages, as well as lack of professional development training for authors and publishers in developing high-quality digital books. Given the low threshold for entering the digital 'bookshops' on Apple and Google Play market, many children's digital books get published without any educational oversight of their value. The commercial interest of Apple and Google is reflected in placing e-books alongside children's entertainment media, this is dominated by large entertainment companies who provide content familiar to mass market, such as Disney or Peppa Pig. So highly creative e-books and niche productions are unlikely to make it to the top of the charts. Therefore, Nigel's strategy of relying on expert reviews and reputable awards in selecting e-books is very important.

Hoel and Jernes (2020) investigated the use of digital books in Norwegian classrooms and developed an easy-to-use evaluation framework of children's digital books for teachers. Based on their research, they encourage teachers to download the digital book first and answer some questions for themselves in a short questionnaire. The questionnaire is intended as a reflection prompt about the match between the specific title and the purpose of the classroom session, as well as the specific characteristics of children who will access the book. The questionnaire does not provide direct recommendations, but it generates some considerations for teachers to make before they let children browse the book. The English version of the digital version of the questionnaire is freely available from the VEBB project website.

Another strategy for ensuring good content is to focus on e-books that have been pre-selected by reliable committees as Nigel has done. Even more, teachers can adopt the judging criteria used by judges of book awards and thus establish whether a given title meets the highest quality standards. Teachers can become directly involved as judges of children's digital books by participating in the annual United Kingdom literacy Association Children's Digital Book Award. If they choose to participate, they need to commit to using a shortlist of digital books in their classrooms and provide their verdict on the books within three months. Teachers who took part in the judging process before reported not only increased knowledge of children's digital books but also children's enthusiasm around their use, especially when the children's views on the titles were solicited as part of the evaluation process.

Future directions

As the design of children's media gets more sophisticated, the possibilities to cater for individual profiles of readers become more realistic. Notably, the use of personal data and adaptive algorithms allows for dynamic adjustment of content in relation to pre-established reading profiles (for example based on the students' reading scores supplied to the system). While the use of personal data needs to be treated with extra caution to avoid the exploitative nature of targeted advertising already present in many adult digital media, it offers a genuine possibility to support the reading process through personalised feedback and personalised reading motivation techniques. For example, a digital reading system could recommend to children reading titles based on their own interests as well as titles based on the school curriculum and/or family history. The reading difficulty could be gradually advancing as the young person progresses in selecting and reading the individual titles.

Another exciting possibility that teachers might consider is to combine multimedia with print and connect reading of various media through one story arc. For instance, internet of toys could employ more strategically the use of texts and use print texts together with apps for augmented reality experiences that bring story characters to live. For example, Mobybou is a storytelling platform that allows children to interact with digital content through the manipulation of physical blocks. It is such features that make e-books an enriching and novel experience in reading and that pave the way for preferred reading futures.

Conclusion

In conclusion, to achieve educational objectives, a close collaboration with teachers, educational professionals, librarians and literacy researchers is essential. Designers need to collaborate with children's authors and illustrators to achieve a synergy between innovative content and innovative format of story representation. Furthermore, collaboration with families is vital. Teachers, together with parents, act as gatekeepers when it comes to facilitating children's access to reading materials. Digital books can be a great way for bridging home-school reading cultures and diversifying the content children access. For example, illustrations and images can be supplied by children and voice-overs, especially those in foreign languages, supplied by parents. Another exciting possibility is to collaborate with teachers who can contribute ideas for content. During the pandemic, several families and teachers created their own digital books about the corona virus and their experiences of the lockdown. Sharing the digital books online was an emotional experience for both the young and old, across borders and across screens. The future of children's digital reading is bright if adults and children join forces in sharing authentic stories as one community.

Recommended reading

Gamble, N. and Yates, S. (2002) *Exploring Children's Literature: Teaching the Language and Reading of Fiction*, 1st ed. London: SAGE Publications (CA).
The International Collective of Children's Digital Books. Available at: www.childrensdigitalbooks.com/
Kucirkova, N. (2018) *How and Why to Read and Create Children's Digital Books: A Guide for Primary Practitioners*. London: UCL Press.
The UKLA Children's Digital Book Award Scheme. Available at: https://ourfp.org/research/page/ou-ukla-digital-book-award

References

Cambria, J. and Guthrie, J. T. (2010) Motivating and engaging students in reading. *New England Reading Association Journal*, 46(1): 16–30.
Courage, M. L. (2019) From print to digital: The medium is only part of the message. In *Reading in the Digital Age: Young Children's Experiences with E-books*, pp. 23–43. Cham: Springer.
Furenes, M. I., Kucirkova, N. and Bus, A. G. (2021) A comparison of children's reading on paper versus screen: A meta-analysis. *Review of Educational Research*, 91(4): 483–517.
Hoel, T. and Jernes, M. (2020) Samtalebasert lesing av bildebok-apper: Barnehagelærer versus hotspoter. *Norsk pedagogisk tidsskrift*, 104(2): 121–133.
Korat, O. and Falk, Y. (2019) Ten years after: Revisiting the question of e-book quality as early language and literacy support. *Journal of Early Childhood Literacy*, 19(2): 206–223.
Korat, O., Graister, T. and Altman, C. (2019) Contribution of reading an e-book with a dictionary to word learning: Comparison between kindergarteners with and without SLI. *Journal of Communication Disorders*, 79: 90–102.
Kucirkova, N. (2016) iRPD-A framework for guiding design-based research for iPad apps. *British Journal of Educational Technology*, 48(2): 598–610.
Kucirkova, N. (2018) Personalised learning with digital technologies at home and school: Where is children's agency? In *Mobile Technologies in Children's Language and Literacy*. London: Emerald Publishing Limited.
Petrocchi, S., Marciano, L., Annoni, A. M. and Camerini, A. L. (2020) 'What you say and how you say it' matters: An experimental evidence of the role of synchronicity, modality, and message valence during smartphone-mediated communication. *PLoS ONE*, 15(9): e0237846.

Rvachew, S., Rees, K., Carolan, E. and Nadig, A. (2017) Improving emergent literacy with school-based shared reading: Paper versus ebooks. *International Journal of Child-Computer Interaction*, 12: 24–29.

Sari, B., Takacs, Z. K. and Bus, A. G. (2019) What are we downloading for our children? Best-selling children's apps in four European countries. *Journal of Early Childhood Literacy*, 19(4): 515–532.

Scardamalia, M. and Bereiter, C. (1991) Higher levels of agency for children in knowledge building: A challenge for the design of new knowledge media. *The Journal of the Learning Sciences*, 1(1): 37–68.

Schugar, H. R., Smith, C. A. and Schugar, J. T. (2013) Teaching with interactive picture e-books in grades K–6. *The Reading Teacher*, 66(8): 615–624.

Shamir, A., Korat, O. and Fellah, R. (2012) Promoting vocabulary, phonological awareness and concept about print among children at risk for learning disability: Can e-books help? *Reading and Writing*, 25(1): 45–69.

Vieira, E. and Grantham, S. (2011) Perceptions of control facilitate reading engagement. *Reading Psychology*, 32: 322–348.

Wolf, M. (2018) *Reader, Come Home: The Reading Brain in a Digital World*. New York: Harper.

Chapter 3

Exploring gender and reading for pleasure

Amelia Hempel-Jorgensen, Tom Brassington and Megan Dixon

Introduction

Gender inequality affects many classrooms in contemporary primary schools. This chapter focuses on gender differences in Reading for Pleasure (RfP), why they occur and the implications for children's engagement with reading. In particular, it discusses how and why girls and boys may engage with RfP to different extents and with different types of texts. These inequalities matter because readers' engagement and the frequency with which they read impacts on educational attainment (Sullivan and Brown, 2013), in addition to well-being and identity formation (Rothbauer, 2004). Likewise, the type of texts children choose to read (e.g. whether fiction or non-fiction), also has an effect on educational outcomes (Jerrim and Moss, 2019). The more a child reads for pleasure, the better their reading skills become and vice versa; there is a bidirectional relationship between reading will and skill (Morgan and Fuchs, 2007). There are potentially many reasons why different children engage minimally with RfP, although, when it comes to gender, boys are known to engage less than girls internationally and historically (OECD, 2010a). However, girls may also experience inequality and this chapter focuses on boys who rarely choose to read for pleasure and girls who are engaged readers but do not engage with

DOI: 10.4324/9781003215615-6

non-fiction and therefore miss out on the specific benefits of this text type. The chapter discusses the issues around these RfP gender inequalities through case studies by Megan Dixon and Tom Brassington, both Reading Teachers.

Gender is understood as socially constructed and the differences between girls and boys as readers are therefore shaped by social structures, beliefs and practices. Differences between boys' and girls' reading attitudes and practices are thus due to dominant beliefs that boys or girls should conform to certain characteristics or behaviours (McGeown, Goodwin, Henderson and Wright, 2012). For example, reading is often seen as a more feminine activity and may therefore be viewed as a more acceptable practice for girls than for boys. Stereotypes about girls and boys can have a powerful effect on children as readers; in their research, Jones and Myhill (2004) found that teachers held stereotypes of girl readers as high achieving and compliant, and boys as underachieving and troublesome. This influenced their interactions and their teaching practices with both boys and girls as readers. Teachers' perceptions, which may be based on stereotypes, can have a notable effect on children's self-perceptions as readers and their engagement with reading. To understand gender reading differences and inequalities we therefore need to understand wider societal constructions of gender, as well as more local attitudes and relationships, including in classrooms.

Why do boys engage less with RfP?

It has been argued that boys' lower engagement with RfP is because reading for enjoyment is seen to be at odds with dominant ideas about masculinity and is more in line with feminine gender roles (McGeown et al., 2012). One of the key differences found in this research between girls and boys as readers relates to the motivation to read including: curiosity and interest, the enjoyment of texts and deeper immersion in reading. These were all seen as feminine characteristics by their study participants. Children can internalise such stereotypes, shaping their gender identities and in turn their reading attitudes and behaviours. This could be a reason why boys are less motivated to read and are therefore less engaged with RfP. Previous research reviewed by McGeown et al. (2012) also highlights the role of gender identity in reading engagement.

Another reason for gender differences in engagement is how reading is supported and taught in schools. A study carried out in four primary schools found that boys' lower engagement with reading, compared with girls, was due to their different response to school reading curricula (Moss, 2007). Boys disengaged particularly from reading fiction texts because these were overtly banded by reading ability and the boys didn't want their place in the ability hierarchy to be visible to others. They therefore chose non-fiction texts which were not ability banded. This was in contrast to girls who were much more willing to engage with fiction and were not discouraged by their position in the ability hierarchy being on display to their peers. A further explanation also related to school reading curricula is that boys have different reading interests to girls and that schools' reading curricula cater more for girls in terms of reading materials (Clark, 2012). Again, this may be related to the perception that reading is primarily a feminine activity.

It is likely that both gender identities and stereotypes, and school reading curricula and teaching practices, influence boys' lower engagement levels. Hempel-Jorgensen and Cremin (under review) found that teachers' perceptions of children's multiple social identities (gender, social class and ethnicity) had a significant effect on their teaching practices and interactions with children. Some teachers had negative perceptions of boys of colour from working class backgrounds as readers, and this affected their teaching practices and impacted negatively on the boys' engagement with reading.

Reading Teachers

Reading Teachers (Cremin, Mottram, Collins, Powell and Safford, 2014), through their understanding of reading and children's literature, can have a positive effect on children's development as readers and engagement with RfP. Tom describes his approach:

> As a teacher who reads, I consider it a key part of my role to be aware not only of how often or how well a child reads, but also what it is they choose. In my experience, once you know a child as a reader, you begin to build up a picture of their likes and dislikes. This, coupled with a broad knowledge of age-appropriate children's literature, enables a teacher to recommend and encourage children to trial new books or experiment with a different genre.

Here Tom describes his role in relation to supporting children in choosing books, but what is also important about being a Reading Teacher is how he learns from his own experience of being a reader. This includes how to talk about reading and discuss texts in a way that interests children and engages them as readers. This will become clearer in Tom's case study.

For the purposes of this chapter, Tom, a class teacher, and Megan, a head teacher, were invited to observe gender patterns to reading in their schools' contexts, to identify any patterns of concern and design a way to change this. Tom, who identified gender patterns related to girls' choice of text types, describes his school context as follows:

> Within my class of 7- to 8-year-olds, there are 26 children, an even split of male and female learners. Our school's strategic focus (post-pandemic) holds RfP as a core thread because of its importance for children's educational success.
>
> Our trifold aim is to ensure children:
>
> - Have access to books that they enjoy;
> - Have access to books from a wide range of authorship and genre;
> - Have the freedom to be able to develop their own RfP habits.
>
> It is our school's hope that, by placing RfP as central to our vision for the students in our care, we will develop readers for life who embrace a wide range of literature and thus open themselves up to different worlds of opportunity.

Megan focused on the relationship between the will and the skill to read, particularly in relation to the intertwining of engagement and skill in reading. She describes her chosen context:

> This case study is in a secondary school with 11- to 12-year-olds in a low socio-economic area in the North West of England. The library is well stocked with a range of fiction, non-fiction, graphic novels and other interesting reading materials.

The school has been working hard on providing high quality books and book clubs for all children.

Fostering girls' engagement with non-fiction

Turning to Tom's classroom, whilst girls are less often identified as experiencing reading inequalities than boys, he observed them almost only choosing to read fiction at the expense of non-fiction. Tom describes his process of observation and reflection on what might influence the girls' choices.

> Regularly in my classroom, I will give opportunity for the children to read freely, with a range of reading materials available. Book blankets (where a range of texts are spread out on a blanket for children to browse and discuss) are a great way for readers to browse the class collection, supporting later choices. During Spring term 2021, I observed in my class a pattern of reading behaviour that seemed almost exclusively linked to gender. Given the free choice of fiction or non-fiction, only 15% of the girls in my class chose non-fiction. This was a stark contrast to the 66% of boys who chose a non-fiction book. I continued to track this for a number of weeks with consistent results. When I asked the girls in my class about their decisions, their responses ranged from, 'I like books about people, not things' to 'I just like reading stories', and perhaps the most damning to my reading ego, 'But, you don't read fact books Mr B!'
>
> Reflecting upon these observations, I was left with a number of questions:
> Chiefly, why were non-fiction books not engaging the female learners in my class?
>
> - Was the narrative nature of fiction, with exploration of character and plot, more appealing?
> - Does non-fiction need more scaffolding?
> - How much of a child's reading choices are dependent on their peers?
> - Is my expectation as a teacher that girls and boys would prefer different books? Is that assumption accurate?

While Tom did consider there might be an issue around the nature of the available non-fiction texts, his conversations with the children indicated that their reasons for choosing fiction were social. The girls spoke of the important role of the social networks they were part of in choosing texts. This limited what they were likely to choose. The solution, which Tom developed, was therefore of a social nature, designed to make non-fiction texts a part of the girls' networks at school and a viable choice for RfP. Tom describes the two key changes he made to his practice:

> **Actively raise the profile of non-fiction.** Initially, I decided to host a non-fiction book blanket. The books were placed on the classroom carpet with tables and chairs moved aside. The children were able to discuss and try out any books from the blanket in small 15-minute sessions. These were done in an informal, 'comfy reading' style where the children could sit alone or with their friends and choose any spot in the classroom.
>
> In addition, as I'm aware teachers hold a privileged position in the primary classroom and for many students, their teacher is a hero, someone to aspire to, or impress, whose example they might follow, I modelled my passion for non-fiction reading. I

created a poster on my door 'What is Mr B reading?' to entice children into discussing the book I'm reading as well as what they were reading. I also updated my class fortnightly via our online communication systems about what non-fiction I was reading. Additionally, I created a Non-fiction 'book of the week': This book was displayed in a frame with a brief blurb about the book written by me. We'd usually share this together during register time one morning a week.

Observe and utilise peer-to-peer recommendations. After carrying out discussions in my classroom, another pattern emerged: girls in my classroom were twice as likely to listen to their peers and teachers' reading recommendations than the boys. The opportunity that book blankets (and similar book talk activities) present, to observe reading behaviours and choices is extremely valuable. I would encourage others to continue to consider their role as a teacher who reads and the impact this has on their classroom. Why would a child pick up a new genre of book, if they never see their teacher doing the same? How do your recommendations affect the readership patterns in your class?

Tom reported that non-fiction became part of the girls' social connections with one another, and generated book talk based on non-fiction topics:

Before the summer holidays, the girls were more likely than before to share non-fiction texts as they seemed to have discovered that they make for a great communal reading opportunity – the chance to share information/learn together. I do wonder whether this is something to do with the diversity of experience our children have: each child bringing something different to every book they read? Reading non-fiction seems to have a snowball effect whereby children's existing knowledge is built into their growing understanding. The girls mentioned that they wanted to see more non-fiction options in our school library that matched the quality in our class library, and also made it clear that it was 'easier to pick up' a non-fiction text without the baggage of characters/setting/plot in a narrative.

Over the summer, a number of parents commented on seeing a shift in the books their children asked to buy and some girls even chose specific visits they wanted to go on, or activities they wanted to complete, that linked explicitly to their non-fiction reading. I still believe that in our setting it is more likely a child will be exposed to a majority fiction reading diet both in lessons and free reading. However, I do believe that some of the girls are now more confident to explore non-fiction than they were before and that they have a different understanding of the non-fiction genre that goes beyond just lists of facts.

This case study illustrates how Tom, as a Reading Teacher, became conscious of how book choices for RfP were gendered as a social practice. Not only did he observe text choices made by boys and girls, but he also spoke to them to help him understand the reasons. Focusing on the girls' choices, their conversations enabled him to appreciate they were influenced by their social networks, they were socially motivated to read (an issue discussed in more depth in Chapter 4). He therefore developed small scale practices to open up possibilities for choosing non-fiction. Tom's inquiry indicates that there was a clear gender pattern in the classroom which excluded some children (in this case girls) from accessing a major text type.

Engagement with non-fiction as part of RfP practice has been found to lead to enjoyment. Based on empirical research with boys and girls aged 8–18, Alexander and Jarman (2018) found that reading science books for pleasure involves both cognitive and affective engagement, which often overlap. Such intellectual pleasure can be related to the 'joy of finding out' and 'wonder' and 'awe' at a range of phenomena (2018: 84). An important aspect of learning which can be generated through engaging with non-fiction, and can stimulate engagement, is curiosity. Children's interest in and passion for a very wide range of topics can be satisfied by contemporary non-fiction texts. It can deepen readers' knowledge leading to an increase in their intrinsic motivation to read. The benefits of reading non-fiction may also overlap with many of those in fiction, such as identity development through reading texts about the country of origin of one's family which could foster a sense of connection. One unique aspect of contemporary high-quality non-fiction books is their attractive and interactive designs with flaps and fold outs that reveal information. In Alexander and Jarman's (2018) study they found that most children enjoyed reading non-fiction texts when offered rich examples and many changed their minds about this genre if they had previously been prejudiced against it.

Aside from developing an understanding of how choices were gendered, Tom's inquiry indicates how other RfP practices might also be gendered. Building on this, it could be that further observations and conversations with children might identify other gender patterns and potential inequalities. Such an approach to RfP would make this a more equitable practice where both boys and girls are able to access the benefits of RfP. This work suggests that recognising that RfP may be gendered and understanding children's individual reading preferences are important. For this reason, teachers need to have a good knowledge of children's texts and of individual readers, so that they can make recommendations and offer choices related to individual's interests. This can help children to develop and identify their own preferences *and* their own dislikes and nurture their volition as readers. However, they should all be given opportunities, role models and texts that tempt them to try something different, to read beyond their comfort zone. It appears from Tom's inquiry and research, that once girls do engage with non-fiction they may well find texts which they enjoy and from which they can benefit.

Connections between the will and the skill

The next case study focuses on inequalities experienced by boys in relation to their engagement with RfP (their 'will' or desire to read) and the consequent implications for their reading attainment (their reading skills). Megan's school is in a low-income context so the link between will and skill is arguably even more important to consider because boys in such contexts (eligible for Free School Meals), tend to have lower reading attainment than boys in higher income circumstances (OECD, 2010b). Nevertheless, the link is important for all children and is key to understanding the benefits of RfP in all contexts.

Megan describes how she identified the gender patterns present in her school. Her process started with measuring the young people's reading skill and then ascertaining their engagement with RfP.

> The introduction of new online assessment practices provided another lens onto the reading attainment of the students, complementing the insights of their teachers. [We used standardised word recognition and comprehension tests.] As a starting point, all

students who scored within the lowest percentiles were identified for further intervention and support. It became evident there was a gender discrepancy, with more boys being identified for support than girls. Seeking to explore this further, it was decided to administer further reading fluency assessments and a brief interview to gain an indication of their views on reading.

The additional individual assessments provided another rich source of information and supported the teachers' knowledge and understanding of these readers. Very few of these students appeared to read independently for pleasure when not in school. Once again, there was a disparity between the genders. The boys interviewed reported that they preferred to play outside, or games online, such as Minecraft or Warzone. The girls were more likely to report spending time on their phones, sometimes engaging in activities they would describe as reading. When asked about reading during their lessons, one boy reported that the reading in Science and English was hard as he did not know the words. Another suggested that he had enjoyed reading The Vampire Diaries by L.J. Smith but had not finished the book; he had read the first few pages, but then had not continued.

The pattern for the boys is stereotypical because they report reading for pleasure very little and have low reading skill attainment. Both these factors are likely to interact to sustain the status quo at a low level. Megan's approach to alleviating this situation was to work with the young people within both these domains in the hope that they would positively affect each other, and help the boys become more skilled as readers and engage more volitionally in reading. She explained her conceptualisation of the issues in terms of the will and skill relationship and likened it to a vicious cycle of underachievement and under engagement:

> The students' challenges appeared to rest not only with the skill of reading, but the volume and complexity of the texts they read. For many, the difficulties they had in tackling texts with more complex language and construction resulted in a lack of sustained engagement with reading. Without extended engagement in texts that interested and excited them, they were not having the opportunities to develop a self-sustaining interest in reading outside the confines of the school environment. This was particularly evident for the boys involved – their lack of interest in any wider reading for pleasure or information was stark. We theorised that attending to the skill of reading would result in a short burst of accelerated progress (the skill), but changes to the self-directed volitional reading behaviours (the will) would also be needed to maintain and sustain further growth.

Therefore, the interventions Megan initially developed simultaneously aimed to improve the will and the skill, although they were more successful at enhancing the latter. She then recognised that a new response was needed to develop students' engagement with RfP more effectively. Megan's two stranded approach involved two interventions for the skill (although there are some weaker 'will' elements here too), and one clear RfP strand.

> Two interventions [as part of the first strand] were initially developed to respond quickly and appropriately, building both the skill and the will of the students. To support the development of reading skills, the students were allocated to either a small

group intervention designed to boost their word recognition and fluency, or a small group intervention that was aimed at supporting them to develop and apply reading comprehension strategies. Both small group interventions placed the use of 'real' text [as opposed to extracts or reading scheme books], often in the form of short stories or non-fiction of interest, as a central component of the teaching. In both intervention groups, the students were encouraged to become part of the selection of the texts, in order to develop interest in choosing texts to read.

The impact of these approaches was carefully and systematically monitored and adjustments to the provision made. As many of the students indicated that they read most frequently in school, it was decided to begin with an approach that was designed to encourage self-motivated volitional reading there. Time, during the day and within each subject, was identified for reading and discussion. The English Department took the opportunity to revisit their curriculum with these challenges in mind. They audited the texts they used, from the perspective of the students – with a clear focus on texts that would engage. As new texts were introduced, the teachers systematically sought the opinions of the students and small targeted focus groups of students provided further insight and understanding.

Gradually, a range of shorter novels, short stories and other bitesize texts that students could read quickly and with enjoyment were selected to introduce them to a broader range of texts and more contemporary authors. Over time, the teachers planned to explicitly extend the length and challenge the texts presented, focusing on both the literary and literacy challenges each offered. Every book taught was accompanied by a list of other texts around the same subject, or from the same author, as a way of introducing students to wider choices, including reading online and through apps.

The second strand of Megan's approach involved an enhanced RfP pedagogy involving dedicated time for reading. This included providing a more varied, broader selection of texts, supporting students' choices and involving them in book audits. These practices introduced the young people to diverse text types as well as authors and writing styles. Megan also suggests that book talk was encouraged for students to deepen their engagement, although this may also have covered literacy curriculum objectives at the same time. Nevertheless, the RfP elements of this second strand seem to be much stronger than the literacy skills aspects. Megan's account of her schools' practice and how it evolved illustrates her role as a Reading Head Teacher reflecting on the school's pedagogy as it unfolded. In particular, she thought about text choice and the ways in which it could be facilitated by teachers. She attempted to infuse the first two interventions with RfP practices which included young people choosing texts and the use of 'real' texts. Yet after analysing the nature of these two groups in relation to RfP pedagogy, she decided that it was not sufficiently conducive to RfP. This reflects her understanding of the complexity of RfP and the conditions needed to foster a reading space that is informal and social and in which children can be as autonomous as possible as readers.

The impact of social class and income on boys' engagement with reading

While this chapter has primarily focused on gender inequalities, there are likely to be other factors which impact on children and young people's reading attitudes and level of engagement, hence causing further inequalities. Some of these relate to their social identities such as social class, or their life circumstances including their family's income and the local economic conditions. Boys whose families live on lower incomes are likely to be less technically skilled at reading because their language skills are less well developed from an early stage (Moss and Washbrook, 2016). However, it cannot be assumed that this applies to individual children, as they will also have the potential to enjoy and become skilled at reading and indeed may have books at home and at school.

It has been found that boys from working class backgrounds in low-income areas are more likely to be perceived by their teacher in deficit terms because of their gender and social class, and that in turn this influences the opportunities and reading provision offered to them (Hempel-Jorgensen, Cremin, Harris and Chamberlain, 2018). As a result, it was very difficult for the boys to be seen as engaged or successful readers despite their efforts to achieve this. The effect on their engagement with reading was negative and is likely to be a contributing factor to their lower attainment. This was even more marked for boys who were from different ethnic groups which the teacher also saw in deficit terms (Hempel-Jorgensen and Cremin, under review).

In Megan's school context, a high proportion of students live in poverty and boys in particular are overrepresented among lower attainers. Arguably, improving their reading skills is an essential part of improving their engagement with reading for pleasure and vice-versa, improving their motivation to read is also likely to increase their skill. It is therefore possible that RfP can play an important role in these young people's reading journey. Another likely factor to be affecting some of the boys in this setting is their social class. The group of students from lower income backgrounds are almost certain to overlap with being working class boys, although not all working class families will necessarily be on a low income.

Both working class boys and those whose families live on low incomes are often assumed to be 'non-readers', although recent research challenges this notion (e.g. Scholes, 2019). In this Australian study of 9- to 11-year-old boys from both working class and low-income families, Scholes found that some loved to read and read frequently at school and at home on a daily basis. The factors which supported their attitudes and practices included positive experiences at school with boy peers who also loved reading, and parents who encouraged them to read at home. Scholes (2019) suggests that these two factors interact to reinforce positive attitudes and reading practice in each setting. Her later work also highlights that boys' reading volition may be constrained by a lack of professional understanding of the wide range of their preferences in reading and the ways these change as boys develop as readers (Scholes, Spina and Comber, 2021). This again reinforces the value of Reading Teachers avoiding stereotypical assumptions based on gender or any other aspect of young readers identities, and of spending time getting to know individual readers' interests and preferences.

Conclusion

This chapter has focused on gender reading inequalities in schools. These are most widely known for affecting boys but there are many exceptions and boys vary in ways other than gender which also influence their engagement with reading. As the chapter has shown, girls, even those who are avid fiction readers, may have a low engagement with other text types, perhaps as a result of assumptions made on their own part or their parents or teachers.

However, as Tom's responsive RfP provision indicated, it is more than possible to encourage girls to try non-fiction, and many found that they valued and enjoyed the opportunity.

Megan's case study reveals the importance of motivation within students' reading journeys and that this sits alongside the skills of reading. Attending to both skill and will is essential in developing successful readers and may be particularly appropriate in schools where reading skills and volitional reading rates are low. In both cases, Tom and Megan used their understanding of their role as Reading Teachers/head teachers to spend time closely observing and reflecting on children's reading practices. Instead of making assumptions about what these children would respond to or what motivated them, they talked to the children and documented their responses and then planned accordingly. In this way, Tom and Megan used reflection on the processes of and motivation for reading to guide their decisions and to innovate practice that overcame inequality for both boys and girls.

Recommended reading

Harris, B. (n.d.) *Book Blankets*. The Open University RfP website. Available at: https://ourfp.org/eop/book-blankets/

Moss, G. (2007) *Literacy and Gender: Researching Texts, Contexts and Readers*. London: Routledge.

National Literacy Trust (2012) *Boys Reading Commission*. Available at: https://cdn.literacytrust.org.uk/media/documents/2012_06_01_free_other_-_boys_commission_report.pdf.pdf

Scholes, L., Spina, N. and Comber, B. (2021) Disrupting the 'boys don't read' discourse: Primary school boys who love reading fiction. *British Educational Research Journal*, 47(5): 1–18. https://doi.org/10.1002/berj.3685

References

Alexander, J. and Jarman, R. (2018) The pleasures of reading non-fiction. *Literacy*, 52(2): 78–85.

Clark, C. (2012) *Boys' Reading Commission 2012: A Review of Existing Research Conducted to Underpin the Commission*. London: National Literacy Trust.

Cremin, T., Mottram, M., Collins, F. M., Powell, S. and Safford, K. (2014) *Building Communities of Engaged Readers: Reading for Pleasure*. Abingdon: Routledge.

Hempel-Jorgensen, A. and Cremin, T. (under review) Understanding boys' (dis)engagement with reading: An intersectionality perspective. *International Journal of Qualitative Studies in Education*.

Hempel-Jorgensen, A., Cremin, T., Harris, D. and Chamberlain, L. (2018) Pedagogy for reading for pleasure in low socio-economic primary schools: Beyond 'pedagogy of poverty'? *Literacy*, 52(2): 86–94.

Jerrim, J. and Moss, G. (2019) The link between fiction and teenagers' reading skills: International evidence from the OECD PISA study. *British Educational Research Journal*, 45(1): 181–200.

Jones, S. and Myhill, D. (2004) 'Troublesome boys' and 'compliant girls': Gender identity and perceptions of achievement and underachievement. *British Journal of Sociology of Education*, 25(5): 547–561.

McGeown, S., Goodwin, H., Henderson, N. and Wright, P. (2012) Gender differences in reading motivation: Does sex or gender identity provide a better account? *Journal of Research in Reading*, 35(3): 328–336.

Morgan, P. L. and Fuchs, D. (2007) Is there a bidirectional relationship between children's reading skills and reading motivation? *Exceptional Children*, 73(2): 165–183.

Moss, G. (2007) *Literacy and Gender: Researching Texts, Contexts and Readers*. London: Routledge.

Moss, G. and Washbrook, L. (2016) *Understanding the Gender Gap in Literacy and Language Development*. Bristol: University of Bristol.

OECD (2010a) *PISA 2009 at a Glance*. Paris: Organisation for Economic Cooperation and Development (OECD).

OECD (2010b) *PISA 2009 Results: Learning to Learn – Student Engagement, Strategies and Practices (Volume III)*. Paris: Organisation for Economic Cooperation and Development (OECD).

Rothbauer, P. M. (2004) 'People aren't afraid any more but it's hard to find books': Reading practices that inform personal and social identities of self – identified lesbian and queer young women. *Canadian Journal of Information and Library Science*, 28(3): 53–74.

Scholes, L. (2019) Working-class boys' relationships with reading: Contextual systems that support working-class boys' engagement with, and enjoyment of, reading. *Gender and Education*, 31(3): 344–361.

Scholes, L., Spina, N. and Comber, B. (2021) Disrupting the 'boys don't read' discourse: Primary school boys who love reading fiction. *British Educational Research Journal*, 47(5): 1–18. https://doi.org/10.1002/berj.3685

Sullivan, A. and Brown, M. (2013) *Social Inequalities in Cognitive Scores at Age 16: The Role of Reading*. CLS Working Paper 2013/10. London: Centre for Longitudinal Studies.

Chapter 4

Supporting readers' social motivation

Marilyn Mottram, Katharine Young and Kiran Satti

Introduction

Helping children to blossom into readers who choose to read for pleasure is one of the most important things teachers can do. It is also one of the most challenging. The expert Reading Teacher, almost intuitively, finds ways to finely balance the two sides of reading: teaching the 'skills' of reading while simultaneously fostering children's 'will' to read. How do the best teachers model, entice and invite children to become readers, even when a child is making a shaky start to learning the skills? How do these teachers create classrooms that cultivate children's love of reading: their desire and will to read? What role does the teacher's personal 'reading self' play in the process?

In this chapter, we foreground two crucial ingredients that help children to become readers: one is the skilled Reading Teacher who reads and reflects, the other is the teacher's clear understanding of motivation. Motivating young readers is core to nurturing volitional reading and whilst intrinsic and extrinsic motivation are considered, we focus in more detail on the social motivation to read – that desire on the part of young children to connect to others, their friends, peers and teachers. Children and adults often find reading satisfying because it enables them to interact with others, to share 'books in

DOI: 10.4324/9781003215615-7

common', create reading networks and relationships and belong to a community of readers. We reflect on the ways in which this happens in classrooms and how children reveal their desire to relate to others through reading. We consider the relationship between Katharine Young and Kiran Satti's roles as Reading Teachers and their capacity to nurture new reading relationships with children.

To do so we draw on socio-cultural theories of reading, recognising that reading is relational and affective, and highlight the critical role that the social context (climate and ethos in the classroom) plays in shaping young readers. In this chapter Kat and Kiran use 'professional noticing' to formatively document the reader dispositions and identities of children and track how these develop and progress over time. There is much we can learn from their observations and reflections about the influence of social motivation in Reading for Pleasure (RfP).

Introducing reading motivation

Fostering intrinsic motivation, the enjoyment and fulfilment in reading, is a key teacher goal because in part it determines whether a child becomes a reader. The child that finds pleasure in reading, and does so early, has an in-built advantage. Sadly however, nurturing the 'will' to read has often been the neglected half of the reading curriculum.

The relationship between reading motivation, reading engagement and achievement has a long history of research interest. Much of this stems from the work of Guthrie, Wigfield and colleagues who argued that reading motivation produces reading engagement, which promotes achievement (Wigfield and Guthrie, 1997; Guthrie and Klauda, 2016). These scholars integrated research findings from both general motivation theory and literacy motivation to identify what they saw as the most important aspects of reading motivation. Originally these included: involvement, social, efficacy, curiosity, competition and recognition (Wigfield and Guthrie, 1997). Each aspect was aligned to either intrinsic or extrinsic dimensions of motivation. This theoretical framework and the corresponding Motivations for Reading Questionnaire (MRQ) have been hugely influential.

Distinguishing between intrinsic and extrinsic reading motivation is worthwhile. The former, relates to internal reasons for reading, such as deriving enjoyment, involvement and satisfying one's curiosity. The latter relates to external reasons for reading, such as reading for rewards and recognition. RfP is more closely associated with intrinsic than extrinsic motivation (Hebbecker, Förster and Souvignier, 2019), although of course children choose to read for many different reasons and their motivation can be both intrinsic and extrinsic at the same time (McGeown, Osborne, Warhurst, Norgate and Duncan, 2016).

In synthesising 20 years of research in this area, Schiefele, Schaffner, Möller and Wigfield (2012) identified 'seven genuine dimensions of reading motivation'. These were: curiosity and involvement (intrinsic motivation) and competition, recognition, grades, compliance and work avoidance (extrinsic motivation). Elements such as self-concept and self-efficacy were deemed 'antecedents of reading motivation' rather than aspects of motivation itself. Social motivation for reading was excluded in this synthesis, as it was in a later paper by Conradi, Jang and McKenna (2013) who also described reading motivation as individualistic.

However, more recent psychological research has begun to look at social motivation for reading and at how children interact with each other and with adults in their reading practices. There is growing awareness that reading is situated within the social practices of child-rearing and education (McGeown et al., 2020). This recognises that reading is a social act, since talking about, listening to and engaging in reading experiences involves other people and reflects their social, cultural and historical contexts. Within this framework, it is easy to see how social contexts can catalyse motivation and how skilled Reading Teachers can be significant social agents in the classroom. Reading Teachers explicitly identify as readers and also involve children in reading, not only as a social practice, but also as a reader identity position.

We therefore argue that the social motivation to read arises from relationships with others and that social contexts play a critical role. Neugebauer (2016) suggests that

> Classroom contexts that create opportunities for students to interact with each other around texts such as sharing texts, discussing texts with each other or exchanging writing about texts, have students who are more motivated to read than those without these more interactive classroom routines.
>
> (2016: 395)

This echoes findings from the *Teachers as Readers* research (Cremin, Mottram, Powell, Collins and Safford, 2014) in which reciprocal relationships around reading – between teachers and children and between children and other children – were found to be a critical factor in motivating children to want to read.

Social determination theory

To take this more child-centred, socio-cultural approach further, we draw on social determination theory which is an approach to human motivation. This focuses on volitional or self-determined behaviour and the social and cultural conditions that promote it. It argues that people are driven by three innate and basic psychological needs: competency, autonomy and relatedness (Deci and Ryan, 1985; Ryan and Deci, 2000a). This allows us to adopt a more learner led, nuanced and complex view of motivation. Research shows that where these three basic needs are fostered, there is a marked difference not only to the frequency of children's reading engagement behaviours, but also to their language comprehension (Orkin, Pott, Wolf, May and Brand, 2018). There is an interplay between what we know about RfP and social determination theory which relates to the interrelatedness between the three humans needs and aspects of RfP (see Table 4.1). For example, research shows that feelings of competence will not enhance intrinsic motivation unless accompanied by a sense of autonomy (Orkin et al., 2018).

This interrelatedness is especially significant for those young readers who fall into the '20%' of lowest achievers. Very early in school-life, children form beliefs about what they can and cannot do. This affects their sense of self-efficacy, autonomy and motivation. According to the 'Matthew effect' able young readers who are motivated to read, read more, are more persistent in coping with difficulties, and so become better readers (Stanovich, 1986). By contrast, those who initially struggle, experience low achievement which reduces their intrinsic motivation to read, and this in turn further lowers their achievement and self-efficacy. So, the reading 'rich get richer and the reading poor get poorer' (Stanovich, 1986) and the disadvantaged gap gets wider. How then do Reading Teachers cultivate intrinsic motivation for reading, especially for those reading 'disadvantaged' young people in their classrooms?

Table 4.1 Applying social determination theory to reading for pleasure

Social Determination Theory (SDT)	Reading for Pleasure (RfP)
Three basic psychological needs necessary for self-motivation, well-being and growth	Conditions necessary for the development of young readers who choose to read and read widely
Autonomy The need to feel free and self-directed.	*Volition/agency* The need to foster children's self-direction and volition as readers who can exercise agency, discrimination and choice.
Competency The need to feel effective. When an individual feels competent they feel able to interact with their environment.	*Competency* The need for a positive attitude to reading, positive reader identity and high sense of self-efficacy.
Relatedness The need for a sense of belonging, connected to others in nurturing and reciprocal relationships.	*Relatedness* The need to be part of vibrant communities of engaged readers with trusting reader-relationships rooted in friendship and affect.

Classroom conditions that cultivate intrinsic and social motivation

Research highlights the continuity between Reading Teachers (teachers who read and readers who teach) and children as engaged and self-motivated readers (Commeyras et al., 2003; Cremin et al., 2014; Cremin, 2020). Such teachers model being readers and create classroom conditions that foster children's intrinsic motivation to read even for those children who are finding reading difficult. As Kiran notes:

> As a Reading Teacher, I aim to cultivate an environment where reading is joyful, enables connections to be made and curates a sense of community. This is my role. My classroom is blanketed with books and opportunities for children to become thoughtful readers, to be free and imaginative. As I have evolved as a teacher and leader my understanding of humanising pedagogy has strengthened. Talking with the child about their reading and offering something of myself as a reader to this is a joy. It's about respecting every young reader for their uniqueness.

Kiran's comments indicate the importance she places on fostering a sense of community in her classroom and the deep association that this has with the concept of belonging. Her belief in a humanising or relational pedagogy positions her as a teacher who aligns her practice with children's learning experiences and perspectives, honouring their cultures and worlds. These principles and beliefs are closely aligned to those underpinning RfP which tends to be learner/child led, and learner/child owned. The following study from Kiran brings this to life as we consider one child, Declan, who initially does not show any signs of self-determination or sense of belonging. We can learn a great deal from closely observing how such children engage with reading when they are free from the restraints of having to do what other people tell them. This is revealed in Kiran's reflections on 6-year-old Declan's reading journey.

Declan's reading journey

Declan had just moved up a year when I was seconded to his school as part of my leadership development and progression. I regarded Declan as a disadvantaged reader. By this I mean: he is not often read-to and does not share books with others beyond school. He is also falling behind in his reading skills, including phonics. In our first reading lesson he told me: 'I can't read'.

In the wise words of Margaret Meek – 'Learning to read . . . at seven is no more and no less of a problem than learning at any other stage with one difference: the learner's view of himself now dominates the process' (Meek, 1982: 114). This was true of Declan. His negative self-concept was influenced by a complex range of factors associated with his ability and self-efficacy. He knew that he had fallen behind others in his class. He knew that he was stuck on books from the previous phases of reading. I told him with conviction, 'You will love reading soon enough'. I often remind him of this moment as he is now a child who reads well and loves to read. More importantly, he enjoys reading and chooses to spend time reading. I quickly got to know the other young readers in the class. Rhys is an avid reader and loves reading about anything scientific. Lana and Callum are beginning to widen their reading through their library choices. Many of the children are inspired by Rhys – including Declan.

Exploring social influences

To encourage the class to think and talk about reading, Kiran routinely holds small group reading conferences. She makes sure that Declan is part of conversations with other children, some of whom are avid readers and uses this social interaction to encourage Declan to engage with his peers around reading. In this way, Kiran is building a bridge between Declan and other more competent and confident readers in the class. This is especially important for those children who are finding reading difficult as they may never realise that reading is something that others choose to do for pleasure. This is a short extract from a reading conference:

TEACHER: Am I a reader?
ALL: YES!
TEACHER: How do you know?
LANA: Because you love books!
DECLAN: You have loads of books on your shelf
CALLUM: You write a lot
RHYS: You know lots of words
TEACHER: Are *you* readers?
CALLUM: yes, yes. I read lots of big books – by myself
LANA: yes – I just am
DECLAN: I want to be a reader
RHYS: yes, I like being a reader and learning interesting things.

The conversation about reading continued. Declan was quiet, so Kiran posed another question: Do you have to be good at reading to be a reader? Declan replied 'Yes, that's why you always tell us to read. You have to learn to read and then you have to be good at it'.

As a skilled Reading Teacher, Kiran knows the powerful impact that positive attitudes, beliefs, desires and motivations exert on learning to read. She makes sure that Declan is talking to children, such as Rhys, Lana and Callum who are intrinsically motivated readers. Kiran carefully orchestrates these shorts conversations and interactions because she wants Declan to feel comfortable, respected and heard. This transcript reveals that Declan has noticed Kiran's bookshelf 'you have loads of books'. He has concluded that Kiran is a reader and enjoys reading. This is symbolic. We know that books do not play a big part in his world beyond school. Indeed, it may be the first time that he has realised that some people choose to read purely for pleasure. It seems that for now Kiran is the main player with a chance to catch Declan and draw him into the world of reading.

Kiran believes that seeing and hearing other young readers, like Rhys, Lana and Callum, is a form of social persuasion and will encourage Declan. Without these thoughtful interventions, Declan might spend most of his reading time surrounded by other struggling readers. Kiran recognises that these conversations and interactions around reading are beginning to work as Declan is participating, listening and contributing. However, she also understands that there is more to do to build his self-efficacy.

The concept of self-efficacy refers to an individual's belief in their capacity to execute behaviours necessary to produce the specific performance needed for a given task (Bandura, 1977, 1997, 2006). Consider the interest that Kiran takes in the children's perceptions about their abilities and about reading identities, as well as self-efficacy. Declan states, 'I can't read'. He does not say 'I can't read *yet*'. This stems from his past experiences with reading tasks including phonics sessions. Children with poor self-efficacy do not feel in control and do not believe that they have the capability for success.

As self-determination theory posits, the need for growth drives human behaviour; people are always seeking to grow and improve (Deci and Ryan, 1985). So gaining mastery over challenges (both new and old) is essential for developing a positive sense of self. This is hard for Declan (and for the rest of the 20% in our classrooms). We move back to Kiran's next steps as she engaged in more 'professional noticing'.

Noticing

> Declan arrived in school and, independently started reading his class book. He read this to me the previous day and needed support in parts. To help him, we used a 'fluency tree' as a way of breaking sentences down, adding a word at a time to support reading confidence and fluency. I noticed that Declan fetched the fluency tree that we had used previously and read through the words and phrases. He then went back to the book and reread the pages from yesterday and then read on, independently using his reading skills to decode, decipher, self-correct and reread. He later asked me, 'Can this class book be my home reader book now?' I agreed. I asked him why and he replied, 'I like it more now. It was hard at first, but I kept reading and – it gets easier'.

This short observation shows Declan exercising agency and choice within an enabling environment. He chose to fetch and use the fluency tree to support his independent reading. He asked to take his class book home instead of his home reading book. As an expert Reading Teacher, Kiran keeps the balance between the 'skill and the will' and has a holistic view of the child/the reader in the round in her mind. This is the bread and butter of teaching – being in tune with the child/the learner and in this case the young reader.

Over time, Kiran noticed and documented Declan interacting with reading activities and demonstrating more autonomy within the classroom. On one occasion, realising that Kiran has one-to-one reading time, he fetched his book and home/school diary and placed them on her desk: a clear signal. When Kiran called him over, he told her, 'I love this book because it has loads of pages and I can read them'. Here he was exhibiting belief in his own competence, exercising autonomy and expressing trust in his relationship with Kiran. Kiran's intuitive care for Declan's basic psychological needs is strengthening his self-determined motivation, well-being and growth. Later in the term, Kiran noticed Declan interacting with the wider culture and ethos of the classroom and becoming more engaged and connected to reading and readers. The next extract captures this.

Reading as a social and relational act

> During one rainy lunch time, the children went into the library with the dinner ladies, but Declan came into the classroom. He asked if we could read, Who Will Play With Me by Michelle Coxo which had been one of his class readers. It is the story of a friendship that grows between a boy and a cat. The story is told from two perspectives. From the front is the cat's story: from the back is the boy's story. The stories meet in the middle. Declan told me that after he read it, he had passed it to his friend, Azeera, because she loves cats.

As a Reading Teacher, Kiran recognises the significance of this small act. For the first time, Declan has loved a book enough to want to share it with another reader. We know that for Declan book recommendations do not happen beyond school. He extends his enjoyment of this book further by inviting Kiran to share it with him. Kiran's next extract shows how this little act grows into something very significant.

> Declan was still reading with me when the rest of the class began to trickle back. They sat quietly listening to Declan reading. Many of them knew and liked the book. Declan gradually realised that he was reading to more and more of the class. He started to read very quietly so I began to support him and we read parts together as the class listened. There was a lot of smiling as the friendship between the boy and the cat's stories began to weave together.

Declan was experiencing a sense of mastery. He was reading well, was very proud of himself and clearly felt a sense of belonging and trust in the class community of readers. This positive achievement experience was intrinsically motivated and socially supported. As a result of many complex factors at play in this classroom, Declan's 'will' or motivation to read is blossoming within this social context.

Hamid's reading journey

We turn now to learn from Katherine's observations as she notices, documents, reflects and acts upon her growing understanding of 9-year-old Hamid.

> As a Reading Teacher there are things that I notice intuitively that I don't consciously think about or even realise I am doing. I think there are moments in time for children as readers – moments that could flick them either way. It is a privilege to have time to do close observations because that's how you get a deeper understanding. Noticing the tiny little things about the way a child behaves around reading when they have some choice and thinking 'Why is that happening? I'll explore it'.

The child in this case study is Hamid. Katherine is not Hamid's class teacher, but she taught Hamid's older brother and sister a few years ago. The class teacher describes Hamid:

> Hamid is nearly 9 years old. He is an avid reader who has historically good attainment in terms of reading test scores for in-school assessments, achieving slightly above the expected standard for his age. I class him as an avid reader. He has a level of 'resistance' when he is asked to stop reading. For example, I had to 'prize Percy Jackson and the Lightning Thief out of his hands' during a maths lesson! I'd say he is socially motivated; he talks to friends about his reading and I know that they make recommendations to each other.

Exploring social influences

Katharine believes that noticing how children interact with texts and with other readers gives powerful insight. As she says:

> It helps us to keep the child at the centre of our thinking and shape our RfP pedagogy to meet their individual needs and interests. Although I do not teach Hamid, he is the younger brother of two pupils that I have taught in previous years. They were both very able and avid readers. His sister was a particularly keen reader. I know that the family value education and reading highly and have high expectations of their children. Like his siblings, Hamid tells me that there are hundreds of books at home, and that lots of them are the Qu'ran! He said that they had recently moved house and that there were boxes and boxes of books yet to be unpacked.

Katharine's interest in children's reading lives, beyond school, is intuitive. She knows that RfP takes place in Hamid's home where reading is also seen as a serious activity associated with work or religion. This respect for books and reading is part of Hamid's social and cultural world beyond school. Knowing this enables teachers to build on these 'funds of knowledge' (Moll, Amanti, Neff and Gonzalez, 1992) and offer appropriate encouragement and challenge as we see later in the chapter.

Noticing

After teaching this class one day, Katharine described an incident when, during whole-class teaching of the text *King Arthur* (by Benjamin Hulme-Cross), the children were asked to read the last few pages of the story independently. Towards the end, she noted that Hamid looked up and burst out to the class, 'Sir Bertilak **was** the Green Knight!' He looked at her, almost surprised at himself and clapped his hand over his mouth as if to stop himself. He then looked at her apologetically and turned round to see whether others had noticed.

It seemed that Hamid had been so absorbed in the story at the moment when he shouted out, that he hadn't realised what he was doing until it was too late. It was interesting too, that he looked around the classroom after his outburst, demonstrating that he wanted to share with others the moment of discovery, but also aware that he might have spoilt the ending for them!

Katharine captured this lovely moment in Hamid's reading. Hamid's relationship with the text had been intense and interactive. He was totally immersed in the world of King Arthur's world, creating meaning, experiencing joy, discovering new understandings. As an active member of the reading classroom, he immediately wanted to share the denouement. Perhaps Hamid realised that he had broken a reciprocal obligation to fellow-readers by voicing this 'spoiler'! In this class, social interactions around texts are a common part of the dynamics of the classroom. Hamid's immediate desire is to share his response with his peers, to see what they think, to consider and create new understandings with them. Noticing this, Katharine noted it down and sought to find out more about the social influences on Hamid's reading, as we see in the next extract.

> In one lesson, we were taking part in a Zoom call with a partner school in Ghana as part of a British Council Project. Throughout the call, Hamid kept flicking through his book *Space Boy*. When the Zoom call ended, the class moved into reading time. Hamid immediately jumped up and exchanged *Space Boy* for *Planet Omar: Accidental Trouble Magnet*. I asked him about his choice and he said he had already started *Planet Omar* and wanted to read it. He said 'I've seen other children reading it and wanted to try it myself'. I asked what helped him to choose books and he told me, 'When someone else is reading a book, it makes me want it. That's what happened with *Planet Omar*. I also read things that my teacher recommends to me'.

Katharine noted that Hamid had at this point chosen to read any books that she had recommended to him, but does reads books recommended by his teacher and his friends. This suggests that accepting a recommendation is conditional for Hamid, based on trust and relatedness and indicating Hamid's autonomy and assurance as a reader. In order to find out more about the social interactions at play in the class, during independent reading time, Katharine invited the children to write some answers to three questions about reading so that she could 'get to know them even better as readers'.

Reading as a social and relational act

Katharine commented that Hamid completed these questions very quickly and then turned to a pile of picture books borrowed from his teacher's book box. This is her personal collection of books and is available for children to choose from, in addition to the class books. Hamid had chosen *Ssshhh* by Chris Haughton, *Oi Aardvark* by Kes Gray and Jim Field, *Triangle* by Jon Klassen and *The Blue Giant* by Katie Cottle. She asked him about his selection, 'Are you in a picture book mood today Hamid?'

> Hamid replied, 'Yes I love picture books'. I commented that he had read a number of them in a short time. He said 'I read them so fast that other people don't think I'm reading them properly, but I am'. I asked him what got him into reading picture books. He said, 'I read picture books to my cousin-sister [female cousin]. I read these to her all the time [*Oi Frog!* and *Oi Goat!*]. But she is two and is quite naughty. She rips the pages'. We then talked about how I read to my daughter every day too, and how it's a lovely bonding experience. He agreed with this and went on to talk more about his 'cousin-sister' and the things that she likes to do.

Here I saw another example of the social interactions around reading in Hamid's extended family. It struck me as interesting that other children in the class don't think that he's reading 'properly' because he reads picture books so quickly. This shows that children have their own conversations about each other's reading practices. Hamid spoke in a very animated manner about the reading he does at home with his cousin-sister. This contrasted with the previous occasions when Hamid has been less inclined to talk about his reading.

Katharine's observations show a classroom where relational support and peer interaction around reading are powerfully working away beneath the surface. We note that Hamid is advantaged as a reader. His home is full of books and there are many different social interactions around reading beyond school. He relates *Oi Aardvark* (on the teacher's bookshelf) to books at home in the same series which he reads to his sister-cousin. He enjoys the delights of many different text-types with his family and friends, including religious books and digital texts. His motivation to read is complex and multidimensional, but the social and relational aspects are clearly significant. Katharine as his skilled Reading Teacher keeps a light hand on his shoulder. She pays attention and notices his behaviours, sustaining Hamid's motivation by challenging the breadth of his reading with recommendations and discussion.

Conclusion

The disparity between Declan and Hamid in terms of their reading experiences beyond school is stark. It is not only the range of reading and access to reading books that is different. Social interactions and social motivation encouraging reading have been part of Hamid's world from early in his life. This gives in-built advantage. He is already an assured reader who articulates his reading preferences with discernment. On the other hand, Declan has made a shaky start to learning the skills of reading. He lacks enabling social interactions, events and motivations around reading beyond school. This furthers his disadvantage. However, both children have been moved on by the skilled Reading Teachers who engage in the act of professional noticing to find out more about how to best support, encourage and challenge young readers.

In Declan's case (a disadvantaged reader) the act of professional noticing and reflection in which Kiran engages adds to her information about his reading. It reveals that Declan's motivation for reading is low and his reading avoidance is high. She notes that read aloud sessions are not making enough of a difference. Her understanding of the relationship between motivation, achievement and self-efficacy (his belief in himself) is critical. So is her awareness of Declan's basic human need to feel a sense of belonging, in this case to the class reading community. These are key factors in moving Declan forward. Kiran knows that improving Declan's self-efficacy requires very incisive skills teaching so that he experiences success. She gently guides Declan into reading relationships with others in the class, recognising that such relationships are new. This is a Reading Teacher effectively balancing the skill and the will.

In contrast, for Hamid as an avid reader, the culture of shared thinking and talking about books is a powerful motivator and keeps him moving forward. It allows him to enjoy meaning-making, both as an individual and as a joint, creative endeavour – captured in his shout out to others about the Green Knight. Katharine carefully broadens Hamid's repertoire through informed recommendations and by cultivating an ethos of peer-to-peer recommendations in class. This is perhaps most powerfully exemplified by the exchanges and informal talk about reading so alive beneath the surface. These social interactions keep reading vibrant in Hamid's life. Her professional noticing and reflection reveals that he is influenced by social interactions around texts and how he too influences others. This informs Katharine about 'where next' for Hamid, and others. It feeds into her actions, incidental conversations and recommendations that support and challenge the children as readers.

What are the implications of these case studies? First, they show that motivation is complex, and multidimensional. In both, social interactions around reading, at many levels, play a significant role in fostering children's 'will', their enjoyment and fulfilment. Given that it is the child's willpower that determines whether s/he grows into a reader, these Reading Teachers do not wait for motivation to 'happen'. They make it happen and build bridges so that all children, including the most disadvantaged readers, have opportunities to belong, to feel connected and respected as readers. We need a deeper understanding of this, especially for disadvantaged readers. Secondly, this work shows that the use of professional noticing is a powerful lever to support young readers. Such noticing triggers small scale documentation, (to retain the insight), prompts reflection, and then leads to responsively attuned actions. Professional noticing thus helps teachers to understand individual children's experiences around reading, their interactions, interests and preferences and informs their conversations, support and recommended readings. It is clear that as Reading Teachers Kiran and Katharine place the well-being of the whole child at the centre of their teaching. Their classrooms cultivate young readers who are connected to others and exercise agency, discrimination and choice.

Recommended reading

Cremin, T., Mottram, M., Powell, S., Collins, R. and Safford, K. (2014) *Building Communities of Engaged Readers: Reading for Pleasure*. London and New York: Routledge.

McGeown, S., Bonsall, J., Andries, V. V., Howarth, D. and Wilkinson, K. (2020) Understanding reading motivation across different text types: Qualitative insights from children. *Journal of Research in Reading*, 43(4): 597–608.

McGeown, S., Osborne, C., Warhurst, A., Norgate, R. and Duncan, L. (2015) Understanding children's reading activities: Reading motivation, skill and child characteristics as predictors. *Journal of Research in Reading*, 39(1): 109–125.

Children's books

Cottle, K. (2020) *The Blue Giant*. London: Pavilion Children's Books.
Cox, M. (1992) *Who Will Play with Me?* North Carolina: Carson-Dellosa Publishing.
Gray, K. and Field, J. (2015) *Oi Frog! (Oi Frog and Friends)*. London: Hodder Children's Books.
Gray, K. and Field, J. (2018) *Oi Goat! (Oi Frog and Friends)*. London: Hodder Children's Books.
Gray, K. and Field, J. (2021) *Oi Aardvark! (Oi Frog and Friends)*. London: Hodder Children's Books.
Haughton, C. (2015) *Shh! We Have a Plan*. London: Walker Books.
Hulme-Cross, B. (2020) *King Arthur*. London: Bloomsbury Education.
Klassen, J. and Barnett, M. (2018) *Triangle: 1*. London: Walker Books.
McCranie, S. (2021) *Space Boy Volume 10*. London: Dark Horse.
Mian, Z. and Mafaridik, N. (2019) *Planet Omar: Accidental Trouble Magnet Book 1*. London: Hodder Children's Books.
Riordan, R. (2013) *Percy Jackson and the Lightning Thief* (Book 1). London: Puffin.

References

Bandura, A. (1977) *Social Learning Theory*. Englewood Cliffs, NJ: Prentice Hall.

Bandura, A. (1997) *Self-efficacy: The Exercise of Control*. New York: W. H. Freeman.

Bandura, A. (2006) Towards a psychology of human agency. *Perspectives on Psychological Science*, 1: 164–180.

Commeyras, M., Bisplinhoff, B. S. and Olson, J. (2003) *Teachers as Readers: Perspectives on the Importance of Reading in Teachers' Classrooms and Lives*. Newark: International Reading Association.

Conradi, K., Jang, B. G. and McKenna, M. C. (2013) Motivation terminology in reading research: A conceptual review. *Educational Psychology Review*, 25(4): n.p.

Cremin, T. (2020) Reading for pleasure: Tensions and challenges. In C. Daly and J. Davison (Eds.), *Debates in English Teaching*, pp. 92–102. London: Routledge.

Cremin, T., Mottram, M., Powell, S., Collins, R. and Safford, K. (2014) *Building Communities of Engaged Readers: Reading for Pleasure*. London and New York: Routledge.

Deci, E. L. and Ryan, R. M. (1985) *Intrinsic Motivation and Self-determination in Human Behaviour*. New York: Plenum.

Guthrie, J. T. and Klauda, S. L. (2016) Engagement and motivational processes in reading. In P. Afflerbach (Ed.), *Handbook of Individual Differences in Reading: Reader, Text, and Context*, pp. 41–53. London: Taylor & Francis/Routledge.

Hebbecker, K., Förster, N. and Souvignier, E. (2019) Reciprocal effects between reading achievement and intrinsic and extrinsic reading motivation, scientific studies of reading. *Scientific Studies of Reading*, 23(5): 419–436.

McGeown, S., Bonsall, J., Andries, V., Howarth, D., Wilkinson, K. and Sabeti, S. (2020) Growing up a reader: Exploring children's and adolescents' perceptions of a reader. *Educational Research*, 62(2): 216–228.

McGeown, S., Osborne, C., Warhurst, A., Norgate, R. and Duncan, L. (2016) Understanding children's reading activities: Reading motivation, skill and child characteristics as predictors. *Journal of Research in Reading*, 39(1): 109–125.

Meek, M. (1982) *Learning to Read*. London: Bodley Head.

Moll, L., Amanti, C., Neff, D. and Gonzalez, N. (1992) Funds of knowledge for teaching: Using a qualitative approach to connect homes and classrooms. *Theory into Practice*, 31: 132–141.

Neugebauer, S. (2016) Stable or situated understandings of adolescent reading engagement across readers and raters. *The Journal of Educational Research*, 109(4): 391–404.

Orkin, M., Pott, M., Wolf, M., May, S. and Brand, E. (2018) Beyond gold stars: Improving the skills and engagement of struggling readers through intrinsic motivation. *Reading & Writing Quarterly*, 34(3): 203–217.

Ryan, R. M. and Deci, E. L. (2000a) Self-determination theory and the facilitation of intrinsic motivation, social development, and well-being. *American Psychologist*, 55(1): 68–78.

Ryan, R. M. and Deci, E. L. (2000b) Intrinsic and extrinsic motivations: Classic definitions and new directions. *Contemporary Educational Psychology*, 25: 54–67.

Schiefele, U., Schaffner, E., Möller, J. and Wigfield, A. (2012) Dimensions of reading motivation and their relation to reading behavior and competence. *Reading Research Quarterly*, 47(4): 427–463.

Stanovich, K. E. (1986) Matthew effects in reading: Some consequences of individual differences in the acquisition of literacy. *Reading Research Quarterly*, 21: 360–407.

Wigfield, A. and Guthrie, J. T. (1997) Relations of children's motivation for reading to the amount and breadth of their reading. *Journal of Educational Psychology*, 89: 420–432.

My reading practices

Helen Hendry

In the morning and at night I read and update my things to do lists for work. It helps me to feel calm and organised.

I read social media on my phone, especially memes. I like to read the best ones out loud to my husband – he doesn't think they are funny! I often start and end my day with some memes.

I like to read fiction or poetry in bed just before I go to sleep. I must finish a chapter before sleeping! I often fall asleep whilst reading and have to reread the next day.

I have a pile of books beside my bed. I am usually reading several things at the same time. I keep my place by lying the books inside each other to mark the page I've reached.

I often read academic texts or fiction whilst my husband is watching TV or talking to me. I don't hear anything because I'm so engrossed in reading!

Sometimes I read obsessively. I really can't put the book down and will read it in a day or two. I might lie on my bed in the daytime to finish a book at the weekend.

I will read an old favourite once every few years. I return to familiar funny books and collections of poetry if I am feeling sad or overwhelmed.

I buy or borrow books to take on holiday, usually three or four for a week. I worry about running out and sometimes buy emergency books at the airport. I try to take something to read with me even on short journeys, just in case!

I keep some of my favourite recent reads and give them to my sister. She does the same for me.

Sometimes I get distracted by something that looks interesting to read online and I start to read it instead of carrying on with the task in hand.

If I need to really think about something I am reading online, I will print it off. Reading on paper helps me to concentrate and remember. I like to move away from the screen to read.

I read the lyrics to songs I am learning in choir and sing along to the music on my phone. I like to do this when I'm cooking. It's a good time to practice.

Reflection on my reading practices

When I reflect on my own reading practices, several elements offer potential learning for my work with children. Firstly, **the variety of reading media** that I like to access during the day includes print and on-screen media, short webpages and much longer reads. My reading style adapts to suit these purposes in that it is sometimes short-lived, at others engrossed and sustained. Children too may appreciate this varied diet and acceptance of different reading 'modes'. Some may like to dip into comics or joke books or read a webpage about an area of interest. In the classroom I would, therefore, incorporate shorter reading opportunities, including those on screen, in reading time, alongside a variety of other texts. Similarly, as I like to **reread old favourites**, children may have their own favourite texts that give them comfort and enjoyment to read again. These old favourites might offer a starting point for some interesting discussions with children, and I would like to offer older children the opportunity to talk about and reread favourites from previous years, including those normally associated with younger children. I might arrange for them to look at the classroom collections lower down the school to select favourite picture books to read and discuss.

I also notice how I like to share my reading, reading things that I find funny to my husband, and saving books to give to my sister. In sharing, I enjoy the texts more as I can talk about them and re-engage with them through chat, finding out others' responses. These experiences are also important for children. Opportunities to **share and discuss favourite reads** by reading aloud snippets or suggesting a friend reads a book, are ways of reading that I would want to support in school. I could encourage children to sometimes read in friendship pairs, and to build in time for recommending books to one another at the beginning or end of reading time. For me, RfP is often functional – such as when I read lyrics to practice singing, at other times much more about my emotional response – such as when I read old favourites for comfort, or books to relax on holiday. **Discussing what, where and why we like to read** is another way to help children think about their reading identities and could lead to children collating their own 'holiday reads', or 'reading that cheers me up' and sharing them with one another.

My reading choices highlight that **RfP does not conform to a traditional view of reading at school**. My reading is not solitary, or quiet. I am happy to read when there is noise around me, even in front of the television, and I like to involve others in my reading and talk about what I read. I also **like to read several things at the same time**, keeping collections of books to read and moving from one to the other. Equally I sometimes like to read for long uninterrupted periods. Reflecting on my reading shows me that I need to ensure children can access quiet spaces and enough time to become immersed in their reading as well as more social opportunities. I would timetable uninterrupted quiet reading and chatty times. Children could be allowed to keep a small 'reading pile' of their current reading choices, rather than being expected to complete a book before borrowing another one. It is also clear how much my reading takes place at home throughout the day so, finding ways to talk about and value children's reading at home is a key element I would want to build on through discussion with children and asking them to keep a reading diary through pictures or even video.

Section 2

Reading for pleasure pedagogy

Introduction

The previous chapter illustrated that to inspire all children to want to read for pleasure, opportunities must be created to support social motivation, and to nurture children's sense of belonging and sense of agency. However, as Mottram, Young and Satti stressed, this does not just happen; supporting and enhancing children's reading engagement must be carefully planned for. Indeed, research in the USA (Moses and Kelly, 2018, 2019) found that research-informed shifts in pedagogy in one first-grade classroom led to better support for the 'development of joyful reading' (Moses and Kelly, 2018: 330). The authors documented the ways in which the teacher modelled enjoyment of reading, encouraged pupils to share and discuss texts, supported book selection and built a 'social atmosphere of a community of readers' (Moses and Kelly, 2019: 335) amongst other things. Children's desire and inclination to read is not predestined, nor is it static – with careful support and encouragement, even the most reluctant readers can find enjoyment and inspiration.

This section explores four elements that, together, have been found to be the cornerstones of a robust Reading for Pleasure (RfP) pedagogy (Cremin, Mottram, Powell, Collins and Safford, 2014). The following chapters will discuss reading aloud,

DOI: 10.4324/9781003215615-9

informal book talk and recommendations, independent reading and the importance of social reading environments. However, it is vital to stress that these four elements are not isolated, each aspect is interconnected and interdependent, and to be effective they must be an integral part of the classroom culture. Furthermore, RfP pedagogy cannot be thought of as a package; effective Reading Teachers do not simply 'do' RfP activities in their classroom. In this section it will become clear why it is not enough to just allocate 15 minutes to reading aloud or independent reading time in the timetable; likewise, it will explore how an occasional class book discussion does not constitute informal book talk, nor do a few soft toys and cushions in the book corner generate a rich, social reading environment. Developing a rigorous and comprehensive RfP pedagogy requires teachers to have an in-depth understanding of each aspect, how they work together, and to appreciate that the efficacy of this pedagogy is dependent on teachers' detailed knowledge of their children, and of literature and other texts. Tracking the consequences of this integrated pedagogy on children choosing to read is also essential.

Developing RfP pedagogy that is both robust and responsive matters. Whilst some children have abundant access to exciting texts at home, are supported to read and have family members who engage in reciprocal dialogue around a book – many children do not have these opportunities at home. For some children, the classroom may be the only place in which they are supported and inspired to read. Hence, developing a robust, research informed RfP pedagogy is a matter of social justice, and the role of knowledgeable and enthusiastic Reading Teachers in levelling-up children's opportunities to become engaged readers cannot be overstated. However, Bernstein (2000) proposes that 'performative pedagogy', involving high levels of teacher control and a strong focus on 'attainment', is more prevalent in schools in lower socio-economic status (SES) areas. Indeed, research by Hempel-Jorgensen, Cremin, Harris and Chamberlain (2018) in four low SES schools from across England, found that children's volition and social interaction was restricted by the pedagogical approach deployed, particularly for struggling readers. The study further illustrates the need to developing a rich, research informed and responsive RfP pedagogy.

The case-studies in the chapters that follow exemplify RfP pedagogy in action, detailing how knowledgeable Reading Teachers reflect on their practice and provision, how they continually notice how children engage, listen to children's views about their reading and take action to adapt practices in response. The examples show how Reading Teachers also model practice, inspire others and are able to share their research informed practice and pedagogic principles with confidence and authority.

References

Bernstein, B. B. (2000) *Pedagogy, Symbolic Control, and Identity: Theory, Research, Critique*. London: Rowman & Littlefield.
Cremin, T., Mottram, M., Powell, S., Collins, R. and Safford, K. (2014) *Building Communities of Engaged Readers: Reading for Pleasure*. London and New York: Routledge.
Hempel-Jorgensen, A., Cremin, T., Harris, D. and Chamberlain, L. (2018) Pedagogy for reading for pleasure in low socio-economic primary schools: Beyond 'pedagogy of poverty'? *Literacy*, 52(2): 86–94.
Moses, L. and Kelly, L. (2018) 'We're a little loud. That's because we like to read!': Developing positive views of reading in a diverse, urban first grade. *Journal of Early Childhood Literacy*, 18(3): 307–337.
Moses, L. and Kelly, L. (2019) Are they really reading? A descriptive study of first graders during independent reading. *Reading & Writing Quarterly*, 35(4): 322–338.

Chapter 5

Reading aloud

Teresa Cremin, Ben Harris and Matthew Courtney

Introduction

Do you remember being read to? Do you recall a sense of comfort and connection, intimacy even as the sound of the adult's voice conjured words and worlds in which you were suspended in another space and time? As co-authors we do. Ben remembers the feelings evoked by the sound of his father's voice, Matthew recalls listening to audio recordings of Lucy Daniels' *Animal Ark* series, and Teresa has strong memories of an English teacher bringing Greek myths to life. Under the umbrella of reading aloud, a range of practices have always existed in homes and classrooms. Different terms, including shared reading, joint reading and dialogic reading describe this activity and highlight the adults' contribution in a reading engagement which is potentially jointly constructed by the reader, the listeners/participators and the text. In school, both adults and children read aloud in classes, groups and one to one. Most commonly, adult-led reading aloud occurs within:

- Comprehension instruction
- Writing instruction

DOI: 10.4324/9781003215615-10

- Cross-curricular lessons
- Dedicated timetabled slots
- Assemblies

In each of these situations, reading aloud is used for different purposes. In English lessons and across the curriculum for instance, the teacher's intention in reading an extract or chapter may be to scrutinise it for the purposes of comprehension, develop inference and deduction skills, or share new knowledge and introduce subject specific vocabulary. Such teacher-led practice is not however focused on developing the habit of free voluntary reading and whilst it may be an enjoyable experience, it will not necessarily lead to this. Studying rich texts in English is no guarantee of children choosing to read such texts or authors in their own time, and although teacher-led read aloud may trigger some children to read the next book in the series, or another by the same author, much will depend upon staff knowledge, text availability and the young people's identities as readers. Keen able readers are far more likely than their less experienced peers to follow up texts that they are introduced to in English, so paying close attention to the consequences of reading aloud is critical if the goal is to nurture choice-led reading. Reading Teachers notice children's responses to reading aloud, particularly those who are not yet keen readers and act upon what they observe in ways that seek to maximise the impact on children's engagement and desire to read.

As the DfE (2021a: 1) state, 'high quality reading aloud *for pleasure* is in addition to reading aloud as part of literacy teaching'. This is the focus of the current chapter which, through combining research and practice, highlights the benefits, challenges and underpinning principles of reading aloud in order to nurture voluntary reading. Reading Teachers Matthew Courtney and Ben Harris both dedicate substantial time in school to sharing stories, non-fiction, poetry and other texts for pleasure with children and also offer opportunities for the young people to choose to read aloud to one another. Whether dedicated read aloud time motivates children to choose to read in their own time depends on multiple factors, including the text, the reader, the others involved and the wider social context. Summarised in Figure 5.1, these factors indicate the complexity of reading aloud as a socially shared reading experience.

Worryingly, data suggest that reading aloud in UK homes is declining, particularly around the age of eight once children can read to themselves (Farshore, 2020). In school, the pressure of curriculum coverage and the reading for proficiency agenda also constrain this practice, but when sensitively combined with the other strands of RfP pedagogy (Cremin, Mottram, Powell, Collins and Safford, 2014), reading aloud can inspire and encourage the habit of reading in childhood.

The benefits of reading aloud for pleasure

It is widely claimed and generally accepted by practitioners, policymakers, publishers and scholars that reading aloud has both cognitive and affective benefits (e.g. Trelease, 2013; DfE, 2021b). The research literature that examines reading aloud to children at home predominantly uses quantifiable research methods, such as surveys, for example Bus, van IJzendoorn and Pellegrini (1995), highlighted that irrespective of family income, reading

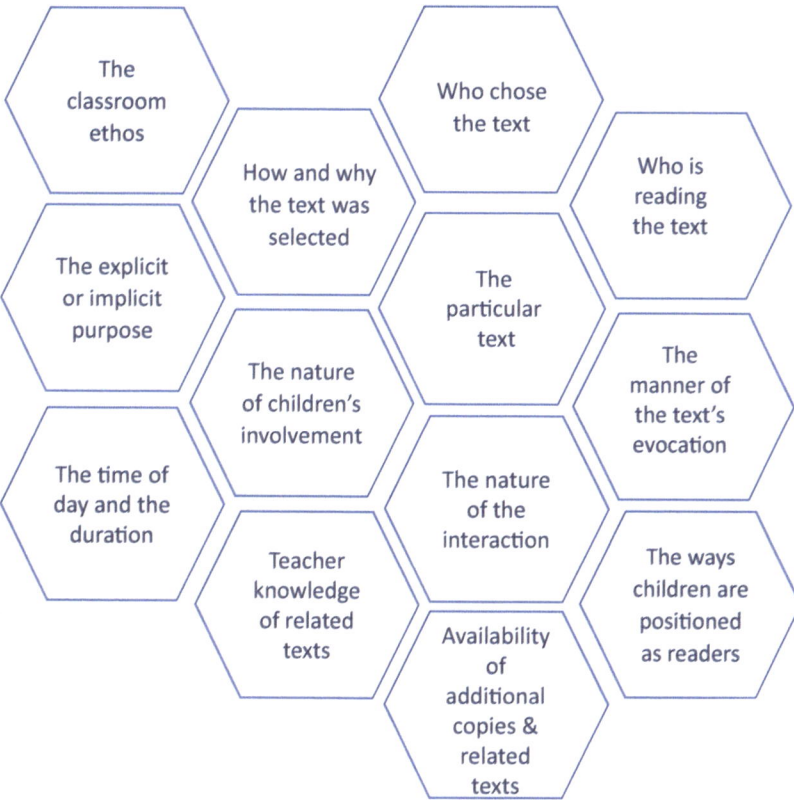

Figure 5.1 Factors influencing the impact of reading aloud on volitional reading

aloud positively impacts on children's oral language acquisition, emergent literacy and reading. Later studies affirm this Stahl, 2003) and, drawing on a longitudinal study of Australian children, Kalb and van Ours (2013) found an association between reading aloud recurrently to 4- to 5-year-olds and the reading, mathematics and cognitive skills of these children age 8 to 9.

Reading aloud research also tracks impact on vocabulary (Lenhart, Lenhard, Vaahtoranta, and Suggate, 2018) and on decontextualised language, showing for example, that 'extra-textual talk' (i.e. conversations around reading aloud that are not solely word focused) are associated with vocabulary gains (Zucker, Justice, Pentimonti, Cabell and Kaderavek, 2013). Other studies conclude that children must *use* the words in the text, as well as hear them for vocabulary gains to persist (Wasik and Hindman, 2014). In this latter work, teachers' use of contextualised text talk (in the book) and decontextualised text talk (beyond the book), as part of read aloud was seen to be advantageous in enhancing children's vocabulary. However, it is challenging to isolate reading aloud as a standalone factor influencing literacy learning in homes and classrooms. In many cases, the benefits claimed are deemed to be limited (Swanson et al., 2011), and there is relatively little research which examines read aloud as it happens, or the impact on children's reader identities or later voluntary reading.

In one classroom intervention study, the research team found to their surprise that 'just reading' challenging novels at pace made a marked impact on the comprehension of all the adolescents, but particularly the less capable readers (Westbrook, Sutherland, Oakhill and Sullivan, 2019). Repositioned as 'good' rather than 'struggling' readers, these 12- to 13-year-olds benefitted from experiencing quality novels without interruption. They made 16 months progress on standardised reading comprehension tests over three months and were keen to hear the ongoing narrative. The team suggest that these less experienced readers may previously have received an impoverished reading diet with more time spent on skill development, rather than reading for pleasure. Other work also concludes that hearing cognitively challenging and engaging texts, enables less fluent readers to experience autonomy and fluency and enhances comprehension (Kuhn, Schwanenflugen and Meisinger, 2010).

Additional benefits associated with regularly hearing stories and other texts, relate to potential affective and behavioural consequences, with Kucirkova and Cremin (2020: 77) asserting that 'expressive reading aloud to young children conditions them to associate reading with pleasure', especially if the experience with parents, carers, teachers and classmates is a rich and enjoyable one. Listening to audio books can also be tempting for many young people, with a UK based survey indicating that 59% of children and young people perceived this enhances their interest in reading (Best, Clark and Picton, 2020). Adult readers too often report that being read to impacted on their positive dispositions towards reading (Merga, 2017), and, drawing on observational and interview data, Cremin et al. (2014) argue that developing a shared repertoire of 'books in common' through reading aloud helps build social connections, reader relationships and the development of classroom reading communities. Living through the tensions and delights of narratives or encountering new information together, can create a sense of belonging which is particularly valuable for children from marginalised groups (e.g. those speaking English as an additional language and less assured readers). Reading aloud speaks to their intelligence and capacity to understand complex texts, albeit they cannot yet read these for themselves.

Through in-person read alouds, Reading Teachers model, explicitly and implicitly, the kinds of things readers do – like make connections, respond and voice how a book might sound and feel. This can help children understand more about the experience of reading and provide a model for expressive reading in their own heads. Additionally, reading aloud can offer a foundation for later understanding, enhance prior knowledge, introduce children to the grammar of written language, tune the ear of young writers and nurture more positive attitudes to reading (Moses and Kelly, 2018). It can, research suggests, entice less-able children to want to read (Canoy, van Ours and van der Ploeg, 2006) and can help sustain a love of reading for keen readers (Leung, Moore, Bennett and Alberton Gunn, 2018). In another classroom study, children became more engaged in quiet reading and sustained this for longer periods after daily reading aloud was implemented (Pegg and Bartelheim, 2011). This highlights the interrelationship of the strands of RfP pedagogy and the need to ensure the experience does not create passivity, but offers agency and involvement (Cremin, 2019).

Children's involvement and agency in reading aloud

It is easy however to be guised into thinking that because children appear to be attentive when a teacher reads aloud, everyone is listening. Some children may be choosing not to listen, may be taking a well-earned break or see it as entertainment, not an invitation to engage. Reading Teachers who reflect on their own experience will recognise this; Teresa for instance frequently drives back from work ostensibly listening to the radio yet not hearing a word. Ben and Matthew readily acknowledge that in school assemblies or briefings, their attention is not always 100%. So, seeking child involvement is key. This is particularly important for children who don't see themselves as 'good readers', who lack confidence, dislike reading and may not associate reading with pleasure.

Children's involvement in read aloud can take many forms. In the early years, by balancing 'novelty' with 'familiar' books, teachers encourage participation and joining in with words, chants and actions. This often leads to the book being revisited later during free play. Simple props and puppets are helpful too, enabling children to retell or dramatise the text, supporting sense making and their desire to read more about the characters. In later years, depending on the nature of the text, children's playful engagement can still be invited, for example with picture books such as *The Book with No Pictures* (BJ Novak) or *Click Clack Moo, Cows that Type* (Doreen Cronin). Children can also be involved by drawing if they wish, or connecting with the authors on social media, identifying questions they'd like answered or exploring authors' websites.

Reading Teachers, recognising the importance of choice and agency in their own lives as readers, seek to offer an element of choice – about where children sit or what text is to be read. Many invite the class to choose what they'd like to hear, and encourage voting for the day's picture fiction text using counters. With novels, offering resumes of a few carefully selected texts (e.g. adventure stories, World War II), and giving time for children to discuss these before voting, offers a degree of agency. Additionally, many schools regularly offer 'You Choose' Fridays when children select from a menu of read aloud choices. Drawing on their own preferences and passions, staff focus on particular genres or themes and children select who and what they are going to listen to and discuss. These mixed-age opportunities can help to build reading communities.

Reading Teachers also offer opportunities for children to choose to read aloud to each other in pairs, groups or to the class. Research indicates this supportively positions children as readers, by taking the 'reader's chair' for instance in dedicated reading time (Moffatt, Heydon and Iannacci, 2019) or simply gathering in groups to read books aloud together. Alternatively, children may choose to read aloud during library visits, in the outdoor book area, in Read Aloud assemblies and with reading buddies from different year groups. Ensuring these learner-led occasions are not required or regulated is important if the goal is voluntary choice-led reading.

Children's interaction in reading aloud

During teacher read alouds there are multiple opportunities for interaction, before, during and after the whole text or section of it has been voiced. Some research indicates that when children are invited to make predictions, connections and ask questions, for example, they are more focused and may reap greater benefits (Zevenbergen and Whitehurst, 2008), but balance is key. The danger is that the discourse of comprehension lessons enters the space dedicated to reading aloud for pleasure, resulting in a battery of targeted teacher-led questions that seek to check children are developing reading skills (Hempel-Jorgensen, Cremin, Harris and Chamberlain, 2018). This misappropriation of reading aloud will not fuel children's desire to read voluntarily in their own time.

Social interaction around the text that is low key, informal and relaxed is more likely to invite and retain children's interest and nurture voluntary reading. With novels, a quick recap can help, but quizzes need to be avoided. Conversations about the text that focus on possible meanings and interpretations, without a whiff of assessment or evaluation are both more enticing to participate in and more inclusive. Using drama conventions briefly before a chapter can also enhance engagement. By creating freeze frames of a future event, making sculptures of the text's theme or role playing a previous scene, children revisit and inhabit the narrative and share their views. Such activities operate as focusing tools, increasing the number of listening ears when the read aloud commences. Additionally, using a visualiser to reveal a graphic novel's intricacies, scanning in picture fiction to share in assembly and promoting the author's work or other books on the same theme, can entice children to follow through.

To retain the focus on learner-led read aloud, children's questions will often, though not always, frame the discussion. Professional decisions about if and when to stop and invite comment or questions will depend on the readers, the text and the teacher's experience. Ben, who teaches 10- to 11-year-olds, sees reading aloud as 'the heart blood of the curriculum' and observes:

> I don't stop to check comprehension or the meaning of tricky vocabulary whilst I am reading. I used to but it tampers with flow and to be frank messes up the spell that the author's words are creating. I stop at the end of a chapter and simply ask 'Does anyone have anything they want to say about that bit we've just read?' There is always something.

Most of the time, as he notes, it is thinking and interpretation that no question of his own could ever have elicited. He is conscious that children often simply give their own explanations and comments, but that there are times when debate and discussion begin to develop. He recognises the young people don't see disagreement between themselves negatively and that 'it often produces felicitous delight in how a book has shown two readers completely different things'. Such openness to multiple meanings is not a given however and will have been modelled by Ben. Significantly he also records that in every session he learns something too – about the book itself and the children. When he asked whether it would matter if he just read the book aloud and cut the discussion, his class were adamant that talk was essential to the experience: 'Talking makes you read the book properly', one replied. 'You get to express your feelings about it. And you get to listen to other people's thoughts, so you see their perspective too'. Through hearing others' views the children in Ben's class are learning there is no single story – as Adichie Chimamanda asserted in her seminal 2013 TED talk – no correct interpretation. Like adults, children construct their understandings of texts based on lived experience and vicarious experiences from books, films and TV. They make sense and negotiate possible meanings through making connections, alone and with each other. It is to such connection making we now turn.

Children make connections during reading aloud

Research has found that children from the least advantaged backgrounds have fewer opportunities than their peers to participate in dialogic read alouds (when relaxed conversation and dialogue plays a central role) and are less likely to be viewed and positioned as readers in class (Moffatt et al., 2019). Unconsciously subtle issues of language, culture and class play out in classrooms, but Matthew and Ben both agree, providing the space and time for children to make multiple connections is essential to enrich *all* children's engagement, understanding and the pleasure they derive from the experience. Connections are tools for making meaning and may involve text-to-self, text-to-world and text-to-text connections. As Matthew states, whilst reading aloud is not always teacher-led, it is important to recognise that teachers need to facilitate and encourage children to voice these connections. He suggests that Bishop's (1990) seminal metaphor of books acting as 'mirrors, windows and sliding glass doors' offers a useful framework to explore the role reading aloud can play in fostering and developing children's connections with texts. He highlights how books as mirrors offer text-to-self-connections, and books as windows and sliding glass doors enable text-to-world and text-to-text connections.

Text-to-self connections: Matthew maintains that text-to-self connections increase children's engagement and are the core of many classroom discussions and book blethers. For instance, he remembers reading Alexandra Strick and Sean Stockdale's *Max the Champion*, and the discussion and laughter it prompted about the children's experiences of sports days and a disastrous egg and spoon race. Matthew models such text-to-self connections, for example when reading Jessica Love's *Julian at the Wedding*, he showed the children personal photographs of him at special events, helping them make richer links with the themes of love, belonging and celebration. Matthew considers that the impact of children being exposed to books which reflect their experiences is tangible and finds that when they choose books to read to themselves, children are frequently drawn to those in which they made text-to-self connections. Realising that reading aloud fuels their interests, he capitalises on this by reading related poems and non-fiction and notices these texts are snapped up in the book corner too.

In addition to curating the read aloud collection, Matthew offers rereadings and multiple copies of his core set, so that children can access those they've connected to and can re-visit them later. Such rereading is endorsed by the English government's early years Reading Framework (DfE, 2021b), perhaps because research indicates that as young children become more familiar with a text and its narrative, they engage more deeply, creatively and critically (Rodriguez-Leon and Payler, 2021).

Text-to-world connections: By reading aloud books which offer children 'windows and sliding glass doors' (Bishop, 1990) into others' experiences, Matthew also encourages text-to-world connections that may go beyond children's everyday lives. For example, by reading *It's a No-Money Day* by Kate Milner (a family visit a food bank), or *The Suitcase* by Chris Naylor-Ballesteros (an immigration allegory). He argues that these age-appropriate texts encourage emotive responses and describes how 6-year-old Kazeem connected *The Suitcase* to a Newsround item he had seen about World Refugee Day. In order to develop the children's empathy, Matthew works to mediate the subject matter and structures discussions carefully, modelling this using the sentence stem 'this reminds me of . . .' and positioning himself authentically as a reader too.

Text-to-text connections: Matthew also fosters children making inter-textual connections by reading aloud for pleasure several texts linked to the core English text. For example, when using Simon Bartram's *Man on the Moon* as the core text, he complemented this by reading *Astro Girl* (Ken Wilson-Max), *Look Up!* (Nathan Bryon and Dapo Adeola) and others. The children noticed similarities and highlighted differences and Matthew found that the hybrid nature of *Look Up!*, (which includes facts dispersed through the story) allowed for additional intertextual connections. He argues that in order to facilitate children making connections, teachers need to model this and offer a rich and linked read aloud diet. Wall displays of shared 'books in common' can also support this, nurturing future text-to-text connections as well as connections between readers.

> The books which we live through together for the sole purpose of shared enjoyment represent a rich resource for conversation, for connection and for spinning webs of reader relationships. Such 'books in common' nurture our pleasure in reading and play a particularly resonant role in helping build communities of engaged readers.
> (Cremin, 2019: 5)

Crucially, reading aloud enables children to experience texts above the level they can access easily independently. However, their comprehension will be shaped by the way the text is brought to life.

Voicing texts that tempt

There is no blueprint for reading aloud well, as each occasion will differ, shaped by the listener/s, the text and the reader, but key principles exist which Reading Teachers recognise. The choice of text is one such principle and as noted earlier it is beneficial if children are involved. One year, 88% of Ben's class responding to a survey about read aloud, stated that they wanted more ownership of the book choice, so the novels Ben now reads are chosen by the class from a small selection he offers. He finds picking these shortlists easier as he gets to know his readers, and researches and reads each book first, so he is cognizant of the content and the sensitivities it may trigger. As he observes, this also helps him to 'shape' the narrative with his voice, and plan pacing and prompts for discussion. In many schools, the label 'story time' is used, in others it is avoided to ensure that attention is paid to the power of poetry, non-fiction and other texts that respond to children's interests. Nonetheless, fiction is a vital motivator, creating involvement and challenge, and can lead to increases in voluntary reading (McGeown, Osborne, Warhurst, Norgate and Duncan, 2016).

The texts offered need to tempt the particular listeners so relying on teacher's favourites is inappropriate, especially since professional knowledge of texts tends to be limited, and books from teachers' own childhoods and celebrity authors predominate (Cremin, Mottram, Bearne and Goodwin, 2008; Clark and Teravainen, 2015). A recent survey of UK teachers underscored this challenge, with Roald Dahl being one of the most popular authors for reading aloud online to children during lockdown (CLPE, 2021). In the US too, Conradi Smith, Young and Yatzeck (2022) show teachers rely on fiction texts that are on average, 25 years old! Widening professional knowledge is essential, so that teachers can offer a rich contemporary range, including for example, poetry (perennially a knowledge gap), and the first in a series of books. Both can be effective tools in supporting later volitional reading. Ben regularly finds that even less engaged readers will, when supported, follow up a poet or seek out the next book, particularly when the original text resonated with them.

Although conveying personal pleasure and interest in a read aloud text is persuasive and important, exaggerated dramatics are best avoided; there is no need to over-perform it. Being responsive to the children's reactions and giving life to the text in ways that surface its layers of meaning are far more significant. This requires knowledge of the text and the capacity to sustain the children's imaginative engagement through evoking it effectively and with feeling. Reading Teachers work to develop their inner ear for the poetic language of text and their inner eye for visual details, so that they can tune in to the text's music, the characters' emotions and any pictorial creations. The author's and illustrator's emotional communication with readers needs to be both felt and voiced. Reading Teachers will also notice the children's engagement and will seek, with asides, comments and thinking aloud about the text, to involve the less attentive.

Authentic readings will sensitively deploy pace, pause and intonation to convey emotion, and draw children into an internal and, later perhaps, an external, affective conversation with the text and other readers. Affect is central to the subjective experience of reading and a key driver of volitional reading; it supports children in developing expressive reading in their own heads and helps them connect to the text's themes. Effective voicing of a read aloud thus builds bonds between the text, the teacher and the listeners whose views about the lived experience of reading aloud deserve attention.

Children's perceptions of reading aloud

Ben believes that in his classroom, the reading community develops largely as a result of his commitment to a daily shared read aloud routine of 25 minutes, plus book chat. Each year, he pays particular attention to his class's feedback about the experience, and notes that whilst he used to read at the end of the day, he found this wasn't conducive to quality listening and conversation, whereas after lunch, children are more alert and keener to discuss the book. Some of the most popular books chosen by 10- to 11-year-olds from Ben's shortlists, include:

- *Christmas Dinner of Souls* by Ross Montgomery
- *Ghost* by Jason Reynolds
- *Jelly* by Jo Cotterill
- *When the Sky Falls* by Phil Earle
- *Cloud Busting* by Malorie Blackman

In addition, Ben always asks why the children think reading aloud is important given they can all choose their own books and read for themselves. The responses from a recent class make fascinating reading (see Table 5.1).

Ben grouped their responses into five categories and was interested to note that these range from recognition of perceived affective benefits (related both to individual well-being and to a sense of community) to widening repertoires and skills, as well as his own personal pleasure in the process. Language denoting affective states, including for instance 'happy', 'excited', 'relax[ed]', 'likes', 'love' and 'enjoy' are evident, perhaps because as Ben observes 'The whole feel of the room changes when reading aloud: we are woven

Table 5.1 Response to the question: Why do I still read aloud to you daily when you can read to yourselves?

Well-being	Repertoire/ knowledge	Reading skill	Community	Personal pleasure
Because it's relaxing.	To read stories we maybe haven't heard of before!	I heard online that when someone reads aloud to you it helps your skill to read.	So that we can enjoy the book with him and so we can all discuss about it together.	Because he likes it.
To let us relax.				Because he likes reading a lot.
It makes us all happy.	So we can learn about topics in the book.			He enjoys it.
Because, after lunch, its calming.	To share other stories which we may have not chosen.	To sort of educate us in a way? Like a fun way.	Because he wants to share his love with reading with the class.	Because he likes reading.
To make us happy.		It might not sound as good in my head.	So the whole class can get a reaction of their friends.	Because he likes reading and I am pretty sure that he is better than most people if not all at reading.
		For us to understand more.	Because he wants to share the book and his love for reading with us.	Because he loves reading.
		So we understand the book.	To make us feel excited what is going to happen next, share thoughts and recommend books and films.	

together by the story and by our talk around the book itself'. In exploring more about the children's views of his role during read aloud, Ben was told that his delivery of the text supports their comprehension.

> When you do voices for the characters, it projects the things you're reading into my head. . . . It helps because you can hear what is going on. You get to understand the story much better.
>
> (Mark)

> I can think more deeply into it when you're reading to us. When I'm reading to myself, sometimes I'm not always taking it in, but when you read it, I can understand it and it makes the book better.
>
> (Niamh)

The children's responses to other questions indicate that they are acutely aware that their teacher wants to make the experience enjoyable and that he values and loves reading aloud to them and is a reader himself. For instance, in commenting on what Ben is thinking about during a read aloud session, many children suggested he might be reflecting on how the reading is coming across and if the class are appreciating the narrative 'Are 6BH liking this story? I'm going to ask'. Some children, conscious that Ben sees this as a time when the story is given their full attention, also thought he might be thinking about keeping the class focused 'I hope they're not talking. I don't want to stop in the middle of a good book again' and 'Be quiet or you will put me off reading'. Ben describes his role in read aloud sessions as *'an orchestrator of pleasure in reading'* which these responses also reflect.

In contrast to Ben's class, one Australian survey found that whilst most children enjoyed being read to, nearly a quarter reported disliking the experience (Ledger and Merga, 2018). Their reasons related to a lack of reader autonomy and pace interruptions, behaviour management issues and some resistance to the emotional engagement offered. For these young people, and those interviewed initially in an earlier UK study (Cremin et al., 2014), reading aloud was not a positive shared, social experience. This highlights the value of seeking pupils' views and adapting and adjusting provision in response. In the latter study, once the teachers had stopped tethering reading aloud to written comprehension and had begun to read solely for pleasure as part of planned RfP pedagogy, a sense of trust and community gradually developed.

Reading aloud and community

Over time, in the classrooms of Reading Teachers, children develop more reciprocal and interactive reader to reader relationships with their teachers, these are hallmarks of reading communities. The following conversation between Alyssa and Ben indicates this.

> Have you read 'Pop', Mr Harris?
> No, not yet – it was only published yesterday!
> Well, if we do all choose this one to read as a class, can you not read it first like you usually do? You always ask us about the book you're reading to us, but you know what's going to happen because you've read it first. If you don't read Pop! then you won't know the end either and we can all wonder about it together.

As Ben observes in response, the word 'together' here is key. It takes us back to the ancient art of storytelling, and to our ancestors sitting together while tales, legends and poetry became living breath in the storyteller's mouth. He argues that a felt sense of community arises when groups of human beings are connected together by narratives, and strengthened by the knowledge, history and emotion in the story. In times past, as Ben states, the audience would have been in thrall to the bard, who in recounting the actions of great heroes, would also be improvising and elaborating in the telling, in the way that Scheherazade is now famed. Ben proposes too that as storytellers retold and reshaped tales, they also perhaps enjoyed passing on the emotional charge of *not* knowing – and experienced the heightened thrill of the unknown. This is what he suggests is implied in the fleeting interaction with Alyssa recalled earlier. At this point in the year, his class had deepened their relationships by hearing and discussing 12 'books in common' and now Alyssa was entreating him to step back from guiding them. Ben surmises that the request for him to live through the narrative alongside them indicates there was both a readiness and a willingness to go into the unknown together. Ben was being invited to join the classroom reading community on an equal footing, both as a fellow reader and a living listener to the shared read aloud. A mark of respect.

Conclusion

There is potential magic in reading aloud a brilliant text to a class of children. Moments when everyone, including the teacher, are held within the story's spell, when together the class respond emotionally with laughter, anger or surprise in this affect-driven affinity space. Reading aloud for pleasure can be a powerful shared experience, but it is not a panacea, a solo remedy that turns disengaged readers into keen and eager ones. Teachers need to pay attention to the consequences of this esteemed and valued practice, stay alert to those who may be less engaged and to seek out the young people's views and offer opportunities for them to read aloud also.

However, in the hands of consciously reflective Reading Teachers such as Ben and Matthew, its potential can be realised. When thoughtfully planned and developed in a manner which is learner led, informal, social and with texts that tempt, reading aloud can inspire and motivate choice-led independent reading. When working in tandem alongside the other strands of RfP pedagogy it is an inherently valuable practice, one which makes explicit the very nature of reading, demonstrating that reading is personal, social, affective and relational. Through reading aloud, the inner world of reading is modelled, experienced and lived.

If the teacher's purpose is clear, to nurture volitional reading, then involving the children in making connections between the text and their own lives, the lives of others and other texts, and enabling them to voice these connections and share their views is vital. These connections can fuel further reading and enhance the social and emotional connections between and among children and their teachers. In this way reading aloud builds bonds and a sense of togetherness and community that will last well beyond the pages read.

Recommended reading

Kucirkova, N. and Cremin, T. (2020) *Children Reading for Pleasure in the Digital Age: Mapping Reader Engagement*. London: Sage.

Moffatt, L., Heydon, R. and Iannacci, L. (2019) Helping out, signing up and sitting down: The cultural production of 'read-alouds' in three kindergarten classrooms. *Journal of Early Childhood Literacy*, 19(2): 147–174.

Westbrook, J., Sutherland, J., Oakhill, J. and Sullivan, S. (2018) 'Just reading': The impact of a faster pace of reading narratives on the comprehension of poorer adolescent readers in English classrooms. *Literacy*, 53(2): 60–68.

Children's books

Blackman, M. (2005) *Cloud Busting*. London: Random House.
Byron, N. and Adeola, D. (2019) *Look Up!* London: Penguin.
Cotterill, J. (2018) *Jelly*. London: Piccadilly Press.
Cronin, D. and Lewin, B. (2002) *Click Clack Moo, Cows that Type*. London: Pocket.
Earle, P. (2021) *When the Sky Falls*. London: Anderson Press.
Love, J. (2018) *Julian at the Wedding*. London: Walker.
Milner, K. (2019) *It's a No-Money Day*. Edinburgh: Barrington Stoke.
Montgomery, R. (2017) *Christmas Dinner of Souls*. London: Faber.
Naylor-Ballesteros, C. (2019) *The Suitcase*. London: Nosy Crow.

Novak, B. J. (2017) *The Book with No Pictures*. London: Penguin Random House.
Reynolds, J. (2018) *Ghost*. London: Knights of.
Strick, A. and Stockdale, S. (2013) *Max the Champion*. London: Frances Lincoln.

References

Best, E., Clark, C. and Picton, I. (2020) *Children, Young People and Audiobooks Before and During Lockdown*. National Literacy Trust. Available at: https://cdn.literacytrust.org.uk/media/documents/Children_and_young_peoples_engagement_with_audiobooks_2020_-_before_and_during_ltd-vFpG.pdf (Accessed 2 November 2021).

Bishop, R. S. (1990) Mirrors, windows and sliding glass doors. *Perspectives: Choosing and Using Books for the Classroom*, 6(3): x–xi.

Bus, A. G., van IJzendoorn, M. H. and Pellegrini, A. D. (1995) Joint book reading makes for success in learning to read: A meta-analysis on intergenerational transmission of literacy. *Review of Educational Research*, 65: 1–21.

Canoy, M., van Ours, J. C. and van der Ploeg, F. (2006) The economics of books. In A. Ginsburgh and D. Throsby (Eds.), *Handbook of the Economics of Art and Culture*, pp. 721–761. Amsterdam: Elsevier.

Clark, C. and Teravainen, A. (2015) *Teachers and Literacy: Their Perceptions, Understanding, Confidence and Awareness*. Available at: https://cdn.literacytrust.org.uk/media/documents/2015_11_03_free_research_-_teachers_and_literacy_2015_0EcH766.pdf

CLPE (2021) *Reflecting Realities. Survey of Ethnic Representation within UK Children's Literature 2020*. Available at: https://clpe.org.uk/system/files/CLPE%20Reflecting%20Realities%202020.pdf

Conradi Smith, K., Young, C. A. and Yatzeck, C. J. (2022) What are teachers reading and why?: An analysis of elementary read aloud titles and the rationales underlying teachers' selections. *Literacy Research and Instruction*. DOI: 10.1080/19388071.2021.2008558

Cremin, T., Mottram, M. Bearne, E. and Goodwin, P. (2008) Exploring teachers' knowledge of children's literature *Cambridge Journal of Education*, 38(4): 449–464.

Cremin, T. (2019) *Reading Communities, What Why and How*. Available at: https://cdn.ourfp.org/wp-content/uploads/20210301105855/Reading_Communities_TCremin_2019.pdf?_ga=2.59134382.245682993.1632677737-2008111907.1613423023

Cremin, T., Mottram, M., Powell, S., Collins, R. and Safford, K. (2014) *Building Communities of Engaged Readers: Reading for Pleasure*. London and New York: Routledge.

DfE (2021a) *Reading for Pleasure Audit*. DfE English Hubs. London: DfE.

DfE (2021b) *The Reading Framework: Teaching the Foundations of Literacy*. London: DfE. Available at: www.gov.uk/government/publications/the-reading-framework-teaching-the-foundations-of-literacy

Farshore (2020) *Children's Reading for Pleasure*. Available at: http://s28434.p595.sites.pressdns.com/sitefarshore/wp-content/uploads/sites/46/2021/03/Reading-for-Pleasure-2020-Farshore.pdf

Hempel-Jorgensen, A., Cremin, T., Harris, D. and Chamberlain, L. (2018) Pedagogy for reading for pleasure in low socio-economic primary schools: Beyond 'pedagogy of poverty'? *Literacy*, 52(2).

Kalb, G. and Van Ours, J. C. (2013 Reading to young children: A head-start in life? *Economics of Education Review*, 40: 1–24.

Kuhn, M., Schwanenflugen, P. and Meisinger, E. (2010) Aligning theory and assessment of reading fluency: Automaticity, prosody, and definitions of fluency. *Reading Research Quarterly*, 45(2): 230–251.

Ledger, S. and Merga, M. K. (2018) Reading aloud: Children's attitudes toward being read to at home and at school. *Australian Journal of Teacher Education*, 43(3): 124–139. https://doi.org/10.14221/ajte.2018v43n3.8

Lenhart, J., Lenhard, W., Vaahtoranta, E. and Suggate, S. (2018) Incidental vocabulary acquisition from listening to stories: A comparison between read-aloud and free storytelling approaches. *Educational Psychology*, 38(3): 596–616.

Leung, C., Moore, L., Bennett, S. and Alberton Gunn, A. (2018) Classroom storybook reading as a dialogic speech event. *Literacy Practice and Research*, Fall 2018, 17–25.

McGeown, S., Osborne, C., Warhurst, A., Norgate, R. and Duncan, L. (2016) Understanding children's reading activities: Reading motivation, skill and child characteristics as predictors. *Journal of Research in Reading*, 39(1): 109–125.

Merga, M. K. (2017) Becoming a reader: Significant social influences on avid book readers. *School Library Research*, 20: 1–20.

Moses, L. and Kelly, L. (2018) 'We're a little loud. That's because we like to read!': Developing positive views of reading in a diverse, urban first grade. *Journal of Early Childhood Literacy*, 18(3): 307–337.

Pegg, L. A. and Bartelheim, F. J. (2011) Effects of daily read-alouds on students' sustained silent reading. *Current Issues in Education*, 14: 1–8.

Rodriguez-Leon, L. and Payler, J. (2021) Surfacing complexity in shared book reading: The role of affordance, repetition and modal appropriation in children's participation. *Learning, Culture and Social Interaction*, 28. https://doi.org/10.1016/j.lcsi.2021.100496

Stahl, S. A. (2003) What do we expect storybook reading to do? How storybook reading impacts word recognition. In A. Van Kleeck, S. A. Stahl and E. Bauer (Eds.), *On Reading Books to Children*, pp. 390–409. Mahwah, NJ: Erlbaum.

Swanson, E., Vaughn, S., Wanzek, J., Petscher, Y., Heckert, J., Cavanaugh, C., Kraft, G. and Tackett, K. (2011) A synthesis of read-aloud interventions on early reading outcomes among preschool through third graders at risk for reading difficulties. *Journal of Learning Disabilities*, 44(3): 258–275.

Trelease, J. (2013) *The Read-Aloud Handbook*. New York: Penguin.

Wasik, B. and Hindman, A. (2014) Understanding the active ingredients in an effective preschool vocabulary intervention: an exploratory study of teacher and child talk during book reading. *Early Education and Development*, 25: 1035–1056.

Westbrook, J., Sutherland, J. Oakhill, J. and Sullivan, S. (2019) 'Just reading': The impact of a faster pace of reading narratives on the comprehension of poorer adolescent readers in English classrooms. *Literacy*, 53(2): 60–68.

Zevenbergen, A. and Whitehurst, G. J. (2008) Dialogic reading: A shared picture book reading intervention for preschoolers. In A. Van Kleeck, S. A. Stahl and E. B. Bauer (Eds.), *On reading Books to Children Parents and Teachers*. London: Lawrence Erlbaum Associates Publishers.

Zucker, T. A., Justice, L. M., Pentimonti, J. M., Cabell, S. Q. and Kaderavek, J. N (2013) The role of frequent, interactive prekindergarten shared reading in the longitudinal development of language and literacy skills. *Developmental Psychology*, 49: 1425–1439.

Chapter 6

Informal book talk and reader recommendations

Lucy Rodriguez Leon and Jon Biddle

Introduction

The popularity of book clubs is testament to the joy people find in talking about a book with likeminded folk. Reading can be an intense experience; there may have been a time that something you read affected you so deeply that you felt compelled to tell someone immediately. Whilst reading tends to be thought of as an individual and solitary endeavour, our desire to talk about the books, and other texts we read, exemplifies the social nature of reading. As Evans (2009) states, 'Many children read books alone without sharing them or talking about them; this is hardly ever enough to enable in-depth, meaningful understandings to take place' (p. 5).

The significance of book talk in promoting children's enjoyment in reading and in developing their critical thinking has been evidenced in research (Cremin, Mottram, Collins, Powell and Safford, 2014; Roche, 2015; Moses, Ogden and Kelly, 2015). A study in the United States examined strategies to facilitate pupil-led book talk, finding that peer discussion enhanced engagement in and motivation for literature (Moses et al., 2015). These authors also noted that as book talk became established, children began creating opportunities to use comprehension strategies learnt in class, they appeared to take greater responsibility for their own learning, and they supported each other. Similarly, the Teachers as Readers (TaRs) study developed Chambers' (1993) conceptualisation of book talk and illustrated how informal conversations around books and reader recommendations were key strands of Reading for Pleasure pedagogy (Cremin et al., 2014). The teachers participating in the research noticed a difference between book talk that was teacher-directed and that which was child-led. Reflecting on their practice, they also realised that the majority of talk around books in their classrooms was teacher controlled and tended to focus on skill acquisition and assessment. Children had little space for informal and spontaneous book chat; opportunities for children to discuss aspects of the book that really mattered to them were few and far between.

However, through discussing their own reading with others, these teachers came to fully appreciate the motivational power of book talk, and how such talk underpins reader-to-reader recommendations (Cremin et al., 2014). They committed to create time and space in their classrooms to nurture talk that was free from assessment criteria and unconstrained by curricula goals, they sought ways to nurture the kind of talk that emerges from children's own interests or concerns. Furthermore, these teachers soon noticed that when they showed genuine interest in what children had to say, and when they engaged in reciprocal dialogue with children, book talk became more sophisticated. Over time they began to discuss characters, plots and scenarios in greater depth and detail, and they began to discuss their own preferences for genre, authors and poets.

Book talk and reader recommendations go hand-in-hand. Book talk has the potential to raise the status of books in the classroom, it can make reading 'cool' (Moses et al., 2015). The motivational power of hearing peers talk about a text with real enthusiasm and passion cannot be overstated. In addition, teachers who have well-developed knowledge of children's literature and other texts, and who have good knowledge of individual children as readers are well placed to recommend appropriate books to children (Cremin et al., 2014). This is essential in teaching, because being able to put the right book in the right child's hands at the right moment, can change that child's relationship with reading forever (Collins and Safford, 2008).

In this chapter, we rethink traditional views of what engaged reading looks like; whilst the image of a child engrossed in a book, oblivious to all going on around them, remains a vision of a highly engaged reader, we propose that it is not the only way that children can be deeply involved in a book, or other text. In this chapter we explore different types of talk around texts and discuss some of the theories that underpin the educational, social and emotional benefits of book talk. Drawing on examples from Jon's classroom with 10- to 11-year-olds, we will consider a range of strategies to promote book talk and reader recommendations in schools.

What do we mean by 'book talk'?

Informal book talk is quite distinct from the teacher-led classroom talk that you might use to develop and assess children's reading comprehension. The informal talk that emerges responsively from, or around engagement in a book (or other text) takes many different forms. These conversations might involve a brief exchange or might be sustained over a longer time. It might be a conversation that is revisited on multiple occasions over the course of days or even weeks. Book talk might involve a few surface level passing comments about the text, or the discussion might be complex and profound. In the classroom, book talk can emerge spontaneously between readers, or it might originate in a planned, teacher-initiated activity. Furthermore, when a group of children are all familiar with the same book, the talk may continue spontaneously in the corridors and playground, and the narrative may be re-enacted in child-initiated dramatic play or games. However, informal book talk is so much more than frivolous chatter, it not only enhances children's enjoyment and motivation, but it also boosts social, emotional and language development and it is part of the process of constructing meaning and expanding thinking. These aspects of children's development and attitudes to reading are not easily measured or quantified, but they are evident in observation and can be documented. Yet it is important to note that the nature of talk around books differs considerably. Talk that involves reasoning, questioning and analysis of the text, rather than a literal recall of events, offers the greatest opportunities to enhance meaning and thinking (Roche, 2020). This distinction is exemplified in the following brief transcripts from Lucy's research in a nursery classroom.

The transcripts are extracts of video data that capture 4-year-old Bobby's participation in book talk in two different contexts (Rodriguez Leon and Payler, 2021). All children's names have been changed.

Transcript 1 – teacher-led read-aloud

This first transcript captures a snapshot from a teacher-led group read-aloud of the traditional tale, 'The Little Red Hen'. It begins midway through the reading, when the teacher altered her reading style to phrase the story as a series of questions, encouraging the children to join in. The transcript includes only the teacher's and Bobby's words, other children also participated.

TEACHER: What do you think the duck said?
BOBBY: No
TEACHER: Not I, quacked the duck
TEACHER: What do you think the dog said?
BOBBY: Not I
TEACHER: Not I, barked the dog – what do you think the cat said?
BOBBY: Not I
TEACHER: Not I, meowed the cat – what do you think the pig said?
BOBBY: Not I
TEACHER: Not I, grunted the pig – you're right they all said no – so what do you think the little red hen did?
BOBBY: Chop it down all by herself
TEACHER: She did

Transcript 2 – child-led book sharing in the book corner

On Bobby and Phoebe's request, the adult joined them in the book-corner where Bobby had selected a familiar book, *Shark in the Dark* (Nick Sharratt). Once settled and comfy, the adult began reading and both Bobby and Phoebe joined in, rhythmically reciting the memorable lines. After a few pages, Bobby initiated the following brief dialogue.

BOBBY: There's that bird again
ADULT: Oh yes
BOBBY: And there's the moon again

ADULT: The moon's shining brightly
PHOEBE: And the lighthouse is shining
BOBBY: Why is that bird there when there's the moon?
ADULT: Well . . .
BOBBY: Cos do birds come out at night-time?
ADULT: You know, I'm not sure if seagulls do come out at night-time.
BOBBY: No, I don't think so.

These brief transcripts highlight the difference between recall and book talk in the early years. In the latter episode, Bobby begins to question and critique the book in relation to his own developing knowledge of birds. As Roche (2020) notes, reading-aloud and book talk are not the same thing; however, this is not to underplay the importance of read-alouds, which are fundamental to children's engagement with literature and can be powerful entry points for book talk. However, these transcripts exemplify that when opportunities are created, even very young children can be encouraged to engage critically and creatively with books through talk. Similarly with older children, the aim of informal book talk is not to assess pupils' ability to answer question from a passage of text in preparation of reading comprehension tests. Spontaneous and responsive conversations around books and other texts will indeed boost comprehension, however it is not the central purpose of such informal book talk. A transcript from Jon's class of 10- to 11-year-olds later in this chapter demonstrates how the sophistication and depth of book talk can develop throughout the primary school years.

Social and emotional aspects of book talk

The wide-ranging social and emotional benefits of being a childhood reader, such as developing empathy and self-understanding, are discussed in other chapters in this book, and there is no need to reiterate these in detail here. However, relevant to this chapter are the ways in which these aspects are potentially amplified by talk. For example, book talk can prompt children to question or challenge social injustices and develop an understanding of the inequality of peoples differing life circumstances. Similarly, for a child grappling with understanding their own situation, reading about a character in a similar position and discussing the book in a supportive environment creates an opening to express themselves. Book talk fosters relationships: being metaphorically and literally 'on the same page' as others and coming to a consensus creates a sense of affinity and belonging. Yet, book talk is also an opportunity to distinguish oneself from others and express individuality. Firstly, children can express their own preferences and unique reader identity; in addition, by supporting, opposing and critiquing the ideas presented in the text, they construct and express their perspective and position on the subject. Through book talk in a supportive environment, children discover similarities and differences in views, and come to respect and accept differing perspectives.

It is not just the individual that benefits. For example, the talk and sense of camaraderie that potentially emerges from discussion of a book on biodiversity loss or environmental issues can be a powerful impetus for collaborative action and change of behaviours. Book talk around reliable information gives the sense of being a part of an environmental movement, fostering children's sense of agency and self-efficacy. As Kelly, Ogdan and Moses (2019) propose, 'without these conversations, we miss opportunities to address social injustices, share life experiences and express compassion and empathy' (p. 36).

Book talk and inter-thinking

Book talk and text comprehension are complementary, that is, the more deeply the reader understands what they are reading, the better placed they are to talk about it, and through talking about the text, meanings are developed and refined (Serafini, 2009). However, readers are not simply consumers, or receivers of information contained within a text, rather, each reader brings their own unique lived experience and perspective to the narrative and actively constructs meaning. Interpretations may be influenced by the reader's experiences with other texts, film or TV, for example (Rosenblatt, 1994). Through book talk, meaning is co-constructed; thoughts and ideas are shared, explored, negotiated, questioned and affirmed. This process creates opportunities for deeper, more complex, multilayered thinking and interpretations to be generated.

Sociocultural theories offer an explanatory framework to understand the relationship between book talk and thinking. Building on the work of the Russian psychologist Lev Vygotsky (1962), sociocultural theorists study how learning, thinking and language development emerge through social interaction and are shaped by cultural forces (by cultural we mean peoples' 'ways of life'). It was also Vygotsky who firstly recognised, hypothetically, a link between language, social interaction and individual cognitive activity. More recently, the pivotal role that language plays in the relationship between social interaction and thinking has been corroborated by research evidence (Mercer and Littleton, 2007). These scholars developed the concept of 'inter-thinking' to illustrate how people use language to think together in a creative and productive manner; Littleton and Mercer (2013) state

> [interthinking] means using talk to pursue collective intellectual activity. It represents an important and distinctive strength of human cognition, whereby people can combine their intellectual resources to achieve more through working together than any individual could do on their own.
>
> (p. 111)

The authors explain that through inter-thinking with language, people co-construct knowledge, they share and build upon each other's ideas and collaboratively problem-solve. Hence, inter-thinking not only plays a key role in the development of human knowledge and understanding at an individual level, but it has also been vital to the advancement of our species.

However, not all talk is conducive to inter-thinking; talk that involves a lot of dispute and antagonism or talk in which people passively agree with one another are less favourable. It is the sort of talk described as 'exploratory talk' that Mercer and Littleton (2007) found to be most beneficial for thinking productively and creatively together. Exploratory talk involves reasoning and questioning; it also involves people engaging respectfully, constructively and sometimes critically with each other's ideas. When people share relevant information, give reasons for their views and opinions and acknowledge others' perspectives, then two (or more) minds become better that one (Littleton and Mercer, 2013).

However, we know that not all children grow up in environments that promote exploratory talk. Whilst the vast majority of children competently learn to speak at least one language, not all children experience rich discussion, or have role models who use language for reasoning, to elaborate or embellish, to manage emotions or to find consensus of opinion. For some children, the classroom may be one of the few places in which they can develop their capacity for exploratory talk and inter-thinking, and rich book talk plays a vital role. Opportunities to participate in this kind of talk about books 'can induct children into new ways of literacy thinking' (Smith, 2005: 23).

Whether adult–child, peer to peer, in small groups or a whole class, informal book talk underpins reciprocal reader relationships and builds wider networks of engaged readers; as such, book talk also goes hand-in-hand with reader recommendations.

Reader recommendations

Enjoyment of reading is dependent on book selection, and a key aspect of fostering reading for pleasure in the classroom is ensuring children can take ownership of their reading choices (Cremin et al., 2014). However, even in a well-stocked library, deciding what to choose can be tricky! Without guidance, children have no other choice than to 'judge the book by its cover', and inexperienced readers can find it difficult to make an informed choice. We know that finding books that personally resonate with the reader is crucial to nurturing childhood reader; therefore, tailored recommendations, both from peers and teachers, are valuable for helping children to select engaging reading materials.

Through book talk, teachers and pupils get to know each other's reading habits and preferences for genre, authors and text types. Teachers and peers might then recommend texts on the same subject, by the same author, or that are in a similar style to those previously enjoyed. Equipped with good knowledge of children's texts, teachers can make carefully tailored recommendations that do not simply offer more of the same, but rather, tempt children to expand their reading repertoires. Thus, frequent and vibrant book talk in the classroom exposes children to a wider range of texts than they may otherwise be exposed to (Merga, 2018).

Jon notices that when peer recommendations become established in his class each year, it has a positive impact on the quantity and range of book borrowed from the class library. As momentum builds and more children are inspired to read the same texts, the talk is enriched by more voices and perspectives. As he notes, the more children talk about books the more they find out about each other's tastes and preferences, enabling more tailored recommendations. Book talk and recommendations are mutually sustaining! This culture of reciprocal reader relationships supports individuals' reader identities, but importantly, it enables an inclusive class reading identity to emerge.

Informal book talk and reader recommendations in practice

Developing a culture of spontaneous, child-initiated book talk can take several weeks, sometimes months, to establish in a class. In Jon's classroom, book talk is re-introduced at the start of each school year with a significant amount of teacher modelling and scaffolding. Opportunities for child-led book talk are created almost every day, either as a whole class or in small groups.

The following transcript is of a conversation that took place midway through the school year in Jon's class. The conversation documented here involved Jon and six pupils (pseudonyms used). It was initiated when Jon shared his thoughts on the book *How to* research with reading groups in secondary schools that 'shadowed' the judging of two well-known book awards (Cremin and Swann, 2016), the informality of the discussion and children's obvious deep engagement with the books contributed to reader relationships and a social space to share their enthusiasm.

Fostering a classroom culture of informal book talk

The theory, research findings and examples from practice discussed in this chapter render visible the significance of informal book talk and reader recommendations. Depending on age and previous experiences, some children and young people will be accustomed to, and well-versed in, the art of dialogue; for these youngsters, peer book talk might emerge quite spontaneously during independent reading time, in the playground, or in the lunch queue, for example. Other children need opportunity, time and support to develop the motivation, language and social skills to engage in the vibrant book talk exemplified in the transcript from Jon's classroom. A good starting place is to begin by reflecting on the ways in which the ethos and culture of the school and classroom shape how children can participate in informal book talk.

Talk in classrooms and schools is governed by rules and conventions which differ in different contexts. Children are not typically expected to chat to one another during a school assembly, for example. During some lessons, there may be an expectation that children raise their hand to speak; in contrast, the playground tends to be a space in which children's voices are mostly unconstrained. Informal book chat tends to fall somewhere in the middle, therefore, across all age group, establishing guidelines is important for children to understand how to participate. This will ensure that the group is not dominated by just a couple of individuals; more confident, talkative children are invaluable in group discussion, but they too may need some support to contribute constructively. For those pupils that are more reticent and possibly concerned about 'getting it wrong', ensuring book talk is a non-assessed activity will help to alleviate performance pressure.

Teacher-scaffolded small groups are ideal for modelling an ethos of reciprocal care and respect around book talk; with frequent opportunities, children will quickly come to know what is expected. As children's capacity for productive discussion develops, the teacher begins to play a lesser role, as exemplified in Jon's classroom example. Based on Littleton and Mercer's (2013) guidance for productive group discussion, there are some key principles for fostering productive, but informal child-led book talk. Rich book talk requires fluent, free-flowing conversation, in which participants respectfully listen to one another; everyone should have an opportunity to participate. Children should be encouraged to share relevant information and give reasons for their ideas. They should be encouraged to build on each other's responses and check understanding by asking questions, which will enable book suggestions to be tailored to the recommendee's preferences, rather than the recommender's. Each participant should be expected to listen with courtesy; if they wish to agree or disagree with a point of view, they should be encouraged to explain their rationale. It is important to remember that not all classroom talk is focused on nurturing RfP; in the curriculum, there will be teacher-led talk that is aimed at promoting, for example, knowledge of prefixes and suffixes or evaluating figurative language. However, by making provision and opportunities for informal book talk, children are developing not only cognitively, but developing socially and emotionally as responsible citizens.

Modelling and facilitating productive discussion is not always easy; it takes a reflexive and responsive approach. Of course, teachers will want to gently challenge views based on fake news, inaccuracies or prejudice. However, as an experienced Reading Teacher, Jon is mindful not to exert his position of authority in the classroom and inadvertently 'tell' children what the book is about. Rather, he uses carefully phrased open questions to provoke thoughtful and considered answers. Similarly, salient comments at the right moments can help pupils make connections between the book and their own and others' lives and emphasise that there are multiple ways to respond to a book (Kelly et al., 2019). Such comments and questions provide children with 'interpretive repertoires', that is, tools for analysing and thinking about what they read (Serafini, 2009).

Grounded in these principles, children's capacity to engage in respectful and productive book talk, and other discussion, will thrive. Yet, at the same time, it is important to keep it light-hearted. Informal book talk should also be spontaneous and fun, it should cultivate friendships and reader relationships. So, it's important not to constrain book chat; whether in the classroom, corridors, playground or outside the school gates, at times book talk can get a little silly, as children play with words and funny ideas around the book. As is so often the case in the classroom, book talk requires teachers to perform a balancing act!

Reflections on practice

As with all Reading for Pleasure pedagogy, there is no one single activity or strategy that can be implemented, nor is there a one-size-fits-all set of practices that will suit every child and every class. However, there are multiple strategies and practices that teachers can adopt and adapt to promote book talk that moves beyond recall or a simple question-and-answer session.

Reading Teachers frequently take a step back, notice what's happening amongst readers in their classrooms and reflect on their current practice. The TaRs project (Cremin et al., 2014) suggested a number of points to consider when auditing practice around book talk and recommendations.

- Evaluate how frequently the teacher or other adults in the classroom talk about books with children, other than those being studied in literacy or guided reading sessions. Observe pupils' interactions around books and reflect on the nature of the book chat.
- Review the timetable reflecting upon how frequently book talk opportunities are scheduled.
- Observe and make notes on individual pupils' engagement in reading and their interests and preferences and consider texts to tempt.
- Review how often you or other adults offer specific tailored recommendations to children.
- Observe whether children recommend books to each other (at the beginning of the school year, Jon finds that children tend to recommend only a small selection of books and book series, written by a very limited range of authors. However, over time, the range of books being discussed and recommended expands exponentially).
- Review planned book promotion activities and events for the school year.
- Review classroom book displays and reading areas to consider how they promote book talk and recommendations.

Moving classroom practice forward

There is no blueprint for promoting informal book talk and reader recommendations, your reflections are the starting point for developing practice. However, listed next are a few strategies and ideas that have been found to be helpful.

- **Relaxed reading time:** First and foremost, to promote informal book talk, reading time needs to be deformalised; children need to see classroom reading as a social time where talking and interacting is not only permitted, but also actively encouraged.
- **Teacher-facilitated small groups:** Depending on the age-group, it might be helpful for children to have some time to prepare and think about a book they would like to discuss with the group. At other times, small group book talk might just begin with a teacher prompt, as in the example from Jon's classroom.
- **Reading Buddies:** Pairing older and younger children to read aloud to each other and talk about books can effectively promote in-depth discussion and be a rewarding experience for both children.
- **Narrative role play:** For younger children particularly, providing story props, puppets, soft toys and dressing up clothes that relate to familiar stories will inspire creative retellings and enactments of the narrative. This is an opportunity for children to discuss and negotiate meanings in a playful, informal environment.
- **Shadowing book awards:** Several organisations host annual children's book awards in the UK and internationally, such as the Carnegie Medal and the Kate Greenaway Medal. The class selects an award to shadow; groups of children read books on the short list, then discuss and debate until they decide upon a winner.
- **Class book clubs:** Careful facilitation in the early stages will ensure the book club appeals to less enthusiastic, as well as keen readers. Overtime, children can take ownership of the organisation, choosing their own texts, authors or themes to pursue.
- **Texts to Tempt:** The teacher reads aloud a short opening or the first chapter of a book or comic/magazine, creating a buzz around the text and inspiring children to borrow and read.
- **Book displays:** These might be based on particular genre, authors, poets or newly published texts. Including children in designing and creating book displays enhances classroom book talk and encourages greater depth of thought around recommendations.
- **Weekly pupil-led book reviews:** Every week a 10-minute spot can be allocated for pupils, or groups of pupils to volunteer to give a short presentation, reviewing a book, poem, graphic novel or other text they have read.
- **Teacher's bookshelf:** Reading Teachers make their reading identity and reading preferences visible; displaying the book you are currently reading sparks children's interest and triggers informal book talk.
- **Pupil recommendation shelf:** In this activity, a pupil (or pair of pupils) chooses a selection of books that they have enjoyed and would like to recommend to the class. These books are displayed in a prominent area of the classroom with a sticky note with a mini review. In Jon's class, ownership of the shelf is rotated every couple of weeks to ensure everyone has an opportunity to take part.
- **Technology enabled reader recommendations:** During the Covid-19 pandemic, many teachers creatively used online tools to facilitate book talk and rec-

ommendations. Class Padlets or JamBoards for example, enabled teachers, pupils and parents to discuss and recommend texts. These were found to have great value in promoting home-school reciprocal relationships around reading.
- **Book events:** It is important that book talk becomes an integral part of the culture of the classroom and is not viewed as a standalone activity on events such as World Book Day. However, these sorts of book events can play an important role in building reading communities beyond the school gate and enhancing the status of books and reading.

These are just a few strategies for developing book talk and reader recommendations. However, generating a buzz around books that permeates the entire school community cannot be achieved through one-off activities. The overarching aim is to create communities of engaged readers and a whole school ethos and culture of reading for pleasure.

Children's developing capacity for book talk and the wide-ranging advantages it brings cannot easily be measured or quantified. However, by observing and reflecting upon children's interactions around books, Reading Teachers will become aware of increasing sophistication in book talk, and the enhanced depth of thinking, criticality and creativity with which children discuss books and other texts. Most importantly, individual children's enthusiasm for reading will soon become apparent; acting upon information gleaned from observation enables Reading Teachers to make a real difference.

Conclusion

Independent reading time and regular visits to the school library are typical practices in many primary classrooms, however, informal, child-led book talk is often neglected (Merga, 2018). This chapter has discussed some of the research evidence that underpins the benefits of book talk and reader recommendations. It is clear that this aspect of reading for pleasure pedagogies cannot be thought of as an optional extra or just a time filler, rather book talk and reader recommendations, integrated with other RfP pedagogies, are key aspects of the reading curriculum which need to be timetabled and afforded equal status to reading instruction. However, raising the prominence of RfP pedagogy does not mean formalising their teaching. It is crucial that book talk and recommendations are perceived by teachers and children as a social, relaxed and playful time, rather than assessed activity aimed at skill acquisition.

As this chapter has discussed, book talk is important for multiple reasons. Firstly, it enhances thinking and interpretation of a text; the concept of inter-thinking illustrates how book talk is an opportunity to think together, negotiate and co-construct meaning. Secondly, it builds connections, affinity and relationships and also helps children to recognise that there is more than one legitimate perspective or position on the ideas presented in a text. Thirdly and crucially, book talk is an opportunity to share enthusiasm for reading and recommend texts to others. There is no greater advertisement for a particular book, or for volitional reading than experiencing someone else's passion.

Recommended further reading

1. *Pupil Recommendations Shelf, Example of Practice by Jon Biddle*. Available at: https://ourfp.org/eop/pupil-recommendations-shelf/

2. *Enriching Reading for Pleasure: The CILIP Carnegie and Kate Greenaway Shadowing Scheme*. Available at: https://cdn.ourfp.org/wp-content/uploads/20210205164140/Carnegie_Exec_Summary-1.pdf?_ga=2.168372257.1623898913.1634568456-713727985.1614704238
3. How to Run a Virtual Reading Group with Children. *The Reading Agency*. Available at: https://tra-resources.s3.amazonaws.com/uploads/entries/document/4681/Chatterbooks_-_How_to_run_a_virtual_group.pdf
4. Blog: Penny Slater, Herts for Learning. *Whipping up a Book Frenzy*. Available at: www.hertsforlearning.co.uk/blog/whipping-book-frenzy

Children's books

Hickes, P. and Robinson, K. (2020) *The Haunting of Aveline Jones*. London: Usborne Publishing Ltd.
Hickes, P. and Robinson, K. (2021) *The Bewitching of Aveline Jones*. London: Usborne Publishing Ltd.
Howe, C. (2018) *Ella on the Outside*. London: Nosy Crow.
Howe, C. (2021) *How to Be Me*. London: Nosy Crow.
Rauf, O. (2018) *Boy at the Back of the Class*. London: Orion Children's Books.
Rauf, O. (2019) *The Star Outside My Window*. London: Orion Children's Books.
Rundell, K. (Author) and Horn, H. (Illustrator) (2018) *The Explorer*. London: Bloomsbury Children's Books.
Scott, L. and Westcott, R. (2019) *Can You See Me?* London: Scholastic.
Scott, L. and Westcott, R. (2021) *Ways to Be Me*. Scholastic.
Sharratt, N. (2014) *Shark in the Dark*. London: Random House Children's Publishers.

References

Chambers, A. (1993) *Tell Me, Children, Reading and Talk*. Stroud: Thimble Press.
Collins, F. and Safford, K. (2008) 'The right book to the right child at the right time': Primary teacher knowledge of children's literature. *Changing English*, 15(4): 415–422.
Cremin, T., Mottram, M., Collins, F., Powell, S. and Safford, K. (2014) *Building Communities of Engaged Readers: Reading for Pleasure*. Abingdon: Routledge.
Cremin, T. and Swann, J. (2016) Literature in common: Reading for pleasure in school reading groups. In L. McKechnie, K. Oterholm, P. Rothbauer and K. I. Skjerdingstad (Eds.), *Plotting the Reading Experience: Theory/Practice/Politics*, pp. 279–300. Ontario: Wilfrid Laurier University Press.
Evans, J. (2009) *Talking Beyond the Page: Reading and Responding to Picturebooks*. Abingdon: Routledge.
Kelly, L., Ogden, M. and Moses, L. (2019) Collaborative conversations speaking and listening in the primary grades. *YC: Young Children*, 74(1): 30–36.
Littleton, K. and Mercer, N. (2013) *Interthinking*. London: Taylor & Francis Group.
Mercer, N. and Littleton, K. (2007) *Dialogue and the Development of Children's Thinking*. London: Routledge.
Merga, M. (2018) Silent reading and discussion of self-selected books in the contemporary classroom English in *Australia*, 53(1): 70–82.
Moses, L., Ogden, M. and Kelly, L. (2015) Facilitating meaningful discussion groups in the primary grades. *The Reading Teacher*, 69(2): 233–237.
Roche, M. (2015) *Developing Children's Critical Thinking through Picturebooks: A Guide for Primary and Early Years Students and Teachers*. Abingdon: Routledge.
Roche, M. (2020) Critical thinking and book talk. *Thinking Ahead: Future Edge: New South Wales Department of Education*, 1: 14–32.
Rodriguez Leon, L. and Payler, J. (2021) Surfacing complexity in shared book reading: The role of affordance, repetition and modal appropriation in children's participation. *Learning, Culture and Social Interaction*, 28: 100496.

Rosenblatt, L. (1994) *The Reader, the Text, the Poem: The Transactional Theory of the Literary Work*. Carbondale, IL: South Illinois University Press.

Serafini, F. (2009) *Interactive Comprehension Strategies: Fostering Meaningful Talk about Text*. New York: Scholastic Teaching Resources.

Smith, V. (2005) *Making Reading Mean*. Royston: UKLA Publications, Minibook 20.

Vygotsky, L. S. (1962) *Thought and Language*. Cambridge, MA: MIT Press.

Chapter 7

Time to read

Jo Tregenza, Phoebe Lawton and Sadie Phillips

Introduction

Time is precious. Ask any teacher what is the greatest challenge that they are facing and invariably it is time, everyone wants and needs more. With the ever-increasing demands of a broad and rich knowledge-based curriculum, in which teachers are expected to fill children's minds with facts and then test what they have learnt, time in school is becoming ever scarcer. However, there is a link between positive attitudes towards reading, volitional reading and scoring well on reading assessments (e.g. McGrane, Stiff, Baird, Lenkeit and Hopfenbeck-Oxford 2017) and researchers have endorsed the use of supported independent reading for developing fluency and comprehension (Reis et al., 2008; Reutzel, Jones, Fawson and Smith, 2008). The latter found that for a sample of 8- to 9-year-olds with high levels of deprivation, 20–25 minutes of daily scaffolded silent reading supported not only fluency, but also comprehension (Reutzel et al., 2008). In another study as a result of a focus on teachers as readers, 'teachers reported renewed understanding of the value of independent reading as a planned pedagogic routine rather than something children could do when all other work was completed' (Cremin, Mottram, Collins, Powell and Safford, 2014: 99). It is important to ensure that in the hectic schedule of the day, quality time and space is provided for children to engage of their own volition with reading.

Defining independent reading can be a challenge, so for this chapter we have drawn on Moses and Kelly's (2019: 332) definition: 'Students reading self-selected texts on their own either silently or aloud'. We have expanded this to include the space for children to engage in dialogue with their classmates or teachers as part of the process so there is an element of support and guidance. Without this support, teachers may encounter the challenge of 'fake reading' – children just staring at pages, mimicking the role of the reader, but without engaging with the text.

Through the reflections of two Reading Teachers, Sadie Phillips and Phoebe Lawton, this chapter discusses the importance of offering children time to read in school. It explores how these pedagogues developed strategies to support and monitor children's choices during reading time to ensure that progress and engagement are maintained. As Reading Teachers, they seek to encourage children to look forward to this time which offers them an opportunity to concentrate on reading of their own choosing and to participate in social reading and discussions. Successful reading time provides genuine choices for children and respects the rights of all readers. Hence, we need to weave opportunities into the school day that replicate the sort of conditions that many of us, as experienced readers, might choose when reading. As Ben-Yosef states:

> Isn't school about preparing kids to function in 'real life' adult society? Who tests us adults about our independent reading? To whom do we owe an explanation if we give up on the book after the first chapter? Who controls what, when, how, and why we read independently? Who holds sway over the wandering of our imaginations while reading? In the real world, we control what and how we read, and we are led only by our interests, imaginations, and pleasure.
>
> (Ben-Yosef, 2010: 1)

Drawing on our experience as readers

The challenge is to avoid independent reading time becoming a chore, forced on everyone, a routine that is 'void of authentic reader engagement and interaction' (Cremin et al., 2014: 99). As a child I would devour books at bedtime, never asleep before midnight, and would hide under the covers reading anything from James Herriot's, *It Shouldn't Happen to a Vet* to my all-time favourite, *Little Women* (Louisa M Alcott). I was lucky that my parents acknowledged the value of reading and gave up asking me to turn off the light. Now as an adult, I find I can only really read adult books when am completely relaxed, no pressures or distractions around me and mainly when I am on holiday. Then, once again, I return to my childhood practice of devouring books. It is a very different story with children's books, barely a day goes by when I do not read or buy another of those!

Sadie Phillips too describes how her own personal journey as a reader led her to build quality time and space into classroom routines in which she models and exemplifies how a reader looks and behaves. Sadie volunteers for the United Kingdom Literacy Association (UKLA) in various roles, is the new Head of English at an independent prep school in London, recently had a beautiful baby via surrogacy and is also renovating her first home. So, as she states: 'Finding the time to read for pleasure as an adult is not always easy because work – and, well, life – often get in the way'. As she also notes,

> When I first completed the Open University's (OU) Teachers as Readers self-review questionnaire, it encouraged me to reflect deeply on my personal reading habits, my identity as a teacher-reader and my own knowledge of children's literature. Honestly, I was embarrassed by the results – I rarely found time to read for pleasure, except whilst on holiday and my knowledge of children's literature, like many other educators across the UK, was somewhat outdated. It dawned on me that I was relying too heavily on 'old favourites' and not putting enough time into reading new and exciting children's literature. I acknowledged my shortfalls and set about developing and improving my reading repertoire by allowing more time for reading.

As a teacher, Sadie wanted to foster children's Reading for Pleasure (RfP) in the classroom, but she also had to 'walk the talk' and knew she needed to make time for reading in order to rekindle her own love of literature. One of the first things she did was join an OU/UKLA Teachers' Reading Group as she believed this would give her the added motivation and focus needed to choose to read more often. As she recalls,

> We would share research, quality texts, poems and picture books each session and in-between we'd read the books ready to discuss next time. It was a brilliant way to expand my reading repertoire and support my RfP practice. Through the group alone, I must have read over 20 new children's books that year.

This appeared to have re-ignited her passion for reading. Following on from this, she began to make changes to her daily routine, started getting up earlier and reading for ten minutes with her morning coffee, joined Audible, listened to books on her daily commute and signed up for literature events, conferences and festivals. So, time to read and find joy in reading was effectively plotted into her calendar in advance. As she observes

> My life was so busy, it was important that I found these little pockets of time to read, and I really savoured those precious moments. It was exactly this kind of special, protected reading time that I knew I wanted to instil in classroom life.

Phoebe Lawton, currently in her third year of teaching at a Primary Academy in the North West, is part of the English team with the responsibility for RfP and observes:

> Reading has always been a passion of mine throughout my life. During my Initial Teacher Education, I attended an OU conference at a local Primary School, and this inspired me to 'hold up the mirror' to myself as a Reading Teacher. To begin on this journey, I created my own reading river, this was to explore my own reading identity. I was able to look at the books and other texts I read and enjoyed and those that resonated with me. I wanted to use this as a 'working document' and therefore continue to add to this.

To further examine her own experience of reading, Phoebe made a gingerbread-reading figure. On the inside, she wrote how she liked to read and around the outside how reading makes her feel (Phoebe mostly likes emotional books that make her cry). As she continued to explore the scope of this, she considered her everyday reading habits and practices alongside her preferences and the social nature of her reading. She realised that she is an evening reader and would rather read than watch TV, but also shares her reading with others, in particular her partner's grandparents. Once she considered the nature of her different reading experiences, Phoebe then allowed herself more time to read and used this reflection to change her classroom practice. She invited children to complete their own gingerbread-reading figures to find out about their reading habits/interests and began to design supported independent reading time around this. She also introduced a variety of strategies, including:

- Allowing children to choose where and with whom they might they sit;
- Reading with them on a regular basis;
- Enabling sharing at the end of each session;
- Discussing which kinds of texts children enjoyed, emotional texts and other kinds;
- Recommending texts to children.

The essence of time

The value of setting time aside in school for independent reading has been contested, but there is evidence to indicate an association between reading time and the quality of children's fluency, comprehension and vocabulary (Allington, 2014; Krashen, 2004, 2011). However, the competing challenges on the school timetable mean that it can be problematic for teachers to provide this. Back in 2002, the OECD reported renewed understanding of the value of independent reading as a planned pedagogic routine rather than something children could do when all other work was completed (Kirsch et al., 2002). More recently, with the impact of Covid-19 and time being spent learning remotely, reading time has taken on a new life. It is critical to consider how we can engage children in this space, actively encouraging reading, but also ensuring, as the OECD (2021) allude to in their recent report *21st Century Readers, Developing Literacy Skills in a Digital World*, that children are able to sort fact from fiction and that teachers provide a space to respond critically to texts.

Tinkering with time

Making time for reading can be a significant obstacle to forming positive reading habits – whether for you or your pupils. So, it would be a mistake to view reading time simply as a 'luxury' or an 'added bonus', rather it needs to be seen as privileged, protected time, especially since children may not be choosing to read at home. Whether it is first thing in the morning, straight after lunch or at the end of the school day, putting it on the timetable is crucial. Additionally, identifying and recommending books to capture children's curiosity and enrich their understanding of pollution or Antarctic explorers' for instance is valuable. This can trigger voluntary reading in other curriculum contexts and give additional purpose to reading.

Is silence golden?

Various approaches have been introduced to protect quality, silent time for reading. Drop Everything and Read (DEAR) and Daily Independent Reading Time (DIRT) are named whole school approaches to reading silently at the same time. Whereas more class-based approaches, such as Uninterrupted Sustained, Silent Reading (USSR), and Everybody Reading in Class (ERIC), have been around since the 1960s. These approaches have enabled teachers to protect time for reading, but the quality of this time can be variable with limited real reader engagement as Hiebert and Training, (2014) point out. Including some degree of interaction, encouraging children to make independent but supported choices and teachers' modelling reading behaviours can all help young readers.

In their paper, 'Are They Really Reading? A Descriptive Study of First Graders during Independent Reading', Moses and Kelly (2019) highlight that even 6 year olds in school can read alone successfully when the time is orchestrated by an 'exemplary teacher' and when wider support is offered within the rest of the day. In their study, this was through reading aloud to introduce texts and through book talk activities, both of which helped the children know what they might like to read next and supported them in sharing their own views. This work, in tune with the RfP pedagogy identified by Cremin et al. (2014), highlights the integrated nature of RfP pedagogy and makes clear that independent reading is not a standalone routine, nor indeed necessarily a silent one. Silence may be golden on occasions, but on other occasions children may choose to chat quietly. Reading Teachers monitor children's engagement, noticing in particular the behaviours and involvement of the less engaged or less assured readers and giving support where needed.

Space and time to nestle

As adults we know that many of us like to read when we are comfortable. Research by Reedy and De Carvahlo (2019) explored children's perspectives on reading and found that the 9- to 10-year-olds in their study also preferred a quiet, comfortable environment without distractions. Sadie too wanted to encourage voluntary reading by creating a space where the children could be relaxed and curled up with a book alongside their friends. To reflect the comfort of her home reading she considered resources, lighting and other factors. She collected blankets, cushions and throws from home for the book corner, brought in teddies which the children called 'reading buddies', gave out baskets of torches and dimmed the lights, with a roaring fire on the interactive whiteboard. Sadie also monitored the use of this time and the efficacy of her approaches and used the RfP pedagogy checkLIST, that is she sought to ensure this time was Learner-led, Informal, Social and with Texts that tempt (Cremin, 2019). She also changed the name of independent reading to 'cosy reading time' which she perceived helped some pupils see it as relaxed and informal, their reading time.

Time to choose

Ensuring the learners have choice and agency is key to developing successful reading times. In surveys, children often comment on and value the freedom they have at home to choose what they wish to read and how they approach it (Reedy and De Carvahlo, 2019). They may however need support to choose, as the work of Reutzel et al. (2008) indicates. Reading Teachers provide scaffolding through the careful selection of quality texts, informal modelling, book recommendations and discussion opportunities. For example, Sadie models her book selection aloud, making it clear that she is using the blurb and her knowledge of the author's other books to support her decision. Creating conventions together for comfy reading time can also help, such as not disturbing others, avoiding 'spoilers' and staying in one spot (Sanden, 2014). As previously discussed Sadie also sometimes reads for pleasure herself during this time giving value to the experience.

Planning for independent reading

Due to the pandemic, schools and teachers have been playing a 'catch up' game in relation to reading skills, and experiencing increased pressure to do extra phonics lessons and run skill-based interventions. This can reduce the time for independent reading. Teachers are however planning new opportunities, introducing whole school initiatives, such as reading on the playground, book clubs and early morning 'wake up and read' times. In addition, many are adapting their timetables to fit in more time to read. Table 7.1 offers an example timetable for 6- to 7-year-olds doing a World of Wonder topic using the core text *Here We Are: Notes for Living on Planet Earth* by Oliver Jeffers. It allows for additional time for phonics and maths, English and collaborative work post-Covid and indicates that literacy is taught through a cross-curricular theme linked with the foundation subjects. It signals that making regular time for reading is possible, not only in dedicated times but also in other more liminal moments in the day.

Teachers as time thieves: making time to read

To help her plan class reading time, Phoebe worked to find out more about the children's reading habits and used her analysis of their views to map the available time responsively as well as seizing other moments. As she observed:

> Through observing, surveying and developing an understanding of the children's reading identities, I found that they needed the time and space to really read for pure enjoyment. Each child has their own individual reading habits and needs, I tried to ensure my classroom could cater for these needs. I timetabled free choice reading time in each week and used any 'spare pockets' of time for this too. It is now a common sight to find children choosing to take their books outside onto the playground.

Phoebe notes that when visitors come to school, children often point out the space they like to read in and share their enthusiasm for what they call 'our time' to read. Through developing the children's ownership of this time, she found children who were previously reluctant readers gradually became drawn in and were increasingly intrinsically motivated. Additionally, through encouraging conversations reader to reader, as well as recommendations during this time, Phobe observed that children's confidence to chat about what they were reading grew. Phoebe's work reflects her recognition that a sense of agency, freedom of choice and opportunity to talk about texts informally is important

Table 7.1 An example timetable to indicate possible spaces for reading time

Time	8:45–9:00	9:00–10:00	10:00–10:30	10:30–11:00	11:00–12:30	12:30–13:30	13:30–13:50	13:50–15:00	15:00–15:20
Mon	Wake up to reading	Literacy Class introduction to the text (Here We Are). Class reading and discussion.	Phonics	Break: book club Book club	Maths	Lunch time: playground games club/ book box	Independent reading	Geography: a virtual trip around the world	Parent and child Book Club: a well-being focus
Tues	Phonics fun	Literacy/PSHCE writing focus rules for a better world	Assembly Then class poem Lost by Michael Rosen		Maths		Geography: a focus on our locality (outdoor walk-in local area)		Parent and child Maths Club
Wed	Wake up to reading	Literacy/PSHCE Writing rules for a better world. Letter writing	Reading Club: Guided and independent reading workshop		Maths		Science:		Staff meeting
Thur	Maths club: Playing directional games	Literacy/PSHCE	PE		Maths		Cosy Reading	Geography	Planning meeting
Fri	Phonics fun	Letters read aloud in assembly	Cosy Reading		Maths/PE Let's go orienteering		Art: a world view	Class and family story time	

as children develop as readers. The time became both 'me time and we time' and she developed a stronger RfP culture in her class.

Reading Teachers such as Phoebe are also adept at stealing time when waiting for the inevitable delay to an assembly, or by creating book talk activities such as Book Blankets or Comic Capers which include some time to settle down and read. Phoebe additionally runs summer reading picnics within and across year groups and finds children comment that these offered them a sense of belonging, perhaps through seeing children in other classes reading too. She goes on to say:

> There is ALWAYS the opportunity for reading! We have ensured the children are surrounded by texts and have access to the 'outdoor' reading library, which is often full to the brim during breaktimes. Alongside this, children have their own piles of books within the classrooms, therefore during slack times or when finishing work, as the children come in in the morning, or getting ready to go home; there is a pile of easily accessible books, which children have chosen to read.

Alongside staff reading aloud videos, platforms such as YouTube and Twitter have been used to share stories at Phoebe's school. This has enabled wider access to literature and supported children's own reading choices. During online lessons, staff shared what they were reading (often with a pet) and invited the children to do likewise, and recommendations were made. Phoebe commented 'it was great to see the children sharing their talk about texts – their inside text talk – in this way'.

Developing the children's responsibility, autonomy, perseverance and stamina

As we discussed earlier, one of the significant challenges of providing independent reading opportunities is to ensure that children are actively engaged, and that there is some form of monitoring or progress. As Trudel (2007) notes it is important to monitor reading behaviours without making this onerous or like an assessment, so it needs to be built into the book talk in the classroom. This can be done in part by developing children's reading responsibilities and supporting their autonomy, so that over time they begin to take more ownership of their reading and exert their rights as readers. Equally we need to build their perseverance and stamina as readers, with the strength and determination to read on, to check back as needed and to extend their reading 'miles' (Allington, 2014).

Responsibility

Just as Reading Teachers hold up a mirror to themselves as readers, Phoebe supports children to reflect upon themselves as readers and over time, helps them become more discerning and responsible for their choices. At the beginning of the year, she observes children closely, often exploring why they picked a certain book. Rebecca, a teacher from the South East of England, also encourages children to reflect and take responsibility for their choices; she holds 'behave as a reader' sessions. These start with a provocation, for example, 'The bigger the book, the more difficult it is to read', or 'Is it important to see yourself in the characters in books?' Designed to create a debate, such provocations help children exercise criticality. Another strategy to encourage children to defend their choices responsibly is 'Elevator Pitches'. In a brief presentation, children seek to persuade others to read their recommended book, with the added incentive that when they do a particularly good job, Rebecca will buy a copy of the book for the class; a costly but motivating approach!

Autonomy

Phoebe approached the challenge of building children's autonomy as readers through introducing a more discursive approach.

> Initially, I offered 'quiet reading'. After reviewing my practice, I realised I was preventing this from being child-led, choice-led reading. Subsequently, I assigned time which was not 'quiet or silent reading' but provided more opportunity for children to develop the 'will' or desire to read. I allowed them to make their own selections, as well as make recommendations to others. I modelled sharing comics and swapping picture books. Talking about texts is now a normal and crucial part of the children's independent reading time.

Modelling book talk around self-chosen texts is, as Phoebe recognises, invaluable, as is time to talk in small groups during reading time. This can help forge positive reader to reader relationships both child to child and teacher to child. In encouraging children to choose their own texts, perhaps from genre focused or curriculum book baskets, you will be fostering their autonomy. For example, *The Undefeated* by Kwame Alexander, winner of an array of medals is a lyrical text that could support learning in history, PSHE and citizenship as well as a focus on Black Lives Matter. Children can be invited to add to such baskets and exercise an increasing degree of control over the reading choices in class. As you will see, autonomy and responsibility go hand-in-hand.

Perseverance and stamina

One of the challenges that can inhibit children's engagement in independent reading is if the text is too difficult for them. This might be due to the child selecting the wrong book, so teaching simple strategies such as the 'five finger test' is useful. Children read the first page (or a random page) and if there are five words they do not know, then that book is probably too hard for them. It is also important in the early years, to spend time supporting independent reading behaviours. This might involve making time to sit alongside children as they revisit a text you have previously read aloud. You could discuss the pictures, perhaps taking 'picture walks' through the books. Giving children and parents the opportunity to read and reread books, perhaps providing story sacks to explore in class and at home can also help. Once the appropriate level of book is identified for a child, you may need to provide personalised, spontaneous instruction and scaffolding (Bryan, Fawson and Reutzel, 2003). In order to do this effectively, the teacher needs to be astute, tuning into verbal and non-verbal cues and observing the actions and reading behaviours of children who might perhaps simply be flicking through pages at speed, or staring at an upside-down book!

Some research suggests that when teachers provide direct instruction on text selection, children learn to select books that align with their interests and are at or just above their reading level (Sanden, 2014, 2014; Trudel, 2007). Several studies describe how opportunities to go 'book shopping' and choose books out of baskets, following the teacher's book promotion and read aloud can enable choices to be made and stamina to be built, even in the younger readers (Sanden, 2014; Moses and Kelly, 2019). Engaging children in written responses and reflections (is a more challenging and potentially debatable step (Kelly and Clausen-Grace, 2006; Kelly, Ogden and Moses, 2019). The last thing you want to do is build a culture where once children have read a book, they need to write about it – this can be demotivating. Reading Teachers develop different, more visual means, for example Jon Biddle's bookshelf which allows children to record the books they have read (see Figure 7.1).

When supporting the children in their choice of books, knowing the children as readers is key. During independent reading time, children can make a note about the text they are reading in their reading journals. For early years, photographs of books

Figure 7.1 Bookshelf recording sheet (designed by Jon Biddle, illustrated by Sadie Phillips)

Table 7.2 Teaching strategies to support the development of Responsibility, Autonomy, Perseverance and Stamina (RAPS)

R Responsibility	A Autonomy	P Perseverance	S Stamina
Behave as a Reader	Book talk	Five finger test	Rereading books
Elevator Pitches	Book swaps and shares	Supported book choice	Teacher monitoring
	Book shopping	Picture walks	Teacher instruction

could be used to take away the demand for writing. Some children enjoy doing this as they are motivated by having a list of books to look back on, others may be less keen but it does allow the teacher to see their different book choices and support them further. Some Reading Teachers offer post-it notes for children to add comments or their name inside book covers, which enables the young people to know who else has read the book, and may prompt book discussions. The different strategies discussed can support the elements of responsibility, autonomy, perseverance and stamina (RAPS) (see Table 7.2)

Conclusion

With recent world events it has never been more important to create quality time for children to read independently. As the National Literacy Trust research has shown, for many children, reading is a refuge, a place to be calm, explore possible worlds, make sense of themselves or just escape some of the realities of their own world (Clark and Teravainen-Goff, 2018). The benefits are profound.

The challenges for schools are to prioritise this time, to nurture children's interest, scaffold and support their book choices and build their commitment, engagement and enjoyment. As discussed earlier, focusing on children's responsibility, autonomy, perseverance and stamina can help to deepen engagement. Teachers know time in school is precious. However, ensuring that children have the opportunity to hear stories read aloud, to talk about texts and to participate in child-led independent reading is a valuable use of time. These opportunities combine within a social reading environment to comprise RfP pedagogy. Prioritising time to read and supporting this, can enable children to find pleasure in reading which is intrinsically motivated and self-regulated. There are advantages both for individual children and for the reading culture in the classroom.

Recommended reading

Bearne, E. and Reedy, D. (2018) *Teaching Primary English Subject Knowledge and Classroom Practice*. London: Routledge.

Cremin, T., Mottram, M., Collins, F., Powell, S. and Safford, K. (2014) *Building Communities of Engaged Readers: Reading for Pleasure*. London and New York: Routledge.

Moses, L. and Kelly, L. B. (2019) Are they really reading? A descriptive study of first graders during independent reading. *Reading & Writing Quarterly*, 35(4): 322–338.

Children's books

Alcott, L. M. (2021) *Little Women*. London UK: Puffin Classics.
Alexander, K. (2020) *Undefeated*. London: Andersen Press.
Herriot, J. (2010) *It Shouldn't Happen to a Vet: The Classic Memoir of a 1930's Vet*. Basingstoke: Pan MacMillan.
Jeffers, O. A. (2020) *Here We Are: Notes for Living on Planet Earth*. London: Harper Collins.
Percival, T. (2021) *Ravi's Roar*. London: Macmillan.

References

Allington, R. L. (2014) How reading affects fluency. *International Electronic Journal of Elementary Education*, 7(1): 13–26.
Ben-Yosef, E. (2010) Reading to fly, creative reading as pedagogical equalizer encounter. *Education for Meaning and Social Justice*, 23(1): 1–5.
Bryan, G., Fawson, P. and Reutzel, R. D. (2003) Sustained silent reading: Exploring the value of literature discussion with three non-engaged readers. *Reading Research and Instruction*, 43(1): 47–73.
Clark, C. and Teravainen-Goff, A. (2018) *Mental Wellbeing, Reading and Writing: How Children and Young People's Mental Wellbeing is Related to Their Reading and Writing Experiences*. Available at: https://cdn.literacytrust.org.uk/media/documents/Mental_wellbeing_reading_and_writing_2017-18_-_FINAL2_qTxyxvg.pdf (Accessed 7 November 2021).
Cremin, T. (2019) *Reading Communities, Why, What and How?* Nate Primary Matters. Available at: https://cdn.ourfp.org/wp-content/uploads/20210301105855/Reading_Communities_TCremin_2019.pdf?_ga=2.115863686.1412150920.1649698556-218333398.1633344484
Cremin, T., Mottram, M., Collins, F., Powell, S. and Safford, K. (2009) Teachers as readers: Building communities of readers. *Literacy*, 43(1): 11–19.
Cremin, T., Mottram, M., Collins, F., Powell, S. and Safford, K. (2014) *Building Communities of Engaged Readers: Reading for Pleasure*. London and New York: Routledge.
Hiebert, E. H. and Training, G. (2014) Are students really reading in independent reading contexts? An examination of comprehension-based silent reading rate. In *Revisiting Silent Reading: New Directions for Teachers and Researchers*, pp. 151–167. Newark: International Reading Association.
Kelly, M. J. and Clausen-Grace, N. (2006) R5: The Sustained Silent Reading makeover that transformed readers. *The Reading Teacher*, 60(2): 148–156.
Kelly, R. B., Ogden, M. K. and Moses, L. (2019) Collaborative conversations, speaking and listening in the primary grades. *Young Children*, 74(1): 30–37.
Kirsch, I., de Long, J., Lafontaine, D., McQueen, J., Mendelovits, J. and Monseur, C. (2002) *Reading for Change Performance and Engagement Across Countries*. Paris: OECD.
Krashen, S. (2004) *The Power of Reading: Insights from the Research*, 2nd ed. Portsmouth, NH: Heinemann.
Krashen, S. (2011) Academic proficiency (language and content) and the role of strategies. *TESOL Journal*, 2(4): 381–393.
McGrane, J., Stiff, J., Baird, J., Lenkeit, J. and Hopfenbeck-Oxford, T. (2017) *Progress in International Reading Literacy Study: National Report for England*. London: Department for Education.
Moses, L. and Kelly, L. B. (2019) Are they really reading? A descriptive study of first graders during independent reading. *Reading & Writing Quarterly*, 35(4): 322–338.
OECD (2021) *21st-Century Readers: Developing Literacy Skills in a Digital World*, PISA. Paris: OECD Publishing.
Reedy, A. and De Carvalho, R. (2019) Children's perspectives on reading, agency and their environment: What can we learn about reading for pleasure from an East London primary school? *Education 3–13*, 49(2): 134–147.
Reis, S. M., Eckert, R. D., McCoach, D., Jacobs, B., Joan, K. and Coyne, M. (2008) Using enrichment reading practices to increase reading fluency, comprehension, and attitudes. *Journal of Education Research*, 101: 5.

Reutzel, D. R., Jones, C. D., Fawson, P. C. and Smith, J. A. (2008) Scaffolded silent reading: A complement to guided repeated oral reading that works! *The Reading Teacher*, 62(3): 194–207.

Sanden, S. (2014) Out of the shadow of SSR: Real teachers' classroom independent reading practices. *Language Arts*, 91(3): 161–175.

Trudel, H. (2007) Making data driven decisions: Silent reading. *The Reading Teacher*, 61(4): 308–315.

Chapter 8

Social reading environments

Roger McDonald, Erin Hamilton and Lisa Hesmondhalgh

Introduction

The social reading environment of a classroom, school and wider community is crucial to fostering an ethos of reading for pleasure. In such spaces, children and adults alike can immerse themselves in a safe, comfortable and text rich environment that changes and evolves in response to the experiences of the children who inhabit it. Historically, concepts of the reading environment may conjure up notions of a dedicated reading corner or area in the classroom in which the class library is located. The books within the library may have been passed down from teacher to teacher, rarely being audited, reviewed or renewed. Children would be expected to pick a book, maybe with little choosing time, and read it independently or silently at key points in the day.

However, thinking about the nature of the social reading environment moves our conceptualisations away from the traditional 'reading corner', which is often a fixed space in a classroom, to broader reading spaces located across the school. These spaces may be in the playground, in corridors or in the school hall, for example; they are both richly engaging and dynamic in nature. Research has shown that teachers can transform their concept of the reading environment by reflecting on their own reading practices and

DOI: 10.4324/9781003215615-13

considering their own reading identity, alongside their knowledge of children's texts and crucially, their knowledge of the children as readers (Cremin, Mottram, Collins, Powell and Safford, 2014). This, combined with ample opportunities and encouragement for book talk, reading aloud and independent reading time, helps teachers to generate reading environments which are highly social.

The social reading environment is a vital element of the reading for pleasure tapestry and key to encouraging children into a collaborative environment where texts are discussed, shared and explored. It is pivotal to developing a sense of a reading community, encompassing adults and children alike. At the heart of the social reading environment is the teacher's reflection of their own preferred reading environment, that is, considering where, when and how they choose to read and then reflecting that back into the classroom situation.

This chapter will explore the concept of the social reading environment, identify the key characteristics and principles. Drawing on case studies of classroom practice, it will exemplify how teachers have considered their own reading preferences and practices and the ways in which this influenced their changing conception of the social reading environment.

Principles of a social reading environment

A classroom reading environment reflects the teacher's values and beliefs around reading for pleasure. Reading Teachers who create highly social reading environments will use pedagogical practices which are based on a number of principles and ideologies. Such teachers recognise the importance of:

- A physically engaging space that encourages children to explore books and other texts;
- An interactive space which encourages informal book talk;
- A relaxed culture where reader relationships can flourish;
- Creating dedicated time and space for developing conversations around texts;
- A space where children have choice over the texts they choose to read;
- Providing engaging texts that are relevant to children's lived experiences;
- Providing opportunities for children to choose books based on recommendations.

These principles are grounded in evidence from the Teachers as Readers Research (Cremin et al., 2014) that illustrated that reading environments that were both physically and socially engaging promoted Reading for Pleasure. A well-considered reading environment is not only enticing for children, but it also encourages children's engagement in the reading process, meaning that the environment becomes a learning tool to support reading development (Myles, 2020).

A physically engaging environment

A physically engaging reading environment signifies the value placed on reading (Chambers, 2011) and lays the groundwork of Reading for Pleasure pedagogy (Cremin et al., 2014). Lisa Hesmondhalgh (third author) recalls a conversation in which Alex Seddon, English lead at The Wilmslow Academy, discussed developing her school's reading environments to tempt children into reading by encouraging them to inhabit their reading spaces.

Alex firstly reflected on what the reading environment used to be like in the school. She notes, 'We had a class library, but the children didn't really perceive this to be a space for reading'. In order to investigate this perception further, Alex used a questionnaire to gather children's thoughts and views about their reading environment and found that 'many children said we didn't have a library because they weren't really encouraged to go there and pick books as it was all reading scheme books'. It could be argued that, at this point, the class library was simply a depository for texts which teachers used to assess children in relation to the reading scheme level they had achieved. It was obvious to Alex that the children did not see it as a place for exploration, talk and sharing and that the books within the library were not matched to the children's interests.

Alex's next step was to find out about what the children were reading, what their preferences were and identify their reading habits and practices. She introduced Rivers of Reading (Cliff Hodges, 2010). Reading Rivers are drawings, writing, photographs or snippets of reading material that visually represent someone's reading practices in general, or capture the reading they do over a 24-hour timeframe. The Reading Rivers gave crucial information about what the children read, where they read, the connections they found in their reading experiences and, crucially, which social practices had been influential (Cliff Hodges, 2016). It was important to Alex and the teaching team to ensure that class libraries were reflective of children's interests. Therefore, teachers supported children by introducing them to award winning books (such as the UKLA book awards) and carried out a class voting system for children to hear, discover and vote on new texts for the classroom. Furthermore, Alex notes that, 'we also took our school council to a lovely local independent book shop. The children loved it – they had hot chocolate!' Through the visit the children heard more recommendations which tempted them and excited their interests.

Through the process of exploring the social reading environments within the school, Alex had identified the importance of ensuring children were central to the decision-making process, but guided by the teacher who could prompt, suggest and recommend a range of texts based on the children's experiences. Indeed, teacher guidance is crucial, Renck Jalongo (2007) raises a degree of caution over the notion of random choice, where engagement in reading can actually decrease. Choice, guided by the teacher, was therefore vital for children to have the sense of belonging to a reading community where their input was not only valued but considered essential. Reflecting on the progress made across the school since implementing these changes, Alex identified that

> there are still book shelves, but books are presented differently with many facing forwards so that the children can see them. We have cushions and blankets to make it comfortable for the children. Teachers also have their recommended texts which is something we didn't have before. Children often sit by the radiator because it's nice and warm. They also hide themselves under the coats and bags and make their own comfy space.

Whilst the comfortable space is important, it is the quality of the texts offered to the children which 'capture children's imagination to such an extent that they become unaware of whether they are sitting on a beanbag, an ordinary classroom chair or a bench in the book corner' (DfE, 2021: 33).

Alex identified that the reading environment was, initially, not a space the children chose to inhabit, partly due to the space being primarily teacher controlled and led. The space was not relevant to the children (McGeown and Wilkinson, 2021). The physical changes implemented in the school are important because it acknowledges the physicality of reading. This notion is explored by Mackey (2010, 2011) who posits that although the pages or screens of most texts encountered are flat, reading itself is not flat, it involves 'dragging and meandering and breathing, and clearly entails a kind of journey that happens over time' (Mackey, 2010: 3). Similarly, Wynne-Jones (1998) notes that, when reading for pleasure, we are involved in deep reading where we get 'gut-hooked and dragged overboard down and down through the maze of print and find, to your amazement, you can breathe down there after all and there's a whole other world' (p. 165). This rich description from Wynne-Jones reminds us of the active nature of reading and that our children need a social reading environment which they can inhabit, find space, find stillness or embrace movement.

A socially engaging environment

This section builds further on the idea of reading being an active process and underlines the importance of the social nature of reading where opportunities are created for a range of talk around and about books.

As discussed in Chapter 6, the social nature of reading and the importance of informal book talk has been highlighted in previous literature and research (see Chambers, 2011; Cremin et al., 2014; Kelly, Ogdan and Moses, 2019). In an engaging, safe and comfortable physical environment, and with support from their Reading Teacher, children participate in conversations about texts where recommendations are made by teachers and children alike, building a community of readers with a shared sense of agency.

One teacher's journey of building shared, choice-led social reading environments in her classroom and across the school was exemplified in an interview carried out by Lisa Hesmondhalgh (third author) with Clare Bell who is the reading lead at Victoria Road Primary School. To develop the social reading environment in her classroom, Clare has worked to develop the whole environment rather than the traditional reading corner.

Firstly, Clare created opportunities for children to access a wide and diverse range of texts, to talk about texts they knew and be introduced and tempted into new ones. As a Reading Teacher, Clare knew the connections that could be made through informal book talk, so across the school, they facilitated the mixing of classes. They soon found that groups of children of different ages would be huddled in spaces around the school reading and talking about books. In her own classroom, Clare has ensured there was a wide range of exciting texts for children to choose from. The selection was based on children's interests, which had been discovered through regularly talking with the children. At the beginning of the year, Clare sent a personalised letter to each child enquiring about their reading preferences and was delighted with the children's responses. She noted that 'all the children have written back, and they are absolutely gorgeous answers. I thought they'd write back and say they didn't like reading, but they didn't! They told me they enjoyed reading but didn't know how to choose'. Through diversifying the reading choices and by ensuring that texts reflected the interests and desires of all the children in the class, Clare found that there was a new passion for reading, children were more inclined to browse the class library and engage in book-related discussion.

Clare continued to reflect on the provision; she sought ways to ensure that children had opportunities to hear and see adults choosing texts and she worked to develop support for children to choose their texts. They started a 'We have recommendations' list that children could add to. These books were wrapped up to create suspense and anticipation to the recommendation, and they created attractive displays which encouraged questions, thoughts and opinions to be expressed. The reorganisation of the environment made it a more social space. The reading environment within Clare's classroom was transformed, encouraging children 'to read anything, to read anywhere and to dip in' (Pennac, 2006). Choice, conversation and community were key to the changes made and provided opportunities for social reading spaces which children could inhabit, make their own and explore texts.

Transforming the school environment: a head teacher's perspective

Transforming the social reading environment of a school is an exciting and rewarding challenge for any head teacher. From the perspective of a Reading Head Teacher, Lisa Hesmondhalgh (third author) outlines how she has worked with her teachers to embed the principles of social reading environments and, consequently, has seen a transformation, not only in the environment but in the children's motivation to read. The concept of a Reading Head Teacher is explored in more detail in the next chapter; however, in this section Lisa describes how her school worked through a clearly planned process of transformation, starting from the stance of reflecting on teachers' own reading practices.

Holding up a mirror to social reading practices

Lisa notes that,

> We began our whole school journey by reflecting on our own preferred conditions for reading; we asked ourselves questions such as 'Where and how do I like to read?' As expected, the findings showed that adults across the school unanimously liked to read in comfy, relaxed spaces, giving them time and space away from the demands of a busy life. They preferred to read on the sofa, in bed, in a chair, in the conservatory with a cup of tea, a biscuit or a glass of wine!

Reading in Lisa's school didn't look like this, she commented,

> Throughout my teaching career, my experiences of how children read in school has pretty much been confined to independent silent reading, where children would sit at their own desk or doing the common activity of 'ERIC' (everyone reading in class) silent and solitary. Everyone reading in class seemed to be revolutionary at the time and I'm sure it was enjoyed by many, but it was fundamentally children reading alone, whilst the teacher marked books or, more recently, checked emails. We wanted to change this practice in our school to provide children with a comfortable, social reading environment.

Lisa explained that the school environment was characterised by the traditional book corner. One difficulty the staff encountered was the age of the school building (over 100 years) which placed significant limitations on the space the staff could allocate to a comfy book corner. In addition, their library was, in Lisa's words, 'tired, neglected and more commonly used as an intervention space for additional learning'.

However, through engaging with the Teachers as Readers research (Cremin et al., 2014) the staff were able to make evidence informed changes. Lisa and the staff spent hours auditing books in the school library, ruthlessly throwing away old books; some were well over 25 years old, and staff were horrified at some of the content. The school library was given a lick of paint, some fairy lights, a soft rug and, most importantly, an enticing selection of reading material for children to choose from. In classrooms, teachers revamped their reading corners, positioning books forward facing so children could see the front cover and not just the spine. Relevant and tempting texts were selected and teachers added their own recommendations to the collection. Reading areas were transformed as cushions and blankets were purchased for children to snuggle into. Teachers began making connections to their pedagogic practice and, through reflecting on their own preferred reading environments, began relating to how children experienced reading in school.

Capturing children's space and place

The next stage for Lisa and her team was to capture the children's opinions about reading. As a Reading Teacher, Lisa knew that finding out about what the children read, where they read and why they read was important, indeed 'finding out what motivates students to read is central to inspiring and sustaining reading for pleasure' (McGeown and Wilkinson, 2021: 2). The staff team wanted to extend the reading materials they offered and ensure that texts reflected children's reading habits (Clark and Douglas, 2011). Lisa explains,

> Firstly, we helped our children complete a short survey about their reading habits. Younger children used simple smiley faces or talked to an adult about where they liked to read or what their favourite book was. Older children completed the survey independently and used a simple scoring system. These surveys not only gave us important information about our children as readers, but also provided us with a baseline finding, enabling us to measure progress over time.

The initial surveys resulted in a seismic shift in the way staff planned time for children to read for pleasure (Figure 8.1). The survey showed that children overwhelmingly said they enjoyed reading in comfortable places such as in bed or on the sofa. This was interesting for the teachers as it mirrored their own reading preferences. Lisa exclaimed that

> this was a penny-drop moment! Whilst there is a time and place for sustained silent reading, we were never going to foster a culture of Reading for Pleasure and a relaxed space for book chat without letting children read in a comfy space.

Figure 8.1 Completing survey

The second way Lisa encouraged teachers to find out what the children liked was by simply talking about books. Lisa explains that

> Adults across school talked openly to children about themselves as readers, sitting on the floor and sharing their favourite books, stories and poems. This then opened the floodgates for fabulous blethering across school, enabling teachers to begin to change their conceptions of how the physical layout of the classroom could foster reading for pleasure.

Lisa notes that

> At our school this was easier said than done. In a small classroom surrounded by desks, chairs and classroom clutter it can be difficult to find space. However, we used all areas of the classroom and gave children the time and space to read, gave them permission to be comfy, to share books with friends, to chat and be noisy, and we were completely surprised by the outcomes.

The momentum was clear, as Lisa explains,

From these early stages, blethering about books in our comfy reading spaces snowballed. In our Independent Reading Time, children and staff chatted informally about their reading choices, shared and exchanged books and delighted from each other's recommendations. Some of the books we chose to share were deliberate, carefully planned around the preferences of a specific child, one who may have expressed that they were not a reader or did not like certain books. Other texts were to encourage more avid readers to broaden their horizons and spread their wings to new authors and genres.

Through this case study of the transformation across a school, Lisa has exemplified the way teachers reflected on their own reading experience. They looked at how, when, where and why they enjoy reading, which caused them to reflect on their Reading for Pleasure pedagogy relating to the social reading environment. In addition, the case study foregrounds how it was vital to capture children's opinions about reading, which led to a wider choice of texts which reflected children's interests. Knowing, understanding and acting on the reading preferences of children is paramount, as the reading then connects to their lives and offers children a degree of control (Renck Jalongo, 2007). Increased choice for the children 'enhances their involvement with and enjoyment of reading' (Clark and Phythian-Sence, 2008: 3) and is driven by the intrinsic motivation to read (McGeown, 2013), which is nurtured by the Reading Teacher.

Developing as Reading Teachers

The enhanced social reading environment at Lisa's school has been largely due to the commitment and motivation of staff; over the last few years, Lisa has seen many Reading Teachers emerge and flourish. Regardless of teaching experience, the age of the children they teach, their job specification or their role in the school, teachers and many support staff know the reading habits of the children in their care, they share something of themselves as readers and they know what reading material to recommend (by keeping up to date with texts that tempt).

Lisa encourages all adults to position themselves as readers. She herself (the head teacher), the office manager, midday supervisors, teaching assistants and class teachers all have important roles to play. However, it must be stressed that implementation takes time, and change can be challenging. In Lisa's experience, this is particularly difficult in a standards driven school culture. There is a balance to be found in the teaching of reading; there is a responsibility to ensure that children become both skilled readers and also develop motivation to read for pleasure in their own time and of their own free will. In schools Lisa has worked with, achieving a balanced reading curriculum has been most successful when Reading for Pleasure has been owned by all and driven forwards by everyone.

Interest, choice and motivation

The case studies and discussion in this chapter illustrate that a physically and socially engaging reading environment is rooted in children's interest, choice and motivation. Interest is, according to Renck Jalongo (2007), the most important form of intrinsic motivation; Renck Jalongo identifies three broad topics around interest, namely situational interest, individual interest and instructional facilitation of interest. Situational interest, she argues, is usually short lived and arises through curiosity or novelty. This could be the interest sparked when the teacher introduces a new book to the class, or as children immerse themselves in a new enticing reading environment. Individual interest however is unique to each child and involves an enduring desire to pursue a subject, concept or activity. The examples shared in the previous sections demonstrate how teachers worked to identify the individual interests of the children through surveys and conversations about reading. Individual interest can then build the motivation to read. Through motivation the children recognise the value they gain from the reading they choose to do; hence, they invest in it emotionally. It is this intrinsic motivation which drives children's desire and need to read because they find the reading inherently enjoyable or interesting (McGeown and Wilkinson, 2021). Motivated readers continue to challenge themselves, which in turn, develops their competence as a reader (Cremin et al., 2014). In addition, such motivation activates agency and 'the learners feeling of belongingness' (Renck Jalongo, 2007: 398). For a more detailed discussion of motivation see Chapter 4.

Changes made to classroom practice, which create opportunities for children to pursue their own interest, is as a result of Renck Jalongo's (2007) final category, instructional facilitation of interest. As Renck Jalongo (2007) states, this aspect 'is all about the teacher. It refers to the relative effectiveness of efforts by educators to engage the learners through attention to situational and/or individual interest' (p. 400). From this perspective, Reading Teachers are conduits of children's interest in reading; their role in initiating and sustaining engaging social reading environments in schools is paramount. As illustrated in the case studies, a Reading Teacher knows about children's interests and understands what motivates them to read. This enables them to support children with their reading choices, which nurtures individual interests and motivation. Through rich and engaging social reading environments, children can become hooked on new texts and, with scaffolding and modelling, can develop sustainable reading habits which will empower them as learners.

Developing enriching reading environments across schools

This chapter has identified the ways in which two teachers (Alex and Clare) and a head teacher (Lisa) have developed social reading environments in individual classrooms and throughout the whole school. In the next case study, Erin Hamilton, the reading lead for ASSET Education Trust, discusses how she led school improvement across a number of schools within a multi-academy trust focusing on developing social reading environments.

Working for a multi-academy trust of 14 schools, Erin's role can vary from week to week and from school to school. One thing she aims for in every school in the trust is for students, staff, parents and visitors to see that the school values Reading for Pleasure, and the first visible indicator of this is the school's social reading environment. Erin comments, 'The value a school places on reading is visible in many ways, from a buzz about books in the corridors, lively and engaging displays, a working library and spaces dedicated to books and reading throughout the school and classrooms'.

All the schools embraced Erin's challenge of ensuring there were dedicated spaces for books and reading for pleasure in every classroom. Where there were simple bookshelves or baskets before, staff have enhanced these areas with a greater variety of texts, comfortable seating and room for children to take ownership of the space. Budgets were provided and school staff were encouraged to throw their imagination and creativity into designing and creating spaces ready to welcome students back in the new school year.

As Erin explains,

> I wanted to underpin our work with research; I explained the aims and rationale of the project to staff and supported them to invest time, purpose and passion into the development of social reading environments. Throughout our training, I looked at several factors that needed to be considered in order to create thoughtful, useful spaces. I started by asking staff to consider the sorts of messages that the current environments conveyed about reading and the purpose of these reading spaces. This highlighted the multi-purpose nature of the environments; many were used as additional teaching spaces. Staff agreed to make changes and place reading at the heart of our classrooms. I posed the question, 'does a dynamic reading space actively encourage enthusiasm for reading?' This prompted intense discussion amongst teachers who found themselves on opposing sides of the argument. Comments included, 'The space may be inviting but it is how we use the space that will make the greatest impact' and 'Once children see an inviting reading space, they will immediately want to jump in'. Whilst both statements held a truth, the space itself can only be a starting point for the Reading for Pleasure journey in a classroom or school. Erin found that teachers need to support and guide the children in the reading choices they make. Our conversations continued, addressing the comments of all staff. Using the *Teachers as Readers* (Cremin et al., 2014) research into social reading environments and by studying previous examples of practice, staff began to feel more confident in creating and planning to use these spaces.

The initial training session moved on to discussion around how children could make use of these social reading environments and, from their own analysis of their reading preferences, teachers decided to ensure that the new reading spaces were dedicated solely to reading activities for children and staff. Running congruently, ideas were shared relating to how students could be involved and take ownership of the reading spaces throughout the year. Teachers all agreed that book blether, peer recommendations and visibility of students in the area would be valuable for the entire class. Erin knew that the opinions and views of the children were vital in this development and that plans needed to be dynamic in nature in order to change and adapt in response to children's voices.

As well as changes inside the school, there were notable changes outside with outdoor reading spaces being upgraded in the playground and baskets of books offered each lunchtime and break time for those children who wanted to dip into a book (Figure 8.2). Erin comments that, 'This also extended to Forest School, where teachers are also ensuring that books are very much a part of the outside provision. Links and connections to books are being found and highlighted each day'.

The range of texts available to children and staff also expanded through the way each school audited their reading environments. This resulted in the replenishing of the texts used across the schools through asking teachers for their wish lists based on their knowledge of their children as readers. Erin found that the choice of texts expanded greatly, and more progress was made with texts which reflected diversity in the schools and the wider community. Overall, there was a sustained increase in visible engagement from the

Figure 8.2 Reading shed

children and staff, evidenced through observing children's spontaneous book talk and enthusiasm for reading.

Erin notes how the work across the schools had a notable impact both visibly and pedagogically, evident through changes in the way reading environments are valued and generate a high level of talk. Each school now fully embraces dynamic social reading environments, and the children are loving the renewed ownership they have of the spaces. Across the schools, children take part in adding book recommendations, choosing books and talking about their choices in groups or to the whole class. There are queues of children waiting to read books recommended by peers and there is greater book blether between peers and staff. In addition, Erin was proud of the fact that the reinvigorated social reading environments were generating interest from visitors to the school, who could see how Reading for Pleasure was part of the school's social fabric.

Conclusion

The social reading environment is more than a reading corner or dedicated reading space. It is the way in which children and adults can interact with texts both physically and socially. Social reading environments can be corners children can find to share and recommend books, hideaways made by the teachers where children can snuggle up with a book, open areas where they can spend time browsing and choosing, the list could go on. The social environment will engage children and adults in informal book talk. Talk is the bedrock of personal, social, cultural, cognitive, creative and imaginative development and so its centrality within the reading environment will enable conversations about books to emerge and develop naturally. It is the social reading environment that enables a positive reading experience in which children and adults can immerse themselves in the process of selecting, reading and responding to texts.

The Reading Teacher's role within the reading environment and the reading process is, as we have seen, pivotal. It is important that they are well informed and active in the process; it is their guidance, scaffolding and modelling which supports young readers to make choices and interact with texts. Reading Teachers have a good knowledge of children's literature as well as knowledge of each reader in their class and an acute awareness of the need to offer a physically and socially safe space for children to inhabit as they empower themselves through reading.

Recommended reading

CLPE (2020) *The Power of a Rich Reading Classroom*. London: Sage.
Lockwood, M. (2008) *Promoting Reading for Pleasure in the Primary School*. London: Sage.
Open University. *Reading for Pleasure: Social Reading Environments*. Available at: https://ourfp.org/finding/rfpp/social-reading-environments/

References

Chambers, A. (2011) *Tell Me: Children, Reading and Talk with The Reading Environment*. Stroud: The Thimble Press.
Clark, C. and Douglas, J. (2011) *Young People's Reading and Writing: An In-Depth Study Focusing on Enjoyment, Behaviour, Attitudes and Attainment*. London: National Literacy Trust.
Clark, C. and Phythian-Sence, C. (2008) *Interesting Choice: The (Relative) Importance of Choice and Interest in Reader Engagement*. London: National Literacy Trust.
Cliff Hodges, G. (2010) Rivers of reading: Using critical incident collages to learn about adolescent readers and their readership. *English in Education*, 44(3): 181–200.
Cliff Hodges, G. (2016) *Researching and Teaching Reading: Developing Pedagogy through Critical Enquiry*. Abingdon: Routledge.
Cremin, T., Mottram, M., Collins, F., Powell, S. and Safford, K. (2014) *Building Communities of Engaged Readers: Reading for Pleasure*. Abingdon: Routledge.
DfE (2021) *The Reading Framework: Teaching the Foundations of Literacy* [online]. Available at: www.gov.uk/government/publications/the-reading-framework-teaching-the-foundations-of-literacy
Kelly, L., Ogdan, M. and Moses, L. (2019) Collaborative conversations speaking and listening in the primary grades. *YC: Young Children*, 74(1): 30–36.
Mackey, M. (2010) Reading from the feet up: The local work of literacy. *Children's Literature in Education*, 41(4): 323–339.
Mackey, M. (2011) The embedded and embodied literacies of a young reader. *Children's Literature in Education*, 42(4): 289–307.
McGeown, S. P. (2013) *Reading Motivation and Engagement in the Primary School Classroom: A Handbook for Teachers*. Leicester: United Kingdom Literacy Association.

McGeown, S. P. and Wilkinson, K. (2021) *Inspiring and Sustaining Reading for Pleasure in Children and Young People: A Guide for Teachers and School Leaders.* Leicester: United Kingdom Literacy Association.

Myles, K. (2020) The reading environment. In *The Power of a Rich Reading Classroom*, pp. 71–80. London: Sage.

Pennac, D. (2006) *The Rights of the Reader.* London: Walker Books.

Renck Jalongo, M. (2007) Beyond benchmarks and scores: Reasserting the role of motivation and interest in children's academic achievement an ACEI Position Paper. *Childhood Education*, 83(6): 395–407.

Wynne-Jones, T. (1998) The survival of the book. *Signal: Approaches to Children's Books*, 87: 160–166.

Reflections on the rights of the reader

Lucy Rodriguez Leon

Daniel Pennac's seminal text *Rights of the Reader* was originally published in French in 1992 and has now been translated into English for the second time; the latest edition (2006) has been charmingly illustrated by Quentin Blake.

Like many teachers, I would like to think I'm an advocate for children's rights as readers. As we know, offering children reading choice and mediating their agency and volition are key dimensions of what it is to be a Reading Teacher. Yet, juxtaposing our desire to ensure all children become keen readers with our commitment to respect their rights as readers can surface some tensions. After all, how do we nurture a love of reading whilst respecting the right not to read? Or how do we promote book talk whilst valuing the readers right to be quiet? In this section, I share a few reflections from my years in practice in an Early Years classroom, and consider how we might reconcile RfP pedagogy with promoting the rights of the reader.

The right not to read

During my many years in the nursery classroom, I recall a small selection of children who just didn't seemed to have any interest in exploring books. I would coax them into the reading area in a jolly manner, they may have even picked up a book or two, but the engagement was fleeting, and they just didn't seem interested. Many of these children appeared to enjoy group read-alouds, particularly when the story was of personal interest, but for some, it just didn't entice them to explore books. Yet I recall working with a lively 4-year-old called Tyler, in 2007 or 2008, who never visited the book area by choice. However, he was mad about cheetahs – other big cats also, but mostly cheetahs. Children's books featuring cheetahs are surprisingly scarce; however, after much searching, I duly found one, probably more suitable for upper primary aged children. It contained some wonderful wildlife photos of a cheetah enjoying the spoils of its hunt, which some staff felt were a little too graphic for a 4-year-old!

Tyler loved it – over the following months he spent hours with the book; he took it to adults to describe and explain the photos, and listened intently as they read the accompanying print. On a couple of occasions, he took the book home to discuss with his dad. This is the only book that I ever saw Tyler engage with, other than this, he continued to exercise his right not to read; but I hope that through this one book, he discovered a purpose and some inspiration for reading.

The right to be quiet

Another right of the reader that can be tricky to reconcile with our RfP pedagogy is the right to be quiet. In my practice, talking with children about books could be very enlightening, it offered a glimpse into the connections they made with their lived experience and the inferences they made in interpreting the narrative. Yet Reading Teachers know that deep engagement with a text manifests in different ways, choosing not to share one's thoughts and views does not necessarily indicate lesser engagement. In fact, when profoundly affected by a text, the emotions that emerge might just be too difficult to discuss in that particular moment.

When reading with children, I recall many a time that my commentary around the text was rather one-sided – I would 'think aloud' and draw attention to detail in the illustrations. I always tried to resist the temptation to ask direct questions and in the absence of a verbal response, I would continue interjecting my own reading with my merry monologue. I think an experienced teacher always knows how engaged a child is by their gestures, facial expression and direction of gaze. Indeed, my research on shared reading highlighted the importance of rereading, arguing that, oftentimes, children firstly need time to absorb and digest the narrative before they are ready to talk about it in depth. Whether reading independently, or with an adult or peers, being silent does not indicate lack of engagement. Conversely, we must also accept that there are times that children are not inspired by a text, it may not resonate with them, and they may have no opinion to voice. Whilst enabling book talk is a key element of facilitating reading for pleasure – pressurising children into talking about a text will be counterproductive, rather, at times, respecting their right to be quiet may enhance engagement.

I remember a particular group of children in nursery in 2014 who collectively became passionate about the book *Little Rabbit Foofoo* (Michael Rosen). For over four months, we read, sung, recited and enacted this story as a group at least once a

The right to re-read

week. With very little adult involvement, the children put on shows, they created their own stage and props, and they made tickets for the office staff. On other occasions, children made goblin houses and tiger hide outs in the 'junk modelling' area. Often, children took it in turns to be 'the teacher' and read aloud the book, mimicking my actions and behaviours in their reading (which was both enlightening and amusing at times!). In my view, rereading is an underrated pedagogic strategy. Subsequent readings are never the same experience; we all bring our own background knowledge to our reading and interpret the text in a way that fits our current understanding of the world (Rosenblatt, 1994). On repeat reading, we come to the text with new and different knowledge, we notice different things and create more vivid mental imagery.

In school children are dependent on their teachers to mediate their rights as readers. A great deal of reading that children do in the classroom will be teacher-directed – that is the nature of education from early years to university. However, teachers and schools which value and nurture Reading for Pleasure also recognise and appreciate the value of ensuring children have opportunities to exercise their rights as readers. Pennac (2006: 149-174) set out ten rights as follows:

- The right to not read
- The right to skip pages
- The right to not finish a book
- The right to read it again
- The right to read anything
- The right to mistake a book for real life
- The right to read anywhere
- The right to dip in
- The right to read out loud
- The right to be quiet

My reflections on practice expose some of the tensions that can arise in mediating children's rights as readers in the classroom. However, other rights set out by Pennac are directly reflected in RfP pedagogy. For example, the right to read anything reminds us to refrain from valuing some texts over others, rather it reiterates that all reading is valuable. Rich reading environments include comics and magazines, digital technology and other texts as well as offering books. Likewise, the right to read anywhere illustrates that children may wish to read in the playground in a reading shed, or on the warm grass in summer, or maybe in a homemade den in Forest Schools club.

Pennac's work also helps us to reflect on our own reading practices and consider, for example, when it is that we skip pages or just dip into a text. It prompts us to reflect on which sorts of texts we do not finish, which we reread and why that is; likewise, thinking about readers' rights may evoke memories of reading something in which we were so deeply engaged that we could have mistaken the narrative for real life. Reflecting deeply on Pennac's Rights of the Reader in relation to our own reading and how we facilitate reading in the classroom gives us deeper insights into our own and our children's reading lives and identities.

References

Pennac, D. (2006) *The Rights of the Reader*. London: Walker Books.
Rosenblatt, L. (1994) *The Reader, the Text, the Poem: The Transactional Theory of the Literary Work*. Carbondale, IL: Southern Illinois University Press.

Section 3

Reading communities

Introduction

This section focuses on building and sustaining communities of engaged readers. The chapters offer a thoughtful examination of the research behind the benefits of building a reading community (the 'why'), as well as specific learning and examples of recent practice (the 'how'). The case studies and school vignettes reveal the complexity of this concept. A reading community is one in which all reading practices are equally valued, opportunities for choice-led reading are supported and readers are keen to interact with one another to share and reflect on their reading preferences and practices (Cremin, 2021; Cremin, Mottram, Collins, Powell and Safford, 2014; Watkins, 2020). By positioning reading as pleasurable, reading communities nurture readers and support them to grow (Merga and Mason, 2019). The relationships that underpin a reading community are key. As Watkins found in her study of peer-to-peer read alouds, social interactions within the community

> were sometimes about the text they were sharing, but often deviated from the world of the text and journeyed into more personal, anecdotal discussions about everyday

DOI: 10.4324/9781003215615-15

life. Increasingly, I realised that students were 'getting to know each other' through reading.

(Watkins, 2020: 17)

The establishment of deeper personal connections through reading have also been documented between teachers and children when the former positioned themselves as fellow readers, sharing something of themselves through reading, whilst also getting to know the young readers better (Cremin et al., 2014). The examples in the following chapters show how reading community relationships become reciprocal, encouraging learning and sharing that transcends traditional power relationships in education, child to head teacher, parent to teacher, reader to reader. Each chapter shows that regular book talk and interaction about reading, that is open and without a prescribed agenda, supports readers to develop more confident and positive reader identities. Reading communities also offer challenge and opportunities for readers to read something new or be introduced to reading outside of their comfort zones.

In school, the community can include teaching and non-teaching staff and volunteers as well as children in all age groups and at all reading levels. The TaRs research emphasised that a school reading community is underpinned by teachers' knowledge of children's texts and children as readers (Cremin et al., 2014). Once teachers changed the way they thought about reading by reflecting on their own experiences as readers and spending time talking to children about reading 'they began to reconceptualise reading from the inside out, and more effectively built a reading for pleasure pedagogy and strong communities of readers within school' (Cremin, 2014: 152). School librarians also have a vital role to play in reinforcing this pedagogy (Ahlfeld, 2020).

To fully embed and sustain life-altering changes to children's volitional reading, reading communities connect schools and teachers with parents, carers, public librarians, authors and other organisations in the local area. *The Reading Framework* in England (DfE, 2021) acknowledges the important impact that parents have on their children's interest in reading and their role in developing children's love of reading through interactions at home. However, it focuses on the teacher's role in sharing resources with parents and informing parents about reading activities. Creating a sustainable reading community involves developing new relationships with parents and families – drawing them into the reading community. Teachers need to move beyond traditional interactions about reading with parents to create a more equal, bi-directional relationship between school and home and connect with children's literacy lives beyond the school gate (Cremin et al., 2015).

Whether celebrating reading or building links between schools, libraries and families, the following chapters also illustrate the importance of goal setting and strategic planning for reading communities. Leaders of reading communities offer an important role model and direction for children's volitional reading (Merga and Mason, 2019). They identify school priorities for RfP and work collaboratively, valuing and drawing on the expertise and resources of libraries and librarians and forging genuine partnership with parents and the wider community.

References

Ahlfeld, K. (2020) I'd rather be reading: Creating lifelong readers in school libraries. *Journal of Library Administration*, 60(2): 187–196. https://doi.org/10.1080/01930826.2019.1695472

Cremin, T. (2021) Building reading communities. In A. Gill, J. Stephenson and D. Waugh (Eds.), *Developing a Love of Reading and Books*. London: Learning Matters, Sage.

Cremin, T., et al. (2015) *Researching Literacy Lives: Building Communities Between Home and School*. London: Taylor and Francis. https://doi.org/10.4324/9781315772820

Cremin, T., Mottram, M., Collins, F. M., Powell, S. and Safford, K. (2014) *Building Communities of Engaged Readers: Reading for Pleasure*. London: Routledge.

DfE (2021) *The Reading Framework*. Available at: The reading framework: teaching the foundations of literacy – GOV.UK (www.gov.uk).

Merga, M. K. and Mason, S. (2019) Building a school reading culture: Teacher librarians' perceptions of enabling and constraining factors. *The Australian Journal of Education*, 63(2): 173–189. https://doi.org/10.1177/0004944119844544

Watkins, V. (2020) Reading collaborative reading partnerships in a school community. *Changing English*, 27(1): 15–33. https://doi.org/10.1080/1358684X.2019.1682966

Chapter 9

Reading Head Teachers

Helen Hendry, Sonia Thompson and Andrew Truby

Introduction

Head teachers and school leaders at all levels have an important role to play in developing a reading community in their schools that enables children and young people to read regularly and to be fully engaged by their reading. We know that reading for pleasure (RfP) can positively influence children's reading achievement (Gilleece and Eivers, 2018), but more than this, it has other positive impacts on children's literacy and wider learning including in vocabulary, maths and spelling (Sullivan and Brown, 2015). Consequently, school development that improves children's engagement with RfP can act as a significant driver for school improvement and may positively influence children's attainment across the curriculum.

Reading Teachers are 'teachers who read and readers who teach' in order to support independent RfP (Cremin, Mottram, Collins, Powell and Safford, 2014: 22). They use reflection on their personal reading practices to develop reciprocal reading relationships with children and support independent reading. These relationships draw on teachers' knowledge of children's texts and of children's home and school reading practices. Building on this definition, Reading Head Teachers motivate and support their staff to develop

DOI: 10.4324/9781003215615-16

RfP pedagogy and become critically reflective of their own reading practices. Reading Head Teachers may begin by championing the importance of reading, but they are more than visionaries who set reading as a school priority. Reading Head Teachers are role models, who understand that enabling children to become frequent, recreational readers provides a mechanism for social-justice that offers the potential to change their life-chances. They skilfully navigate the complexity of school leadership to ensure that their whole staff team is part of this journey of transformation. They ensure that RfP, in addition to the technical skills of reading, is a consistent school-development priority, and they facilitate the conditions in which to make this happen. This chapter considers the role of Reading Head Teachers and school leaders, who identify RfP as a focus for school improvement. It highlights key actions and considerations such as motivating teachers, targeting resources and monitoring impact. Additionally, it offers a range of approaches from research and practice with specific examples of overcoming challenges and successful cultural change.

Every educator knows that each school context and culture is very different, with influences from external, local and national priorities as well as internal issues such as staff turnover and children's outcomes. The two case studies included in this chapter draw on the experiences of head teachers of two primary schools in England. Both are situated in areas of economic disadvantage, but at the time of writing were at different stages in their RfP journeys. Sonia, the established head teacher at St. Matthew's, had been focusing on RfP as a core element of school development for over a decade. Andrew, the recently appointed executive head teacher at St. Joseph's, was looking for a catalyst for school improvement. They explained:

> St Matthew's C.E. Primary Teaching and Research School is in Nechells, in the heart of inner-city Birmingham. It is ranked as one of the most deprived areas nationally. There are many challenges but despite these, St Matthew's has developed into a community of evidence-informed educators, we see it as our mission to tackle the pervasive nature of disadvantage.
>
> St Joseph's Primary School serves a former mining community with high levels of deprivation in the North of England. Typically, when we started this focus, the children did not have reading role models at home, and many did not own a book. A recent Ofsted inspection found that many children did not have the technical skills to read independently or the motivation to read for pleasure. It was clear that expectations of staff were too low, and this led to children having low expectations of themselves. The school had been led by six different head teachers in six years, which meant that morale was extremely low, the staff were exhausted and had lost faith in themselves as educators.

Leadership models

Both Sonia and Andrew had a strong conviction that RfP could make a difference to their schools. With this vision, they needed to plan for a fundamental reshaping of school practices to nurture volitional readers. In school leadership research, head teachers have been seen to influence children's achievement in reading both indirectly and directly (Silva, White and Yoshida, 2011; Zhu, Li and Li, 2020). One important way of influencing student outcomes in reading is through 'instructional leadership', that is leadership that is focused on curriculum and pedagogy (Silva et al., 2011). The pedagogy underpinning RfP centres on children's volitional reading rather than the direct teaching of technical skills, or teacher led comprehension activities. However, 'instructional leadership' is still applicable to the way that Reading Head Teachers begin to establish a reading community. Where school leaders aim to tackle unequal outcomes, they need hope, vision and resilience to tackle barriers and resistance (Forde and Torrance, 2017). Therefore, this process requires skills in relationship building and empowering staff as well as the ability to lead change.

Prioritising RfP

Instructional leadership of RfP, begins with creating a shared purpose and establishing specific goals for children's learning (Hallinger, 2005; Day, Gu and Sammons, 2016). First the staff, parents and governors need to understand **why** RfP should be a priority in school development and **what** learning goals RfP could help children to reach. Embedding RfP pedagogy in a school takes time, and so these goals need to be realistic and identified using knowledge of the school context and priorities. Work in the two case-study schools stems from an **understanding of the research base** that evidences the importance of RfP, and the associated effective pedagogy that supports this (e.g. Cremin et al., 2014; Moses and Kelly, 2018, 2019). Both head teachers articulate a clear vision for the overarching benefits of RfP underpinned by research evidence that links into the mission of each school.

> My commitment to reading for pleasure began over ten years ago when I participated in the Teachers as Readers project (TaRs) (Cremin et al., 2014). RfP as pedagogy was never something that I had particularly worked on before. The project opened my eyes to this evidence-informed practice. Involvement in the TaRs study motivated me to drive this forward and set the foundations for identifying and prioritising my next steps when I returned to school. At St. Matthew's, we hold dear to the fact that disadvantage does not equal deficit. We are ambitious for our children and using reading to enhance opportunities for our children is paramount. Reading is our golden thread and is at the heart of what we do as a school community. Our philosophy around about the importance of reading RfP, is simple. We teach maths and we teach English because they are important to a child's education. So, in the same vein, evidence informed RfP is also important to a child's education.
>
> (Sonia)

> It takes bravery to focus on a single area as a driver for school improvement, but if the children cannot read, then anything else that we do around school improvement is a total waste of time and energy. At St. Joseph's, reading became the key priority because the children need to be able to read confidently and fluently to access the rest of the curriculum and being a frequent reader is the most important indicator of future success. Reading became the core purpose for the school and the driver for school improvement. If we can enable all children to learn to read and to choose to read frequently for pleasure, then we can change the course of their lives.
>
> (Andrew)

Effective instructional leadership is not about applying a top-down strategy but involving the school community as equal partners and valuing their knowledge and skills (Marks and Printy, 2003), so 'bringing them on board' by sharing the research rationale for RfP was essential. For Sonia and Andrew, their intention was to use RfP as a lever for change and innovation through including it in their school-development planning. Their leadership approach could therefore be viewed as instructional but also transformational. Instructional leadership focuses on the 'how' and enables communities of learners to establish ways of implementing new strategies. Transformational leadership focuses on the 'why' and involves providing the inspiration, motivation and intellectual stimulation needed to engage teachers with this process. Previous research of schools that combined a transformational approach with shared instructional leadership demonstrated higher pedagogical quality in their classrooms (Marks and Printy, 2003). In other words, the head teachers shared responsibility for curriculum and pedagogical development with their teachers. More recently, Leithwood, Sun and Schumacker (2020: 573) identified that the most influential 'path' to student learning involved a leadership focus on 'staffing, instructional support, monitoring student learning and school improvement progress and buffering staff from distraction to their instructional work'. However, it is important to note that leading this change involved a *change team* of subject leaders, teachers and teaching assistants, who collaborated to develop ways of implementing RfP.

In embarking on an RfP focus, head teachers need to adopt a strategic approach by identifying any potential barriers, strengths, weaknesses and areas for development in terms of staffing, resourcing and environment (Johnson, Whittington, Scholes, Angwin and Regner, 2014). St. Joseph's school had already put a lot of energy into ensuring that systematic, synthetic phonics (SSP) teaching was embedded in the school and this had made improvements to children's decoding skills, but they needed to find a way to balance the SSP progress with their new aims for RfP. Andrew explained:

> The temptation for leaders in this situation is to try to fix everything at once and schools can be overwhelmed by conflicting advice and messages. We began with whole school commitment to the SSP programme, meaning that this happened every day at all costs. I did wonder whether the school would be able to manage being a partner school for the English Hub focusing on phonics at the same time as taking on a 12-month RfP project with the Open University. However, I decided that the RfP pedagogies were going to be crucial, particularly for those older children who simply did not see themselves as a reader and had no connection to books. We really had to rebrand reading across school and find a way to reach these children.

Andrew's use of the word 'rebrand' points to the transformational aspect of this leadership strategy but it was also clear that he assessed the practicalities of time commitments for staff and their ability to maintain the high-quality phonics provision whilst embedding RfP. At St. Matthew's, the strategy for RfP is strongly linked to budget planning and the school development plan because Sonia recognises that expenditure on regularly updated book-stock is crucial to success:

> Our commitment to RfP means that every year, we articulate the benefits to our governors so that we can convince them to allocate a budget. To make our case, we also extol the benefits for developing subject knowledge, academic attainment, and

the links to oracy. We disseminate funds to updating of book stock in the school library, class reading spaces, getting books into homes and finally for individual class teachers to create and update their own personal libraries. These personal spaces are both inside and outside of the classroom and showcase the teacher as a Reading Teacher/Reading Role Model through displaying their reading choices and making recommendations. It also gives them then chance to grow their own knowledge of texts and authors and the discuss texts, they have chosen, with increasing confidence.

Sonia's strategic planning also includes setting high, RfP-focused expectations for all staff to reflect on their own reading practices to inform their work with children. The importance she places on designating space and budget for individual teachers to communicate their recent reading interests to children shows that she is assisting her staff to become Reading Teachers. This is supported by embedding the social reading environment, resources and RfP pedagogy in the school development plan. Sonia aligned the school development plan to the four strands of RfP pedagogy identified as effective in nurturing RfP in the TaRs research (Cremin et al., 2014). St Matthews' stated aims are to:

- Ensure that every child in the school learns within the context of a social reading environment (ensuring pathways to challenge for the most able and support for the less confident);
- Ensure that every child is regularly read to (in acknowledgement of studies showing that children who are regularly read to do better in school socially and academically);
- Ensure that children have access to a wide range of books, from which they can choose to read independently for pleasure;
- Encourage and develop informal book talk and recommendations so children learn to be courageous and discriminating readers.

Overcoming challenges

School leaders are likely to encounter challenges to embedding RfP in their schools. The case-study examples have already illustrated the need to plan for budgetary implications, to consider staff workload and to share evidence of the relevance of this priority with other stakeholders such as the governing body. Sonia and Andrew also highlighted that embedding RfP may require undoing existing staff assumptions about reading. They acknowledge that on any staff team there will be members who are resistant to their messages about RfP, as well as those who agree that it is important but struggle to allocate time for their own reading. In the following example, Sonia explores these issues and underscores how difficult it can be for teachers to adopt a new approach in line with RfP pedagogy. RfP must be child-led, with teachers reading alongside and facilitating choice and book talk, so teachers need confidence and gradual strategies to relinquish the desire to **teach** reading in designated RfP times (Cremin et al., 2014).

> One of my challenges is to ensure that new teachers understand the clear division between RfP and teaching reading, so that children understand the difference and can relax and take the lead. Teachers needed support to be confident enough to 'let go' and really allow this freedom. We developed this confidence through using our

leaders to model what we expected – read and relax meant just that – cushions out, shoes off and tables pushed back was fine. As one teacher said, '. . . you mean no comprehension! I needed to hear that several times before I believed I could actually do it . . . and not get into trouble'. The reading culture has grown as teachers' knowledge has developed, but I am acutely aware that I have had staff whose engagement has been superficial at best. I am conscious though that as teachers prefer teaching one subject over the other, they ultimately know that they must teach their least favourite subject well if children are to thrive. I view their engagement with RfP in the same way . . . they must do it if children are to thrive. It has been amazing to see those teachers that begin in this way then become the most veracious and principled supporters of RfP within their classrooms.

At St. Joseph's, a similar cultural change was needed, requiring all teachers and leaders to review how entrenched practices in the school may have been negatively affecting children's attitudes to reading. Reading Head Teachers must be brave enough to undo accepted practice such as moving away from a reliance on children reading only banded books from schemes. They may need to support staff to ruthlessly review book stock; for example a small bookshelf of carefully chosen, beautifully displayed and varied texts will entice readers more than a library full of old and unloved texts. In this case, Andrew explains how teachers reviewed the way that reading was organised in the school and took a reflective approach to reviewing book stock.

One of the frightening things about developing RfP is when you realise that lots of the strategies in schools have a detrimental effect, for example rewarding children for reading, forcing them to read or asking them lots of questions about what they have read. The school moved away from book banded books completely and any other books in school that were poor quality by applying the Marie Kondo approach (Kondo, 2011) – asking ourselves whether a book brings us joy. The school invested in great books so that the children would only have the very best of experiences when encountering books.

Changing the culture

Gathering a team and identifying priorities

A key strategy for school RfP development involves shared leadership and collaborative work, sometimes with schools convening a specific 'change team' of teachers and teaching assistants across the year groups who take responsibility for developing and sustaining staff development and the use of evidence informed practice. Whilst the vision for making RfP a school priority may start with the Reading Head Teacher an important part of their role involves gathering a team. Once such a team and way of working is established, the priorities for RfP pedagogy across the school can be identified through staff and children's surveys, observations and focus groups. Then different strategies can be implemented with expert knowledge of year groups and key stages, allowing specific ways of working to grow from the whole school priorities. Sonia regularly uses whole school surveys to gauge RfP in the school but supplements these with informal book talk and observations of children and groups of children:

To guide our planning and purchasing, we complete an annual RfP survey of children. We also survey staff. It is crucial to get a sense of what adults and children feel confident about and need support with. It also gives an insight into changing reading choices. Impromptu data collection through book talk and observations around school from Reading Teachers, also allows us to delve into reading habits and agency.

Reading Head Teachers and their change teams then use a range of methods to identify which aspects of RfP pedagogy to develop further or where to start. They might observe the children's use of spaces within the school such as reading corners or the school library (Loh, 2016). They might use surveys for children and staff. In one school in Newham, the English leader used questionnaires and small group interviews to focus on reading practices and interests in Year 5 (Reedy and De Carvalho, 2021). In this case, the children revealed that the school environment was noisy and uncomfortable for reading and that they had limited opportunities to choose what they wanted to read. Following this, staff developed a new library environment with input from children at all stages and led whole school training on children's choice and freedom, which are key to enhancing volitional reading.

Providing a role model

Reading Head Teachers support the process of cultural change by inviting others to share leadership and by providing a **role model of instructional leadership**, perhaps through leading staff CPD in partnership with subject leaders. Leadership becomes 'distributed' between staff members with each agreeing new actions to implement and responsibilities and methods for monitoring and reviewing. The head teacher's active participation in instructional leadership can transform the school culture by positively influencing teachers' commitment, professional involvement and willingness to innovate (Marks and Printy, 2003). At St. Matthew's and St. Joseph's, even the head teacher's office shows the school commitment to RfP where books are proudly displayed and utilised to stimulate spontaneous book talk. This allows Sonia and Andrew to model RfP pedagogy for the benefit of their staff and children in the school.

> RfP needed champions within my school, and I was determined that this began with my leaders and me. I am adamant that if the head teacher does not fully support, endorse, drive and model good practice it will quickly fade away. My office is the place where I celebrate RfP. I display, share and discuss books on a daily basis, with children, adults and visitors alike. No one escapes my book talk!
>
> (Sonia)

> I want everyone to know that we are a school where everyone learns to read and chooses to read and this must be evident everywhere in the school building. I am a role model for promoting reading for pleasure personally therefore I display a number of books in my office and I am always happy to recommend one of them to a child and let them borrow it. In my experience, asking children what they are reading and taking an interest in them as a reader makes the biggest difference when I am visiting classrooms.
>
> (Andrew)

Changing systems

RfP at St. Matthew's is embedded in the school through adaptations to the timetable and planning structure. These school-wide systems build on the head teacher's role model to provide a framework that prioritises voluntary reading and provides spaces for collaborative instructional development. Sonia cautions that developing an RfP community is 'a marathon not a sprint'. Whilst changes to practice are supported by changes to timetabling, planning and organisation it is important to identify where to start and not to instigate wholescale change before staff are ready. As Sonia notes,

> There have been years of development around RfP. Driving it forward in new and innovative ways, has become part of the culture. It is now embedded into everything; timetabled, in all curriculum subjects, environment; and is part of our PD programme. The range of reading practices include:
> - Teacher/SLT reading displays;
> - A two-week timetable for reading, with one week completely for RfP;
> - Wall/library displays;
> - Subject leader reading for subject knowledge displays;
> - Getting involved in national initiatives;
> - Author visits and book fairs.

Time is still given to explicit reading instruction and the technical skills of reading, through phonics, guided and shared reading. However, for 4- to 7-year-olds reading aloud also happens daily and independent reading for pleasure, including book talk, is timetabled throughout the week. For 8- to 11-year-olds, every other week includes three sessions of independent choice-led reading. The teachers read alongside the children and share informal book talk about reading, but RfP texts are not used for class analysis, as a writing stimulus or the focus of comprehension questions.

Planning for the contribution of the school environment is another aspect of instructional leadership. The environment at St. Matthews sends clear messages to the whole community about the priority that is given to RfP, but also the reading areas are carefully designed to be comfortable and welcoming so that they are fully used. The importance of reading for the teachers themselves is also encouraged through reading and sharing books about their subjects. This allows them to model and reflect on reading for pleasure for different purposes and share these experiences authentically with children. School reading events, author visits and book fairs enrich the whole school reading experience. This means that RfP continues to develop and maintains a high profile for everyone.

Empowering staff as Reading Teachers

Whilst the importance of RfP is demonstrated by a wide range of research, teachers may struggle to effectively translate research findings into classroom practice (Cordingley, 2008; Brown and Zhang, 2016). Reading Head Teachers and school leaders have a crucial role to play in demonstrating 'buy in' and introducing teachers to research findings that are related to their current needs (Brown and Zhang, 2016). They also need to help teachers to interpret these findings in their own context (Cordingley, 2008). Both Sonia and Andrew drew on their knowledge of the TaRs research to inform work with their staff

(Cremin et al., 2014). Their whole school development was informed by the EEF whole school implementation process, moving through a cycle of explore, prepare, deliver and sustain (EEF, 2019). Once school needs and priorities for RfP were established in the explore and prepare phases (see previous section), Andrew planned ways to ignite staff interest and encourage them to consider reading from the children's perspectives:

> The RfP programme started with teachers going to a book shop and choosing a wonderful book to read as their class story, which reignited their passion for reading. Book corners were developed to display books with front covers visible and the teachers became experts in children's literature by regularly reading new texts and researching authors. The teachers really focused on implementing the conditions for RfP through choosing great books, developing their knowledge of children's literature, developing book talk and social reading environments.

Andrew encouraged his staff to be Reading Teachers by offering a shared experience and time to read and reflect. The teachers noticed the excitement of being surrounded by new books, the enjoyment of choosing a book and the way that the bookshop enticed them to read using displays. They were able to apply this to the school environment and the way that they tried to engage readers. These reflections enthused the staff to share reading in a different way with the children and Andrew described this as having an 'inspirational effect' on their feeling about the teacher's role in the classroom.

The staff team first needed to develop their own knowledge of children's literature and children's preferences so that they could change their interactions and environment (Cremin et al., 2014). Andrew facilitated this by giving them permission to think differently about reading, new reading resources, time to talk about their own reading and to implement new pedagogy. He therefore 'buffered' them from competing instructional distractions (Leithwood, Sun and Schumacker, 2020). Whilst other curriculum priorities continued, a clear shared focus remained on developing pedagogy for RfP, including the time to talk about reading in a relaxed way in the classroom. One of the teachers at St. Joseph's reflected:

> The most enjoyable thing for myself as a teacher this year is being able to read books with my pupils, as a class together. . . . We are able to have wonderful discussions on what we are all reading and it's a really enjoyable time of the day.

This teacher's comment highlights how the changing culture involved changing relationships for reading so that teachers and children could interact differently and feel different about reading at school.

Reading HTs, families and social justice

During their school improvement work the head teachers maintained a focus on the value of RfP as a means of influencing children's outcomes and life chances. As RfP has been embedded at St. Matthew's over several years, the annual assessment data demonstrates the sustained benefits. For example, annual surveys since 2017 indicate that over 80% of children in Years 5 and 6 like or love reading. Furthermore, data shows a shift in children's perceptions of reading. In 2017, children aged 8–11 referred to reading as a source of self-improvement, for example 'I learn more things, it helps me'. Whereas, by 2020 most responses emphasised their affective response to reading specifically, fun, enjoying quiet time to read and comfortable spaces. Children's reading choices have also become more varied and ambitious including new authors, picture books, poetry and non-fiction. Sonia adds:

> I have no hesitation in saying that a rich reading for pleasure culture within my school had directly impacted on our reading attainment data. We have been consistently well above national averages in our SATs data, in reading, writing and maths, at both KS1 and KS2 for several years. Although I do not feel that I must justify the time we allocate to reading for pleasure, this does help to silence any doubters.

At St. Joseph's, prioritising RfP alongside an already rigorous programme of reading instruction helped to create motivated readers. Following a year of whole school development for RfP, the school was able to move from special measures to good in an Ofsted inspection that included a 'deep dive' into reading. The Ofsted report (2021: 2) highlighted this shift:

> Leaders have made reading a priority. Pupils enjoy reading. They like listening to adults read to them in the daily 'reading for pleasure' sessions. Younger pupils vote each day for the book they would like to read. Parents recognise the improvements in the school, particularly in the teaching of reading.

Andrew explained the transformational effect of RfP on the children, teachers and parents:

> Children are now regularly reading for pleasure, recommending books to their peers and teachers are knowledgeable about children's literature. Books are beautifully displayed around school and there is excitement and enthusiasm when new books are added to the reading corners. In terms of a driver for social change, this is evident with the parents; they have really noticed how reading has transformed their children and their confidence.

A survey of all children in the school (n160) during the year showed a marked increase in children reporting that they independently read for pleasure every day (Table 9.1). Staff observations of changes to the children's behaviour and conversations with children and parents validated these claims.

Sonia and Andrew's case studies were written during the Covid-19 pandemic and this further changed the relationship that the schools had with the families. One part of their role was to keep an overview of the impact of the new RfP practices on the children and the wider school community, reflecting this back to their staff team and noticing unique learning that could inform their priorities moving forward. As Andrew explains:

> As a school community, we learnt a great deal from the pandemic, particularly around working with parents; seeing them respond to technology and being 'included' in reading rather than told how to do it was so powerful. Parents became more interested

Table 9.1 Changes to the percentage of children who read every day for pleasure at St. Joseph's

Year group	September 2020	December 2020	June 2021
EYFS (aged 4–5)	78%	100%	100%
Y1 (aged 5–6)	64%	93%	100%
Y2 (aged 6–7)	65%	96%	100%
Y3 (aged 7–8)	73%	100%	100%
Y4 (aged 8–9)	57%	76%	100%
Y5 (aged 9–10)	54%	63%	78%
Y6 (aged 10–11)	53%	95%	95%

in what happened in classrooms. As reading was a core part of our remote education offer, we built on this by 'showing not telling', for example through sharing a bedtime story for children and parents to tune into with no pressure. This, informal, fun, non-threatening but 'leading by example' approach led to huge success. Parents could visibly see the enjoyment. Books had not previously been part of some homes. However, we were not only delivering food parcels but also book parcels to many of our families.

Sonia also took new meta-learning from her experiences of working with children and families on RfP over the last few years. Taking time to notice children's responses to RfP reinforced her commitment to RfP as a practice for social justice:

> Finding out about children's reading identities has been key in ensuring our engagement with our children and families are authentic. We have to challenge ourselves to make authentic space, value and build on children's agency as readers. This was particularly poignant when a group of boys, who loved reading *The Beano*, then went on to create and sell their own comic to both children and staff. One of these boys said he could not afford comics in his house. We would have never uncovered this without making space for discussions.

In both schools, the impact of well-planned, research informed RfP whole school development work was shown through changes in attitudes and behaviours from individual children:

> I love reading now and I even read with my mum at home. I bought some Marvel books from the shop the other day to read with her. My favourite part of the [school] day is RfP time in the afternoon.
>
> (Luca aged 8)

Reading Head Teachers draw on assessment data but also use their involvement with the whole school community to inform their vision for future pedagogy. They can hold up a mirror to staff practices and emphasise the impact on children and parents, thereby supporting staff motivation and awareness in their continuing work.

Monitoring and maintaining

In both the case study schools the head teachers worked with their staff to implement systems for monitoring the impact of their RfP pedagogy and keeping it on track. At St. Matthew's the RfP focus of the school improvement plan was regularly reviewed but RfP was part of the plan each year.

> The RfP pedagogies became a focus for professional development. I began by embedding one per term which provided the lens through which the school improvement plan could be constructed.
>
> (Sonia)

At St. Joseph's, once the change in the school's reading culture started to have an impact on most children, the staff began to target those children in their class who were not choosing to read. They created an action plan for these children in each class focused on finding out more about their preferences and introducing them to different reading materials that might tempt them to read:

> As the staff grew in confidence, selecting and recommending books moved from being quite adult-led to peer-led and that was a real turning point where reading became 'cool' because everyone was doing it and enjoying it. We eventually got down to a very small number of children who could read fluently but were not choosing to read so we made it part of our raising attainment plans to give this status. Teachers actively sourced books that these children would enjoy and made a formal commitment through the action plan. Slowly but surely, we found a little spark and that was the start of their journey into reading.
>
> (Andrew)

Andrew ensured that work on RfP had specific whole school priorities. These included engaging all children but targeting those who were struggling. In measuring the impact of RfP pedagogy, the Reading Head Teachers considered changes to the whole school environment, relationships, parents and teachers as well as individual children's progress, motivation and confidence.

Both Sonia and Andrew recognised that the impact of RfP may be seen in academic progress but that changes to the community and the relationships within it are equally valuable. One significant shift was the impact on well-being and empathy:

> Children who read for pleasure do well in all areas of the curriculum, have wider vocabulary and background knowledge and are more empathetic. In fact, reading makes the staff more empathetic. The opportunity to read, connect and act, through linking to opportunities/ outside projects, enable us to enhance and sustain our RfP agenda.
>
> (Sonia)

> Being part of the larger project (OU RfP whole school improvement programme), when working virtually during a pandemic supported teachers' mental health. The pleasure that the books brought to them and when books were shared in the sessions,

was therapeutic. The other key aspect about being part of the bigger project was that this made it a national challenge rather than just a school one.

(Andrew)

Conclusion

Reading Head Teachers engage in both transformational and instructional leadership. They present a clear, research-based rationale for RfP that convinces the staff team and wider community of its benefits for the children. They draw together a change team who are invested in this approach and can influence practices throughout the school. They take time to 'undo' unhelpful assumptions and examine existing practices for independent reading and reading aloud. This work is about the hearts and minds of the staff, parents and children starting with changing teachers' understanding of reading and RfP in particular. Learning from research offers a range of specific pedagogical strategies that develop RfP. The head teacher and change team must identify which of these to prioritise at first and keep returning to these, year on year, to drive enhancements. Before commencing any school development work on RfP, it is essential to understand the current practices and experiences of the staff and children in any school. Time should be given for the change team to collect this data through surveys, observations, focus groups, interviews and existing school documentation such as library use and home-school reading records. However, although agreement about whole school priorities and some overarching approaches is needed, there must be space for strategies that are developed across a Key Stage, Year Group or even specifically for one class. This ensures that teachers can respond flexibly to the needs of the children and feel agency and ownership of the strategies they employ.

Reading Head Teachers embed RfP in an ongoing programme of informal and formal professional development such as staff book clubs, RfP newsletters, conferences and twilights. These keep the profile of RfP high and allow time for staff to develop their underpinning knowledge of children's texts and authors. A key element of CPD involves making an emotional connection through shared experiences such as visiting a book shop and listening to stories, poems etc. read aloud. Furthermore, ensuring that RfP is included on the school development plan with an assigned budget can ensure sufficient resources are available. Teachers may be encouraged to select texts for their classrooms or the library that reflect children's interests. They may be gifted children's texts to read themselves and develop their own reading repertoire. Reading Head Teachers highlight the social justice value of this work and appreciate the change to relationships brought about by RfP, but they maintain focus on goals and monitoring impact, especially on those children who do not choose to read. Reading Head Teachers hold up a mirror to staff practices and asks them to examine them anew from a child's perspective. At St Joseph's, this not only improved outcomes in reading, but it also had a transformational effect on all areas of teaching and learning. Focusing on reading and embedding RfP ultimately supported the school to move from 'Special measures' to 'Good' in their most recent Ofsted inspection. At St. Matthew's, their long-term commitment was recognised when they became the proud first winners of the Egmont (now Farshore)/OU/UKLA Reading for Pleasure whole school award. These successes result from sustained changes to practice and the whole school communities' relationship with reading.

Recommended reading

OU. *RfP Strategies for Whole School Development Document*. Available at: https://cdn.ourfp.org/wp-content/uploads/20210211154737/Strategies_for_whole_school_development1.pdf?_ga=2.17054457.1113300486.1630424787-652305418.1613493983

OU. *RfP Whole School Development Webpage Including Surveys for Staff and Children*. Available at: https://ourfp.org/schools-teachers/whole-school-development/

Reedy, A. and De Carvalho, R. (2021) Children's perspectives on reading, agency and their environment: What can we learn about reading for pleasure from an East London primary school? *Education 3–13*, 49(2): 134–147. https://doi.org/10.1080/03004279.2019.1701514

References

Brown, C. and Zhang, D. (2016) Is engaging in evidence-informed practice in education rational? What accounts for discrepancies in teachers' attitudes towards evidence use and actual instances of evidence use in schools? *British Educational Research Journal*, 42(5): 780–801.

Cordingley, P. (2008) Research and evidence-informed practice: Focusing on practice and practitioners. *Cambridge Journal of Education*, 38(1): 37–52. https://doi.org/10.1080/0305764080188996

Cremin, T., Mottram, M., Collins, F. M., Powell, S. and Safford, K. (2014) *Building Communities of Engaged Readers: Reading for Pleasure*. London: Routledge.

Day, C., Gu, Q. and Sammons, P. (2016) The impact of leadership on student outcomes. *Educational Administration Quarterly*, 52(2): 221–258. https://doi.org/10.1177/0013161X15616863

EEF. (2019) *Putting Evidence to Work. A School's Guide to Implementation*. Available at: EEF_Implementation_Guidance_Report_2019.pdf (d2tic4wvo1iusb.cloudfront.net).

Forde, C. and Torrance, D. (2017) Social justice and leadership development. *Professional Development in Education*, 43(1): 106–120. https://doi.org/10.1080/19415257.2015.1131733

Gilleece, L. and Eivers, E. (2018) Characteristics associated with paper-based and online reading in Ireland: Findings from PIRLS and ePIRLS 2016. *International Journal of Educational Research*, 91: 16–27. https://doi.org/10.1016/j.ijer.2018.07.004

Hallinger, P. (2005) Instructional leadership and the school principal: A passing fancy that refuses to fade away. *Leadership and Policy in Schools*, 4(3): 221–239. https://doi.org/10.1080/15700760500244793

Johnson, G., Whittington, R., Scholes, K., Angwin, D. and Regner, P. (2014) *Exploring Strategy: Text and Cases*, 10th ed. Harlow: Pearson Education.

Kondo, M. (2011) *The Life-changing Magic of Tidying Up: A Simple Effective Way to Banish Clutter Forever and Organizing*. London: Penguin Random House.

Leithwood, K., Sun, J. and Schumacker, R. (2020) How school leadership influences student learning: A test of 'the four paths model'. *Educational Administration Quarterly*, 56(4): 570–599. https://doi.org/10.1177/0013161X19878772

Loh, C. E. (2016) Levelling the reading gap: A socio-spatial study of school libraries and reading in Singapore. *Literacy*, 50(1): 3–13.

Marks, H. and Printy, S. (2003) Principal leadership and school performance: An integration of transformation and instructional leadership. *Educational Administration Quarterly*, 39(3): 370–397.

Moses, L. and Kelly, L. B. (2018) 'We're a little loud. That's because we like to read!': Developing positive views of reading in a diverse, urban first grade. *Journal of Early Childhood Literacy*, 18(3): 307–337.

Moses, L. and Kelly, L. B. (2019) Are they really reading? A descriptive study of first graders during independent reading. *Reading & Writing Quarterly*, 35(4): 322–338.

Ofsted (2021) *Inspection Report: St. Joseph's Catholic Primary School*. Available at: Ofsted-Report-St-Josephs-Catholic.pdf (stjosephs-dinnington.co.uk).

Reedy, A. and De Carvalho, R. (2021) Children's perspectives on reading, agency and their environment: What can we learn about reading for pleasure from an East London primary school? *Education 3–13*, 49(2): 134–147. https://doi.org/10.1080/03004279.2019.1701514

Silva, J. P., White, G. P. and Yoshida, R. K. (2011) The direct effects of principal – student discussions on eighth grade students' gains in reading achievement. *Educational Administration Quarterly*, 47(5): 772–793. https://doi.org/10.1177/0013161X11404219

Sullivan, A. and Brown, M. (2015) Reading for pleasure and progress in vocabulary and Mathematics. *British Educational Research Journal*, 41(6): 971–991.

Zhu, H., Li, L. and Li, H. (2020) How school leadership influences Chinese students' reading literacy: A test of the rational, emotions, and organizational paths in rural schools. *Children and Youth Services Review*, 119: 105534. https://doi.org/10.1016/j.childyouth.2020.105534

Chapter 10

Reading Librarians and school libraries

Jen Aggleton, Carol Carter and Mary Rose Grieve

Introduction

There are few places more suited to developing a love of literature than the school library, a place referred to by the Libraries All Party Parliamentary Group as 'The Beating Heart of The School' (APPG, 2014). National Literacy Trust reports repeatedly note that for children from low socio-economic backgrounds the presence of a school library is vital, as they are less likely to have access to books at home (Clark, 2010; Clark and Poulton, 2011; Clark and Teravainen-Goff, 2020). These reports also note that young people who use their school library are consistently more likely to state that they enjoy reading. The librarian is just as, if not more important than, the library itself. Studies from several Anglophone countries have shown that successful school libraries require well-trained, well-supported librarians (see Goodwin, 2017).

Whilst the impact of libraries and school librarians on attainment has been well traced (see Williams, Wavell and Morrison, 2013), there is less research about the role of libraries in developing Reading for Pleasure (RfP). In this chapter, we explore the practice of two school librarians to demonstrate how school libraries, run by Reading Librarians, can form the centre of outstanding whole school RfP provision. By considering professional

DOI: 10.4324/9781003215615-17

practice in the context of the existing literature, we identify key aspects of the librarian's role, as well as the library environment, which offer a pathway to volitional reading which is distinct from, but complementary to, that of the class teacher.

The grounded evidence for this chapter comes from the practice of two school librarians, Carol Carter and Mary Rose Grieve. Carol works as a librarian in a state primary school in Northampton, England, whilst Mary Rose works as a librarian in a private school in Dubai, UAE (for 4- to 17-year-olds). Both exhibit the characteristics of a fully developed Reading Teacher as conceptualised by the continuum in the book's introduction. Not only are they reading role models, sharing their own reading practices, but they also have a deep understanding of the diverse reading practices and identities of their pupils. In addition, both librarians are highly knowledgeable and reflective professionals, who continually consider the pedagogical practices they undertake and how these impact upon children as readers. Crucially, it is their position as librarians, outside of the classroom, which enables them to develop and utilise these characteristics so effectively. As this chapter demonstrates, the role of the school librarian is both complex and highly skilled, and the practices of these Reading Librarians showcase the value that the school library and the school librarian offer.

The themes for the chapter were developed through discussions of our professional practice as librarians and educators. They also reflect existing scholarship drawn from academic studies and professional reports on libraries, education and RfP. Rather than having a separate section exploring the literature, this has been interwoven with the examples offered by Carol and Mary Rose. In doing so we demonstrate how their successful practice reflects or extends our current understandings of the role of libraries and Reading Librarians in the development of RfP, whilst providing rich models that classroom practitioners can draw upon in their own work.

Relationships with children

One of the key principles for successful RfP is the need to create 'diverse, supportive and social reading environments' (Safford, 2014: 90). Both Carol and Mary Rose highlight that the position of the library outside of the classroom, and their roles as librarians rather than teachers, enables the development of these reading environments and positive reading relationships. Research by Shaper and Streatfield (2012) identifies the potential for the positive pastoral role of school libraries and school librarians in the secondary school context, and how the library can provide a safe space where students are able to have agency. The following sections demonstrate how this can also be true within the primary context and provide some key examples of how to develop this positive environment and the impacts it can have on developing a culture of reading.

Library environment conducive to relationship building

The physical space of the library is of key importance when developing a whole school RfP culture. Mary Rose states that:

> An underlying principle of our education goals is to create an environment where curiosity, wonder and inquiry flourish and are promoted. There is nowhere more

fundamental to this than the library; it is both the incubator and the radiator of curiosity and inquiry.

Of great importance to the construction of this environment is that the library is what Goodwin refers to as an 'assessment-free zone' (2017: 49), a feature mentioned by both our Reading Librarians. It is thought common, as Merga and Roni (2018) note, for schools operating within a high-stakes testing environment to inadvertently stress reading for testing rather than RfP. Within that context, the separation of the library from the classroom can lead to the construction of a space which encourages spontaneous, autonomous recreational reading, led by student choice rather than curriculum goals (Merga, 2013; Goodwin, 2017). Beyond this, constructing the library as a 'safe space' away from the pressures of assessment also promotes children's well-being, described here by Carol:

> The library is open to all children from Year 1 upwards, three breaktimes and lunchtimes each week. There are sofas, cushions and comfy corners, as well as 'Book Buddies' – soft toys with name tags saying the types of stories they like to be read. Children can stay as long as they like to read, browse, colour, share stories. While for many, their reason to visit is specific e.g. change their library book, for others the library space is a safe space if they are having friendship issues, or need a break from the hustle of the playground. Many of my visitors are regular – I get to know them well and can spot if things are 'not quite right'. My position outside of the classroom means they can sometimes be willing to share in a way they may not with their class teacher.

As a space with children's well-being, comfort and choice at its heart, the library can offer children the association of books with their well-being and interests, rather than with academic skills and achievements. In addition, as this comment highlights, the library provides time for children to read and browse at their own pace and according to their own interests. In this way, the library environment can bring together the three elements identified by Mallette and Barone (2016) as being the most impactful for developing readers: access to books, free choice of what to read and time to read. However, not all children will come to the library without an introduction, which is where having a librarian who can reach out becomes highly valuable, as described by Mary Rose:

> The Bookeroo service has enabled me to create relationships with students who might not otherwise have visited the library. I can curate a small selection of books to put on the trolley that will appeal to the classes I am visiting at lunch and breaktime. I have found that I have been able to lend books to students who might have been daunted by the searching the bookshelves, not knowing what to look for.

The importance of library resources being easily discoverable by pupils was also highlighted in a study by Larkin-Lieffers (2011) who notes that considerations such as shelf height and organisation can be a barrier to young children meaningfully accessing the library. The expertise of a librarian in organising the library space is therefore a key facet in ensuring a productive environment for reading exploration. As Carol says:

Without a librarian, a library is just a big collection of books – from a child's eye, a jungle of words often hard to penetrate and navigate. With a librarian as guide, the child can have the confidence and support to explore and find the magic within.

Time and expertise to build relationships

As a specialist role, librarians also have the time and a level of expertise to engage in meaningful conversations with individual children which might be difficult to achieve within the restrictions of the classroom. Whilst the expertise of librarians is frequently mentioned in scholarship (see Goodwin, 2017), the importance of time has been overlooked. Carol describes one initiative which draws not only on this time and expertise, but also the environment of the library, to help readers develop a love of reading:

> Teachers can 'refer' a child to me for a Book Conference, maybe because they are a reluctant reader, don't know what to read next, are looking for a book on a specific topic etc. The Conference takes the form of a 10–15 min structured chat in the library, during lesson times, where we collaboratively fill in a form asking questions such as 'What do you like to do outside of school?' and 'What is your favourite book and why?' The Conference enables me to give targeted personal recommendations (the children often leave with a whole stack of books!) and is sometimes followed up with a second Conference 2–4 weeks later. We may also choose a new book to order for the library together (e.g. if they have a specific request such as a book about karate). The combination of having a chance to chat about their interests, habits, home lives etc. and browse when the library is peaceful and there are no expectations has been really successful in engaging children, and gives me the opportunity to suggest reading material they may not have tried before. The relationship is two-way in that I also get useful feedback on gaps in library stock.

Librarians also have the time to be able to build and maintain relationships with readers over several years, offering a level of continuity and development which a teacher is less likely to be in a position to provide. Carol notes:

> While teachers develop intense year-long relationships with their class, the multi-year aspect of my role enables me to nurture children over longer time spans. A child may begin visiting the library café with their parent when in Reception, then visit independently at break time in Year 1 before joining a Book Club in Year 2. Each year, I build on my knowledge of them as reading individuals, considering when they are ready for chapter books, and which author they will love next.

Being in a position to nurture readers over several years, particularly within a non-assessment-based role, enables librarians to make a unique contribution to the development of children as readers. Cremin, Mottram, Collins, Powell and Safford (2014) note the importance of knowing children as readers to building productive and reciprocal reading relationships and practices. Teachers gain a great depth of knowledge into a snapshot of a child's reading but are also embedded in curriculum and statutory requirements to move children's reading 'forward' from a skills-based viewpoint. A librarian can complement this role by drawing on their knowledge of a child's interests and reading habits over a longer period, and can help to encourage a broadening of reading interests in line with the development of RfP. As such, librarians are uniquely positioned to develop RfP by getting 'the right book to the right child at the right time' (Collins and Safford, 2008: 415).

Building community

As well as developing positive reading relationships with individual students, librarians are also uniquely well placed to develop reciprocal and interactive communities of readers. Identified by Cremin et al. (2014) as a key strategy for the development of RfP, communities of readers create social spaces for reading which encourage choice, reader autonomy and equal relationships between members.

Whole-school strategies to build community

Both librarians felt that an important part of their role was their ability to work at a whole-school level, rather than the classroom. They use a variety of methods to develop a whole-school community of readers. Carol discussed some of the strategies she employs:

> I regularly co-present whole-school Book Assemblies with our English Lead. I will usually read a book, but a key feature is a child from each year group sharing a short review of what they are reading. We will also announce competition winners, give out reading certificates, choose Book Bingo winners to collect a book prize etc. – all of which raise the profile of reading within school and allow children to experience reading across year groups.
>
> We also have various ways for children and staff to share their reading likes and dislikes with others within the school. The library has several books/folders where children can write reviews and browse those written by others, but most successful has been a 'Flyleaf Book Review' sheet pasted into the front of each book. Children add their first name, age, star rating and 1–3 words describing the book. The sheet then acts as a record of who has read and enjoyed the book previously.

Carol enables interactions within the community through various pathways, so children have opportunities be involved in ways which are comfortable to them, fostering autonomy and enabling choice, both key aspects of successful reading communities. The value of all readers' views and opinions is also continually highlighted, which maintains a social and dialogic aspect to reading even when readers are not in the same spaces at the same time.

Alongside ongoing initiatives, special events which respond to particular needs can also be very powerful in building reading communities, as described by Mary Rose:

> While we were online in the summer of 2020, I used platforms such as Genially and Canva to create interactive treasure maps, posters and virtual bookshelves to introduce children to the plethora of resources available. All these were accessible from the Library channel on their class Teams, and this became a place for informal discussion, book recommendations and chat. However, the class Teams are not places for whole school involvement, and it was important that we were able to maintain a sense of community when everyone was so isolated from each other.

> So I delivered three Library Live sessions a day to primary pupils. I had to grapple to work out how to ensure that our online reading communities were still characterised by the four principles identified by Cremin (2019): Learner-Led, Informal, Social and with Texts that Tempt. Given that I was delivering the Library Live sessions as a live broadcast and therefore unable to see or interact with the students, I had to find ways to allow the sessions to be directed by the children and to ensure that there were safe, informal ways for them to communicate about the books. I set up a daily Survey Monkey poll with the covers of four books – Old, New, Non-Fiction and Boo! (the last was my choice) – for the children to vote on, and they tuned in live to see which book won. There was a very strong informal online community in the Library Channels in class Teams as children discussed the books we read and made suggestions of books that might be read the next day.

Mary Rose's description of her approach to maintaining communities of readers during online schooling is characteristic of the potential for innovation which comes from having a dedicated and knowledgeable librarian. Working with the whole school, she is able to see trends across classes and year groups and draw on her expertise to prioritise maintaining the key elements of reading communities. As such, her practice is simultaneously strategic, creative and evidence-based, leading to the highly positive RfP outcomes she describes.

In addition to these initiatives, the physical space of the library also plays an important role in developing whole school reading communities, as noted by Carol:

> The open safe space of the library enables children of different year groups to interact in a natural way which benefits both younger and older children. Sometimes this may be an older child reading a picture book to a group of Reception children or recommending a good book as they see a younger child browsing. But just as often the relationship is non-hierarchical, such as several year groups spread on their tummies all spotting 'Where's Wally'.

The position of the library and librarian as serving the whole school creates a rich opportunity to be able to establish, nurture and maintain communities of readers, enabling children to interact with readers beyond their own classes and have a wide range of reading role models amongst both staff and other pupils. A trained, knowledgeable and creative librarian can make the most of this opportunity to ensure that these communities are truly reciprocal, promoting choice, the development of autonomy and social connections (Cremin at al., 2014).

Building community by working with families

When building communities of readers, school libraries are also in a strong position to reach out to families. Merga and Mason (2019) observe that school libraries can be highly effective at connecting local communities with their schools, and through those connections promoting a reading culture in the community as a whole, with the library providing a valued community resource. This role is especially important in areas of low socio-economic status, where children are less likely to have books at home, and cuts to public libraries mean that the school library is often the only local source of free reading material (BMG Research, 2019). Both our Reading Librarians view this aspect of their role as an essential part of widening the community of readers, and implement innovative and creative ways of forging links with the local community. Carol describes one of her ongoing initiatives, the library café:

> The library is open twice a week after school for an hour. Access is as informal as possible – families can pop in for 5 minutes or for the whole hour. There is a different theme each week (superheroes, Ramadan, author focus etc). The general format is that I read 2–3 picture books, followed by drinks, snacks and craft activities. Families are free to browse, read and become comfortable in the setting. We also have a shelf of books for adults, to support parents in modelling the reading habit.

As an ongoing touchstone, the reading café offers a sense of regularity to family reading activities. By including both themes and informality, Carol capitalises on the attractive nature of special events, as well as a need for accessibility by enabling the space to work for families with different reading requirements and at different stages in their reading journeys. As a social time, which includes the provision of books for adults as well as children, the café encourages reciprocity in the reading community, helping to develop equality in reading relationships.

Alongside regular opportunities for family reading, special events can bring a level of excitement about reading to the whole community. One example from Mary Rose was putting on family events in collaboration with other teaching staff:

> One of the ways we did this was though a collaboration with the Art Department on an initiative called Picture A Story. With me in one house, the Art teachers in their respective houses, the producer in another, and four or five hundred families in their own homes across Dubai, we embarked on what was one of our most talked about and successful projects of our online school experience. I read a folk tale, fairy tale or myth from books by Hilary McKay, Kevin Crossley Holland, and others (with their permission) as the art teachers responded to the story in their own unique ways, using a visualiser to film their live painting and drawing.
>
> The families watched and listened and joined in with us, creating some wonderfully imaginative and creative works of art. We displayed the art online, but I think it would have had a more significant impact if we had created a display at school too, which would have generated more talk, memories and connections amongst the students.

By bringing together different members of the school community, Mary Rose was able to create an engaging event which encouraged powerful responses to literature. Her assessment of how the event might be improved also demonstrate another key aspect of the Reading Librarian's role: to take a critical and reflective approach to new initiatives to maximise their positive impact. As a specialist in her field, Mary Rose has not only the time, but also the knowledge and experience to be able to make these assessments and continue to improve upon her practice.

Supporting teachers

Being a Reading Teacher, with a wide knowledge of children's literature, has a powerful impact on developing the habit of reading for pleasure among children (Cremin et al.,

2014). However, as Goodwin (2017) observes, this can be a difficult feat for teachers to achieve given the numerous demands of teaching, and even the most dedicated Reading Teacher benefit from the specialist support of a Reading Librarian.

Curating resources and making recommendations

Both Carol and Mary Rose discuss the importance of curating resources and making recommendations as a way of supporting teachers, both overtly through conversations with specific teachers, and by ensuring library collections include high quality texts and identifying gaps in provision. Carol discusses using her specialist knowledge to support curriculum topics in a way that simultaneously encourages RfP:

> While teachers often have easy access to non-fiction linked to topic learning (through topic boxes, Dewey-decimal shelving etc), a librarian can recommend fiction, picture books, poetry and so forth, linked literally or tangentially, which may not be so easy to find. Librarians can also suggest books linked to subjects that may come up through class discussions or events, such as refugees, bullying, or bereavement.

Carol's support enables children to pursue the curiosity raised by a topic though volitional reading and ensures a range of different text types that are likely to appeal to different readers. Her in-depth knowledge of the collection also enables her to provide appropriate texts on a short time scale, which teachers with classes and busy working schedules may not have capacity to do themselves. In addition, Carol notes that her position as the librarian can also assist with whole class reading choices:

> Librarians will often have an overview of what has been read throughout the school. In September, they may be in a better place to suggest a class reader than a teacher that does not know the individuals yet.

Similarly, Mary Rose uses her expertise to ensure that children have access to a wide range of texts:

> We subscribe to a range of magazines and comics as well as Encyclopaedia Britannica online. We have a smaller collection of Arabic, French, German and Mandarin titles to ensure that all students are able to read books in their own language, but I am keen that our library becomes more reflective of our diverse student population and contains far more multilingual texts.

Mary Rose's approach to collection development reflects Hope's (2017) argument that children need to be able to engage with a wide range of texts which recognise the multimodal nature of reading, as well as the importance of providing children with choice. In addition, this approach acknowledges that a key facet of engaging children with reading is ensuring that books provide them with both 'windows' into the lives of others and, crucially, 'mirrors' for their own experiences (Sims Bishop, 1990). Children from marginalised communities are far less likely to see their own experiences reflected in the literature they read (CLPE, 2020), and so it is important to seek out where a collection has gaps in representation and find resources to address these. Specialist knowledge and time are essential to completing this task, both of which are often in short supply for overburdened teachers.

Sharing and developing good practice with teachers

As professionals with specialist expertise, both Carol and Mary Rose have also taken a role in developing the RfP knowledge and practice of other members of the school community. Carol has worked with her English lead to deliver staff meetings on RfP and has run an after-school session for parents on how to foster the habit of volitional reading. Mary Rose drew on her knowledge of the field to recognise an opportunity to engage more teachers with RfP by starting a Teachers' Reading Group:

> I started the first OU/UKLA Teachers' Reading Group (TaRs) in Dubai in 2018 and it has been perhaps the most significant force in fostering a reading for pleasure culture in school. We have developed a mutually supportive and collaborative group, with each of us learning from each other's knowledge and experience. Leading the group has allowed my role to be seen by teachers as being on a more equal footing to theirs – in terms of academic teaching and pedagogical practice – which goes a long way towards ensuring that the librarian's role is seen less of an administrative one, and hopefully not a luxury, but a necessity.

Developing good practice can serve a dual function – as well as the sharing of expertise, it can highlight to staff the wide range of support they can gain by engaging with the school librarian. This is an especially valuable point as understanding what the role of a librarian actually involves tends to be low amongst non-librarians, and stereotypes can become barriers to engagement (White, 2012).

Support from school

Understanding the role is key to ensuring that librarians are given adequate support in order to be effective. Merga and Mason (2019) note the importance of leadership support, stating that not only do effective school libraries require an adequate budget, but also leadership that explicitly and visibly values the role of libraries in schools. Mary Rose, whilst acknowledging much of the support she does receive from her school, also states:

> As is the case with many librarians both here and in the UK, I am still battling to have the role recognised as an academic, not an administrator and to get the traction I need to be able to make lasting change and to be allowed and empowered to be involved in making strategic decisions.

It is hoped that this chapter will go some way to improving understanding of the complex, multifaceted and powerful role of the school librarian. Both Mary Rose and Carol talked about the importance of working closely with colleagues and being able to have the greatest impact when the extent of what they can offer is understood. In addition, they noted the need to be seen as equal partners when collaborating with colleagues. Carol commented:

A librarian does not work in isolation, but needs reciprocal relationships with a range of staff. Most key will probably be with the English Lead. A librarian needs to be given a balance of support/structure and freedom/trust, so they can work within the school's ethos and development plans with structure, focus and prioritisation, whilst also having the opportunity to develop their own ideas and activities.

This equality of position also extends to the need for training. Both librarians discussed the importance of training and continuing professional development, with Carol stating:

> Librarians need access to high-quality library-specific training, but also to be included in more general events. Falling somewhere between a teacher and a TA, I have sometimes been missed off both lists and missed out on training that would inform my understanding of what happens in the classroom.

Effective communication within the school community, where teachers and leaders are informed of library initiatives and the services the librarian can offer, and librarians are kept informed of what happens in classrooms, is of key importance to the success of their practice. This includes having adequate time to plan, by being informed of budgets and needs in good time to be able to make strategic decisions or order resources. Unsurprisingly, both librarians also noted that they are unable to fulfil their roles without an adequate budget, reflecting a common recurring theme in the scholarship on libraries (see BMG, 2019).

Recommendations for practice

From these reflections and discussions of our experiences, we offer the following recommendations for practice.

Librarians need to:
- Organise library spaces so that resources are easily discoverable, enabling readers to browse purposefully and make autonomous choices about what to read;
- Create comfortable, assessment-free environments;
- Use their positions outside of the classroom to build positive relationships with readers over time, and feedback relevant information to class teachers and senior leaders;
- Build on their overview of the whole school to create reciprocal communities of readers across classes, including staff and families, through both ongoing initiatives and special events;
- Keep up to date through relevant training, reading and networking, and ensure new initiatives draw from evidence-based principles;
- Assess the impact and effectiveness of new initiatives and make changes as required;
- Analyse their collection and prioritise purchases to ensure a diverse range of material;
- Identify related texts to go alongside topics which allow children to follow their curiosity with volitional reading;
- Share their expertise with staff members and families, and communicate their role effectively ensuring everyone is aware of what they can offer.

Teachers and senior leaders need to:

- Ensure the school library environment remains a safe space where curiosity and comfort are equally nurtured. Do not use it as a place for sanctions or assessments;
- Appoint and support a librarian to make strategic decisions across the whole school community by respecting their expertise, creativity and the positive impact they can have on building communities of readers;
- Recognise the librarian's position as complementary to that of the class teacher, and work to maximise the impact that can be gained from having different perspectives;
- Involve the librarian as a full member of the school community, keeping them informed of developments in the classroom and offering them the opportunity to bring their expertise to relevant school policies;
- Provide an adequate budget for resources and initiatives;
- Visibly support and celebrate the school library and librarian by also being a member of the reading community and a positive reading role model for children.

Conclusion

The examples of practice discussed in this chapter demonstrate that a dedicated school library, run by a devoted, well-supported Reading Librarian, can have a powerful impact on developing a whole school reading for pleasure culture. Placed outside the classroom and across all year groups, the library forms the natural centre for the development of a reciprocal community of readers which includes children, staff, families and the wider school community. The potential of the role of the Reading Librarian is best summed up by those in the role.

> A school librarian is invaluable as a bridge connecting and communicating between staff, children and books. The librarian acts as a change-maker, agitator, provocateur, activist, rebel and gentle disruptor. Unencumbered by the demands of a classroom, and of assessment, marking and curriculum, they exist in a space where they are able to take a more strategic big-picture view but also to develop close individual reader to reader relationships with students. Properly supported and trained, they have the time, space, expertise and relationships to find the right book for the right reader at the right time – they perform the wonderful alchemy of placing a book in a child's hands and saying 'Read this!'

Recommended reading

BMG Research. (2019) *National Survey to Scope School Library Provision in England, Northern Ireland, and Wales*. Available at: https://d824397c-0ce2-4fc6-b5c4-8d2e4de5b242.filesusr.com/ugd/8d6dfb_8b8 1a7c94c2c4c4a970265496f42307a.pdf

Clark, C. and Teravainen-Goff, A. (2020) *Children and Young People's Reading in 2019: Findings from Our Annual Literacy Survey*. London: National Literacy Trust.

References

BMG Research (2019) *National Survey to Scope School Library Provision in England, Northern Ireland, and Wales*. Available at: https://d824397c-0ce2-4fc6-b5c4-8d2e4de5b242.filesusr.com/ugd/8d6dfb_8b8 1a7c94c2c4c4a970265496f42307a.pdf

Centre for Literacy in Primary Education (2020) *Reflecting Realities: Survey of Ethnic Representation within UK Children's Literature 2019*. London: CLPE.

Clark, C. (2010) Young people's reading habits and attitudes to their school library, and an exploration of the relationship between school library use and school attainment. *National Literacy Trust*. Available at: https://literacytrust.org.uk/documents/127/2010_06_01_free_research_-_school_libraries_and_reading_in_2009_Zacc2TE.pdf

Clark, C. and Poulton, L. (2011) *Book Ownership and Its Relation to Reading Enjoyment, Attitudes, Behaviour and Attainment*. National Literacy Trust. Available at: https://cdn.literacytrust.org.uk/media/documents/2011_05_21_free_research_-_book_ownership_and_reading_survey_2010.pdf

Clark, C. and Teravainen-Goff, A. (2020) *Children and Young People's Reading in 2019: Findings from Our Annual Literacy Survey*. London: National Literacy Trust.

Collins, F. M. and Safford, K. (2008) 'The right book to the right child at the right time': Primary teacher knowledge of children's literature. *Changing English*, 15(4): 415–422.

Cremin, T. (2019) *Reading Communities: Why, What and How?* Sheffield: NATE.

Cremin, T., Mottram, M., Collins, F. M., Powell, S. and Safford, K. (2014) *Building Communities of Engaged Readers: Reading for pleasure*. Oxon: Routledge.

Goodwin, P. (2017) Becoming a reluctant reader. In J. Court (Ed.), *Reading by Right: Successful Strategies to Ensure Every Child Can Read to Succeed*, pp. 33–50. London: Facet.

Hope, J. (2017) Reading the future. In J. Court (Ed.), *Reading by Right: Successful Strategies to Ensure Every Child Can Read to Succeed*, pp. 189–208. London: Facet.

Larkin-Lieffers, P. A. (2011) *Finding Informational Picture Books for Beginning Readers: An Ecological Study of a Median Income Western Canadian Urban Neighbourhood*. Unpublished doctoral dissertation. Edmonton, AB: University of Alberta.

Libraries All Party Parliamentary Group (2014) *The Beating Heart of the School: Improving Educational Attainment Through School Libraries and Librarians*. London: APPG.

Mallette, M. and Barone, D. (2016) Unite for literacy: An interview with Mark W.F. Condon. *The Reading Teacher*, 69(5): 471–481.

Merga, M. K. (2013) Should Silent Reading feature in a secondary school English programme? West Australian students' perspectives on Silent Reading. *English in Education*, 47(3): 229–244.

Merga, M. K. and Mat Roni, S. (2018) Empowering parents to encourage children to read beyond the early years. *The Reading Teacher*, 72(2): 213–221.

Merga, M. L. and Mason, S. (2019) Building a school reading culture: Teacher librarians' perceptions of enabling and constraining factors. *Australian Journal of Education*, 63(2): 173–189.

Safford, K. A. (2014) Reading for pleasure pedagogy. In T. Cremin, M. Mottram, F. M. Collins, S. Powell and K. Safford (Eds.), *Building Communities of Engaged Readers: Reading for Pleasure*, pp. 89–107. Oxon: Routledge.

Shaper, S. and Streatfield, D. (2012) Invisible care? The role of librarians in caring for the 'whole pupil' in secondary school. *Pastoral Care in Education*, 30(1): 65–75.

Sims Bishop, R. (1990) Mirrors, windows, and sliding glass doors. *Perspectives*, 1(3): ix–xi.

White, A. (2012) *Not Your Ordinary Librarian: Debunking the Popular Perceptions of Librarians*. Oxford: Chandos Publishing.

Williams, D., Wavell, C. and Morrison, K. (2013) *Impact of School Libraries on Learning: Critical Review of Published Evidence to Inform the Scottish Education Community*. Available at: https://scottishlibraries.org/media/1211/impact-ofschool-libraries-on-learning-2013

Chapter 11

Parental and community involvement

Rachael Levy, Julie Doyle and Eve Cairns Vollans

Introduction

Most teachers would agree that the home environment plays a critical role in a child's literacy development, and there is a substantial body of research to support this. For example, studies have revealed that children who read on a regular basis prior to school entry are at an advantage in terms of learning language, vocabulary size and success at reading in school (Bus, Van Ijzendoorn and Pellegrini, 1995; Mol, Bus, de Jong and Smeets, 2008), meaning that there is a positive correlation between the frequency of parents' reading with their children and their child's language and emergent literacy. Over the years research has consistently shown that parental involvement in all aspects of literacy activity has the greatest impact in the early years, however positive educational and literacy outcomes can also be identified into teenage and adult years (Desforges and Abouchaar, 2003).

Yet the home is not just a place where children's literacy skill is supported, it has been shown to be highly influential in shaping a child's literate identity (Cameron and Gillen, 2013) and motivation for reading (Villiger, Niggli, Wandeler and Kutzelmann, 2012). For example, in a study of 4,503 Key Stage 2 and Key Stage 3 pupils, Clark and Hawkins (2010) found that young people who feel that they are being encouraged to read by

DOI: 10.4324/9781003215615-18

their parents, are more likely to develop positive attitudes towards reading themselves. The study also found that young people who report that their parents give them a lot of encouragement to read are twice as likely to regularly read outside of school than those young people who do not get any encouragement. Significantly, Clark and Hawkins (2010) also reported:

> Furthermore, young people who do not get any encouragement to read from their mother and their father are twice as likely to believe that they are not very good readers compared with young people who either get a lot of encouragement or some encouragement.
>
> (2010: 17)

Together this suggests that schools should find ways to work with parents and the local community with the express purpose of encouraging children to develop positive attitudes towards reading. Indeed many interventions have been developed over the years through which schools have tried to encourage parents to engage in activities such as shared reading with their children, however as Justice, Logan and Damschroder (2015) documented, many of these do not work because there is a disconnect between the home and school contexts. This disconnect can occur because schools do not understand the values, beliefs or perceptions of the families with whom they are working. This chapter examines the ways in which schools can promote genuine partnerships with families, in order to promote reading for pleasure in children's homes.

Understanding families and home reading practices

Much research over the last three decades has emphasised the social nature of literacy, and positioned reading as a social practice, associated with different life domains (Barton and Hamilton, 1998) and particular social contexts. For example, Street's (1984) *ideological model of literacy* views reading, and indeed writing, as practices that are embedded in local cultural models of behaviour and identity. The role of the home and the community in shaping reading practices and perceptions of reading, has been well documented in studies such as Heath's (1983) iconic research exploring the literacy practices of three communities in the south-eastern United States, and Barton and Hamilton's (1998) ethnographic study which examined what people in a town in the northwest of England did with literacy and why.

More recently Levy and Hall (2021) conducted research into shared reading practices with 29 families who were from a variety of social and cultural backgrounds, concluding that the ways in which parents perceive shared reading and engage in shared reading activity, are both unique to the individual family and are shaped by social and cultural structures. This was particularly apparent in relation to parents' motivation for conducting and sustaining shared reading activity with their children. Most families in the study reported that child enjoyment was a major aim of shared reading activity, however families from within lower income brackets were more likely to state that they needed to see evidence of their child's enjoyment in order to maintain shared reading activity, than families from within higher income brackets. While the middle-class families stated that they too wanted their children to enjoy shared reading, they were also more likely to report that their goal for shared reading was to promote their children's language development (Levy and Hall, 2021). This suggests that these parents may have been less dependent on gaining positive feedback from their children during shared reading, as they were motivated by the desire to promote learning. To put this another way, findings from this study indicated that while it was important for all parents to gain positive feedback from their children, such feedback may be especially important for some families within lower income groups if they are to maintain shared reading activity with their children.

This shows that the role of the home in supporting children's engagement with reading is complex, and if teachers are to work effectively with parents then they need to recognise this complexity. However, it is also true to say that research has indicated that teachers feel that they obtain limited guidance through teacher education programmes on how to promote parental involvement (Daniel, 2011). What is more, further studies have shown that there are a number of factors that may serve as barriers to parental partnership. For example, Chan and Ritchie (2016) pointed out that schools can sometimes interpret the concept of 'parental involvement' as 'the expectation that parents should follow the teachers' protocols for participating in and supporting the activities and routines' (p. 291) of the school or setting, rather than engaging parents in active decision making with teachers. Moreover they also point out that monocultural teachers from a dominant culture may sometimes struggle to 'recognise the funds of knowledge that children from other ethnic backgrounds bring from their participation in the cultural activities of their families' (p. 291) which take place outside of the school.

Together this suggests that there is a great deal of complexity attached to the concept of partnership between schools and their communities, and it can be challenging for schools to find ways to create genuine partnerships with parents in order to promote children's reading. However, this chapter reports experiences from two UK primary schools who have developed successful strategies to involve parents and communities in reading for pleasure. The purpose of this chapter is to reflect on these strategies, in light of research, to demonstrate how schools can work with parents and communities to create a connected home-school environment that supports children's enjoyment of reading.

What works when working with families and communities

Bearing in mind the issues just raised, the remainder of this chapter reports some strategies and initiatives carried out in two English primary schools, that successfully achieved the aim of working with families and communities to promote children's enjoyment of reading. The first school is Mayflower Community Academy in Plymouth where Eve (third author) is lead for reading and phonics teaching. The second school is Sneinton C of E Primary School in Nottingham, where Julie (second author) works as a Reading Recovery teacher and a Literacy Lead.

Engaging with families and communities

For both of these schools, engagement with families stemmed from a concern to understand them and their needs, so that reading related activities were not only valuable, but fitted into their everyday lives. Mayflower took time to discuss with parents and pupils how they could make reading activities accessible to all families and the local community, including the best days and times for activities to take place. Following this consultation, the school created a *reading calendar* (see Figure 11.1) which presented a snapshot

Community Reading Events 2021-22

NOVEMBER
- Reading Advent Calendar raffle tickets for sale.
- Fireside Read every Thursday 6.30-7pm via TEAMS
- Community Reading Knowledge Organisers- How to create and support reading through selecting and organising

DECEMBER
- Advent Calendar winner announced.
- MCA Staff Online Advent Calendar- via TEAMS
- Fireside Read every Thursday 6.30-7pm via TEAMS
- £1.00 Bargain Book Sale ready for Christmas!

JANUARY
- Create a Story Bag/Story Box- Community sessions.
- Fireside Read every Thursday 6.30-7pm via TEAMS
- New Reading Challenges released
- Phonics Support- Drop-in sessions for families
- Launch of Parent/Carer/Community Book Club

FEBRUARY
- How to read with laptops, Tablets, IPads and Phones- Community Sessions
- Fireside Read every Thursday 6.30-7pm via TEAMS
- Create a Reading Scrapbook Community Sessions
- Phonics Support- Drop-in sessions for families

Reading Community Events 2021-2022

MARCH
- Reading Café- Community Café/Reading Event
- Fireside Read every Thursday 6.30-7pm via TEAMS
- KS1 Phonics Community Workshop
- Phonics Support- Drop-in sessions for families
- Parent/Carer/Community Book Club.

APRIL
- #myfamilyreads – Community event creating "Family Reading Rivers".
- Fireside Read every Thursday 6.30-7pm via TEAMS
- New Reading Challenges released.
- Community Reading Treasure Hunt.

MAY
- Author events- Community event sharing stories/poems/writing workshops with local and national authors.
- Fireside Read every Thursday 6.30-7pm via TEAMS
- Parent/Carer/Community Book Club.

JUNE
- Community Reading Picnic
- Summer Reading Challenges released
- Fireside Read every Thursday 6.30-7pm via TEAMS

JULY
- Reading Festival!

Figure 11.1 Mayflower's reading calendar

of what was happening each month regarding reading activities. The calendar was sent to all families in a variety of formats, including email, paper copy and through social media such as Twitter and Facebook. An example of such activity was a Saturday morning Reading Arts and Crafts Club. These informal sessions invited families to design and create reading sacks that could be used in the Nursery and Reception classes. As well as creating the reading sacks, families were offered hot chocolate and biscuits and a member of school staff concluded the sessions by reading a story to everyone. Other examples of events appearing in the calendar included sponsored reads, author reading and book signing, parent workshops, book swaps, evening reads and Christmas Advent calendar reading. The school found that because parents and members of the local community had received the dates of the activities in advance, engagement was high, manifest in the fact that activities were well attended, but also in offers of help and support from parents in running the events.

Given that 'parental involvement' can often be interpreted as the need for parents to support 'the activities and routines' of the school, as just highlighted by Chan and Ritchie (2016), one of the reasons why Mayflower have had such high attendance at their reading events seems to relate to the fact that the school consulted with families about what they wanted and when they wanted it. This would have had the combined effect of not only ensuring that activities were arranged at times that were convenient for parents, but also sent the message that the school genuinely wanted to develop activities that were informed by the parents and families within the school community.

The concern to consult with families was also evidenced at Sneinton where reading surveys highlighted that many of their families had a limited number of books in homes that could be shared with their children. In response to this, Sneinton set up weekly *Book Swaps*, having managed to acquire a quantity of donated second-hand children's books from Facebook community pages, charity shops and donations from friends and families. This meant that every child, adult and sibling could choose a book from the Book Swap to be taken, read and enjoyed and then returned. Often books were not returned, but the school recognised that the important factor was that books were finding their way into homes. Ongoing donations of books have allowed the school to maintain the Book Swap despite not all books being returned.

Like Mayflower, Sneinton spent considerable time thinking about the needs of families, which resulted in discussion about where best to situate the Book Swap tables and the best time to run this to ensure that they reached as many parents and children as possible. Apart from practical logistics, Sneinton were also conscious of the fact that they had 'harder to reach families' who may have been less likely to actively seek out the Book Swap table. The term 'hard to reach' is used in a variety of contexts to broadly define groups of individuals who, according to Lingwood, Levy, Billington and Rowland (2020) 'are eligible to participate in a service, study or intervention, but who, for a variety of reasons, are difficult to involve or access' (Brackertz, 2007; Cortis, 2012). Although Lingwood et al. were focusing more on the participation of families in reading intervention studies, than school-based activity, the factors that they identified as barriers to participation are relevant to both contexts and include difficulty in establishing contact with families, parents lacking the confidence to participate, parental concerns over being assessed or judged in some way and practical barriers such as lack of time.

Having considered many of the preceding issues and having come to the conclusion that they needed to become an 'easier to reach school', Sneinton were committed to building a community where all parents felt welcomed, comfortable and valued. They found that by positioning the Book Swap table outside at the end of the school day, where all parents had to pass, it was accessible and less threatening. This is important because research has identified that feeling judged or assessed, particularly in relation to one's literacy skills, is not conducive to parental participation in such activities. For example Vanobbergen, Daems and Van Tilburg (2009) found that parents who took part in a book gift scheme, ignored elements of 'support' in the intervention, such as a 'top 10 reading tips' leaflet designed to promote 'reading for pleasure', as this made them feel as though they were being assessed on their ability to read.

In order to avoid any such feelings, Sneinton ensured that the presence of school staff at the Book Swaps was informal. Julie (second author) went on to explain that the Book Swaps had a real impact on the development of relationships between staff and parents due to the increase in incidental and informal chats. In turn, these chats allowed school staff to learn more about parents' and children's reading identities, resulting in staff giving direct recommendations about books that they felt might be enjoyed in the home. Interestingly Sneinton has continued to support many of its 'past pupils' who are older siblings of current pupils, and who still come to collect books from the 'teenage reads' section of the Book Swap. What is more, children regularly ask to take books from the Book Swap as birthday presents for their parents, and staff have been known to help with discreet wrapping! It is also noteworthy that Sneinton decided to run another Book Swap in the morning, recognising that this may allow a different cohort of parents to access the books. This again shows that, as a school, Sneinton are conscious of the need to ensure that the activities they run meet the practical and logistical needs of parents, given that the timing of the event would be barrier for some parents as highlighted by Lingwood et al. (2020).

Sneinton also run a wide variety of other activities designed to encourage the engagement of families in reading. For example *Book Cafes* (see Figure 11.2) have become a popular and regular part of school life. These take place during the first session of the day, and parents are invited to stay for the session having brought their child/ren to school in the morning. A room is set up to look like a café, with checked tablecloths and 'book taster menus'. Books can then be 'tasted', and any favourites can be recorded. Different tables have different genres of books (e.g. comics, non-fiction, poetry, graphic novels, picture books etc) to give families an opportunity to 'sample' a genre that they may not have previously shared with their child. The Book Café is not only enjoyed by families but has allowed the school to introduce parents to a wide variety of children's literature within a fun and informal context. Sneinton's Book Café is another lovely example of an activity that not only promotes the enjoyment of reading, but introduces families to a variety of children's literature within a context that is fun and free from judgement. The concept of 'tasting' books in a 'café' allows families to experience different books and genres without having to commit to a book or display their own reading skills.

Listening to families

What we can see from the preceding examples is that these two schools have found a variety of innovative ways in which to engage families in reading for pleasure with their children. Yet it is unlikely that these activities would have been as successful as they are, if

Figure 11.2 Sneinton's Book Café

the schools had not taken the time and developed strategies to listen to the families and understand them. This is critical if schools are to demonstrate that they want to actively engage parents in decision making, rather than viewing parental involvement as passive compliance in supporting the activities and routines that have been decided by the school, as Chan and Ritchie (2016) warned is often the case. As the preceding examples demonstrate, both of the schools prioritised the families themselves, and sought their views and opinions about reading; these schools also created opportunities for informal 'chats' to take place so that staff could learn more about the interests, reading identities and concerns of the parents. This clearly had an impact on the effectiveness of the reading activities, however these schools also recognised that 'listening' to families involved actively asking for feedback on home-school interactions and, critically, acting on this feedback.

For example, this was evident in relation to the ways in which Mayflower communicated with parents about their child's reading at home. Having recognised that their use of home-school reading diaries needed to be reconsidered, Mayflower stopped sending home the traditional reading diary, which is common in many early years classrooms, and replaced this with a choice of optional reading activities for children to do at home and record in a *Reading Journal*. The children were then invited to share their Reading

Journals on a Friday. Given that Mayflower were keen to develop their partnerships with parents, they asked parents for feedback on the use of the journals and found that some parents felt that it was too much for their child to read regularly at home and complete reading activities. Staff were also struggling to manage the activity as it took so long for every child to share their journals. While this feedback was being considered, the Covid-19 crisis took hold, with most children being home-schooled for a considerable part of their school year. This meant that the school, like many others, had to quickly consider how to work remotely with families. As the children came back to school following the lockdowns, staff spoke to children about their time at home and discovered that many of the children had developed a passion for YouTube; the challenge was then to find a way of capitalising on this in an attempt to bring more pleasure back into home reading, so the school developed #*WatchMeBecomeaReader*. Families were asked to record their child reading at least once per week for two minutes and then send the video to the school via TEAMS or email. If a child was unable to read at home, they were offered the use of an iPad in school to make a recording. Videos were collated and posted on TEAMS. This proved to be a very popular activity with almost 90% of children at Mayflower participating in #WatchMeBecomeaReader.

What is striking about this example is that Mayflower was not content with asking parents for feedback the once, but as they tried out different activities and strategies they continued to seek feedback from parents and children, and the activities were amended accordingly. As highlighted in the introduction, Justice et al. (2015) found that reading interventions to be carried out by caregivers in the home, very often did not reach the levels intended by the intervention developers, because the interventions often did not 'fit' with the everyday culture of family life. The fact that Mayflower succeeded in having almost 90% of its children participating in #WatchMeBecomeaReader suggests that their tenacity in ensuring that the activity was informed by feedback from parents and children paid off.

In an attempt to connect more closely with parents, Sneinton also conducted parent reading surveys, as mentioned earlier, one of which revealed that many parents felt that they were unfamiliar with current children's texts. In response to this, the school invited parents to sign up to be a '*mystery book*' reader. The school then sent these parents a 'mystery book', which was essentially a high-quality children's book that the school thought the parent would enjoy reading and reviewing. All the parents' book reviews and recommendations were shared in the school's regular Reading Newsletter. This again highlights the importance of developing reading activities that are based on what parents actually say they want, rather than schools' assuming that they know what parents need.

In addition to this, Sneinton also actively encourage parents to sign up their new babies to the Imagination Library Scheme, which is run by Dolly Parton. Dolly Parton's Imagination Library is a book gifting programme designed to promote a love of reading in all young children. Every child from birth to five, who is enrolled on the programme, receives a high quality, age-appropriate book in the post every month, free of charge. As Sneinton also receive copies of these books, they share these with families in a weekly 'Breakfast Club' which runs for 15 minutes before the start of the school day. Families can then listen to these stories while enjoying a breakfast bagel. This not only promotes the enjoyment of reading, but also allows staff an opportunity to model shared reading strategies and support parents for whom English may not be a first language. This is important, given that Levy and Hall (2021) expressed concern that some parents may feel that once their children start school, home reading should focus on the decoding of print in reading scheme texts, at the expense of enjoying reading books and stories together. Activities such as the Breakfast Club allowed the staff at Sneinton to demonstrate how to engage children in shared reading in ways that are fun and engaging for both parent and child.

By ensuring that their parents have been listened to, it is clear that Mayflower and Sneinton have both successfully developed reading activities that invite a genuine partnership between school and home. Rather than viewing parental partnership as 'the expectation that parents should follow the teachers' protocols for participating in and supporting the activities and routines' (Chan and Ritchie, 2016: 291) of the school or setting, these schools have tried to understand what parents want in order to work with the school. What is more, these schools have also recognised that if they are to create a connected home-school environment that supports children's enjoyment of reading, then they need to focus on the reading that is taking place in homes as well as in school.

Encouraging reading in children's homes

For both Mayflower and Sneinton, creating partnerships with parents to promote enjoyment of reading meant that some strategies were specifically focused on encouraging more reading to take place in the children's homes. To illustrate, Mayflower offer half-termly Reading Challenges for all pupils and these challenges are carefully designed to involve families in reading together as much as possible. Figure 11.3 provides an overview of the kind of challenges that have been offered to families.

Challenge one Can I make a reading den and read something of my choice inside the den?	**Challenge two** Can I turn the subtitles on when I am watching television and read the subtitles to the programme?	**Challenge three** Can I read a recipe, follow the instructions and make something delicious to eat? www.bbcgoodfood.com/recipes/collection/kids-cooking-recipes	**Challenge four** Can I read a poem by Michael Rosen? https://childrens.poetryarchive.org/poet/michael-rosen/	**Challenge five** Can I read every day on Bug Club AND make sure that I complete all of the quizzes for the books that I have read?
Challenge six Can I call, video message or FaceTime a friend or a member of my family and read to them?	**Challenge seven** Can I make somebody laugh by reading them some jokes? https://learnenglishkids.britishcouncil.org/jokes	**Challenge eight** Can I read some comics (online or paper?) www.bbc.co.uk/bitesize/topics/zkgcwmn/articles/zbk47nb www.marvelhq.com/comics	**Challenge nine** Can I count how many words I read in one day?	**Challenge ten** Can I draw some pictures to show what I have read over the holidays?

Figure 11.3 Mayflower's reading challenges

However the school was aware that not all families will participate in reading together, so Mayflower provides a careful balance of challenges that include activities that the children can complete independently. They also strategically plan the challenges so that they link to the Early Years Foundation Stage Early Learning Goals and the National Curriculum. Each Friday, as part of their Reading Celebrations in class, the children are encouraged to talk about their challenges and bring any texts into school that they are reading at home.

In an attempt to increase the number of books, and indeed reading, that is occurring in children's homes, Sneinton introduced a *Bedtime Story in a Bag* to go home with all their EYFS children. The bag contained a teddy, a high-quality picture book and a laminated card giving tips to parents on how to enjoy a bedtime story with their child. Parents are told that they can swap the book as often as they like. While this initiative is valuable for all families, Sneinton developed the activity to particularly support parents for whom English is an additional language and parents who are not confident with their own literacy skills. In order to support these families, parents are told that they can read in their own language, talk around the pictures or do whatever feels comfortable for them. The emphasis is very much on parent and child enjoying the activity together rather than on decoding printed text. This is critical given that Levy and Hall (2021) found that the parents in their study, many of whom were living in disadvantage, read regularly with their pre-school children because they enjoyed it. These parents were also comfortable reading 'around' the text, and being led by their child in terms of what they read and how they read together; however many of these parents also reported that they would not continue to read with their children if they were not enjoying it. This underlines how important it is for schools to develop strategies such as Sneinton's *Bedtime Story in a Bag*, as it not only encourages reading to take place at home, but ensures that the focus is firmly on promoting the enjoyment of reading together in the home.

Empowering families

One of the essential aims of the *Bedtime Story in a Bag* activity is to encourage parents' awareness of the essential role they play in promoting their child's love of reading; Sneinton deliberately designed this activity to empower parents and encourage them to feel confident in their own ability to foster a love of reading in their own children. Mayflower had similar ambitions to encourage children, families and communities to take ownership of their reading and be empowered by the activities that the school developed. This goal was at the heart of *Fireside Reads* where all children and families were invited to attend an online session on Teams, which began with a member of staff reading a story or poem 'around the fire' at 18:30 on a Thursday evening. These sessions began in the second lockdown and were so popular that they were continued once children returned to school. Following the reading, the children were then invited to share something that they had been reading at home; this could be any text including comics, magazines, non-fiction books, joke books and so on. The majority of families attending Fireside Reads had English as an additional language, suggesting that the activity was particularly valued by this cohort. Mayflower reported that as time went by, parents were invited to lead the sessions and indeed became noticeably more confident in communicating with the group and reading aloud. It should also be noted that as summer approached, the name of the activity was changed to 'Sunshine Reads', given that there were no longer any fires on to read around, but everyone wanted the event to continue!

There is a lot that can be said in praise of Mayflower's *Fireside Reads*. Not only did this work as an effective strategy for the school to connect with children during lockdown, and promote reading for pleasure, but Mayflower used this connection to support the parents' own confidence in reading. In doing so, Mayflower moved 'beyond the hegemonic safe zones of traditional teacher-dominated practices' and succeeded in 'opening up spaces of dialogic, fluid engagement with families whose backgrounds differ from their own' (Chan and Ritchie, 2016: 289). To put this another way, by having the confidence to hand control of the activity over to families, Mayflower sent the message that their contributions, situated within their own home discourses, were valued by the school, therefore empowering parents and encouraging their own confidence in reading.

Engaging with the wider community

The reading-based activities and strategies presented in this chapter demonstrate how committed these two schools are to promoting a love of reading in their pupils, however it is also apparent that both schools recognise that children's engagement with reading is embedded in their home contexts, cultures and communities. Both Eve and Julie as English leads therefore ensured that their drive to promote reading for pleasure was not confined to the school but extended into the community.

Further examples of this were evident in both schools. Having successfully developed a Mayflower Children's Book Club on Padlet, where children could upload pictures of books they were reading, post reviews and share book recommendations, Mayflower decided to create a site for parents and families which they called the Mayflower Community Book Club. This allowed parents and other family members to post comments, reviews, book recommendations etc in relation to their reading, which was shared with other families. School holidays proved to be a particularly popular time for parents to engage with the book club. In turn this allowed school staff to see which parents were interested in forming further book clubs. The school therefore contacted the local library service, and it was agreed that they would attend the book club sessions. The book club meets once a month, and this allows the librarians to make recommendations of reading that suit parents' particular interests; families are also helped to join the library if they wish.

Sneinton involve the whole of their local community in their annual Reading Festival, which they describe as the 'reading for pleasure highlight in the school calendar'. The event is attended by children, families, staff, governors, reading volunteers and other members of the local community, to celebrate the joy of reading. Over the years children have arrived at school all excited and dressed for a festival, complete with glitter and wrist bands, to find that their classrooms have been turned into immersive story worlds overnight! For example the EYFS unit once became the Gruffalo's wood, and Key Stage 1 classes and outside areas become Neverland, complete with the Darlings bedroom, the lost boys camp, the mermaids Lagoon and Captain Hook's ship. Year 3 and 4 children entered their classroom through a wardrobe and found themselves in Narnia, which had become a white snow filled world, lined with trees and a path to Mr Tumnus's house. And Harry Potter's Hogwarts once become the story world for the Year 5 and 6 children, as their classroom was transformed into the magical castle.

After a morning of activities in the various story lands, the children attend the festival in the afternoon. Stalls include a huge book swap, story tents, storytellers, authors, illustrators, book craft activities, a book blind date, book raffles, live music, cream teas and other book/story-related stalls. The festival has grown each year and always creates a real 'buzz' around reading.

What is clear from these examples is that both Mayflower and Sneinton have found highly innovative and engaging ways in which to present reading as an activity that is not only embedded in home and school contexts, but has connections with a child's entire community structure (Heath, 1983). Reading is presented, and indeed celebrated, as a social practice (Barton and Hamilton, 1998) that is valued by communities and rooted in local cultural models of behaviour (Street, 1984). All of the activities presented in this chapter demonstrate that these two schools are committed to working with families and communities to promote children's enjoyment of reading. As these activities have shown, these schools recognised that if they were to successfully engage with parents and families then they had to find ways to listen to them and understand their needs, interests, concerns and motivations for reading, both for themselves and their children. The aim to create partnerships with parents was embedded in a concern to empower families and ensure that they understood that they play a central role in fostering a love of reading in their children. The next section reflects on the implications of this for other schools who may also wish to work more closely with parents and communities in order to promote reading for pleasure in their children.

Implications and recommendations

Many of the implications for practice emerging from this chapter relate to the concept of 'partnership' with parents and families. Having raised the concern that partnership with parents can often be interpreted as the involvement or participation of parents in supporting activities and structures that the school has set, Chan and Ritchie (2016) have argued that 'partnership' with parents is altogether more reciprocal. Schools that work in partnership with parents will have a genuine desire to actively involve their families in decision making and will ensure that they not only listen to them but act upon what they hear. Families will feel that their views are valued and taken seriously and make a valid contribution to the life of the school. This is particularly important in the quest to promote reading for pleasure, given that we know that the home environment plays a central role in encouraging positive attitudes towards reading (Cameron and Gillen, 2013; Villiger et al., 2012; Clark and Hawkins, 2010).

This chapter has presented a variety of activities and strategies from two schools who have successfully involved parents and communities in promoting reading for pleasure. On the basis of this, the following recommendations for schools can be made:

- Cultivate an ethos of partnership with families around reading activity.
- Take time to talk to families about their aims for reading activity in the school.
- Take time to understand the reading practices, attitudes and values of the families.
- Ensure that any planned activities are free from proficiency judgement.
- Ensure that any planned activities fit with the everyday lives of families.
- Ask parents and children for feedback on implemented activity.
- Be creative and innovative in developing activities – make them fun for everyone.

- Build on the everyday literacy practices occurring within the children's homes.
- Find ways to involve the whole community in activities that promote reading for pleasure.
- Focus on promoting enjoyment of reading in the home.
- Develop activities that empower families and ensure that they know that they play a central role in fostering a love of reading in their children.

Conclusion

This chapter has presented a variety of strategies employed by two schools in the UK, to involve parents and communities in promoting reading for pleasure. By reflecting on these strategies in light of research evidence, it becomes clear that successful engagement with parents and families must begin with a school's genuine desire to understand their families, the local community and the ways in which reading operates within homes. Many of the strategies discussed in this chapter worked because the two schools engaged in a dialogue with their families, which meant that the activities and events were informed by the needs, beliefs, values and everyday practices of the families themselves. As a result, these schools not only succeeded in providing activities that gave families what they wanted and needed, but also sent the message that their views and opinions mattered.

In summary, this chapter has provided an insight into some of the ways that schools can work with parents and communities in order to promote reading for pleasure. By finding ways to create genuine partnerships with parents, schools can capitalise on one of the greatest resources in a child's life when it comes to the promotion of reading, and this is the child's home environment. As this chapter has demonstrated, this is not about developing activities that schools believe their families need, rather it is about taking time to listen to families, understand their home reading practices as well as their needs and empowering them to work comfortably and confidently with schools to promote reading for pleasure in their children's lives.

Recommended reading

Compton-Lilly, C. (2009) Research directions: Listening to families over time: Seven lessons learned about literacy in families. *Language Arts*, 86(6): 449–457, National Council of Teachers of English, www.jstor.org/stable/41483574.

Levy, R. and Hall, M. (2021) *Family Literacies; Reading with Young Children*. London: Routledge. Available at: https://ourfp.org/supporting-rah/sharing-the-love-of-reading/www.lucid.ac.uk/resources/for-practitioners/supporting-families-with-shared-reading-activity-in-the-home/

References

Barton, D. and Hamilton, M. (1998) *Local Literacies: Reading and Writing in One Community*. London and New York: Routledge.

Brackertz, N. (2007) *Who Is Hard to Reach and Why?* Available at: http://library.bsl.org.au/jspui/bitstream/1/875/ 1/Whois_htr.pdf

Bus, A. G., Van Ijzendoorn, M. and Pellegrini, A. D. (1995) Joint book reading makes for success in learning to read: A meta-analysis on intergenerational transmission of literacy. *Review of Educational Research*, 65: 1–21.

Cameron, A. C. and Gillen, J. (2013) Co-constructing family identities through young children's telephone-mediated narrative exchanges. *First Language*, 33(3): 246–267.

Chan, A. and Ritchie, J. (2016) Parents, participation, partnership: Problematising New Zealand early childhood education. *Contemporary Issues in Early Childhood*, 17(3): 289–303.

Clark, C. and Hawkins, L. (2010) *Young People's Reading: The Importance of the Home Environment and Family Support. More Findings from Our National Survey*. London: National Literacy Trust.

Cortis, N. (2012) Overlooked and under-served? Promoting service use and engagement among 'hard-to-reach' populations. *International Journal of Social Welfare*, 21: 351–360.

Daniel, G. R. (2011) Family-school partnerships: Towards sustainable pedagogical practice. *Asia-Pacific Journal of Teacher Education*, 39: 165–176.

Desforges, C. and Abouchaar, A. (2003) *The Impact of Parental Involvement, Parental Support and Family Education on Pupil Achievement and Adjustment: A Literature Review*. London: Department for Education and Skills.

Heath, S. B. (1983) *Ways with Words: Language, Life and Work in Communities and Classrooms*. Cambridge: Cambridge University Press.

Justice, L. M., Logan, J. R. and Damschroder, L. (2015) Designing caregiver-implemented shared-reading interventions to overcome implementation barriers. *Journal of Speech and Language and Hearing Research*, 58(6): 1851–1863. https://doi.org/10.1044/2015_JSLHR-L14-0344

Levy, R. and Hall, M. (2021) *Family Literacies; Reading with Young Children*. London: Routledge.

Lingwood, J., Levy, R., Billington, J. and Rowland, C. (2020) Barriers and solutions to participation in family-based education interventions. *International Journal of Social Research Methodology*, 23(2): 185–198.

Mol, S. E., Bus, A. G., de Jong, M. T. and Smeets, D. (2008) Added value of dialogic parent-child book readings: A meta-analysis. *Early Education & Development*, 19: 7–26.

Street, B. V. (1984) *Literacy in Theory and Practice*. Cambridge: Cambridge University Press.

Vanobbergen, B., Daems, M. and Van Tilburg, S. (2009) Bookbabies, their parents and the library: An evaluation of a Flemish reading programme in families with young children. *Educational Review*, 61: 277–287.

Villiger, C., Niggli, A., Wandeler, C. and Kutzelmann, S. (2012) Does family make a difference? Mid-term effects of a school/home-based intervention program to enhance reading motivation. *Learning and Instruction*, 22(2): 79–91.

Chapter 12

Celebrating reading

Sarah Jane Mukherjee, Clare McGreevy and Claire Williams

Introduction

What is more exciting for a primary aged child in the school calendar than a celebration? A time to come together without the pressure of the usual classroom activities, school celebrations often include special food, a non-uniform day, no assessments or difficult work. In short, they are a time for classes and year groups to join in activities together that can bring joy to the whole community, children and teachers alike. This chapter is about celebrating reading. While these events may be liberating for children, for teachers it may be difficult to see how the organisational effort can contribute to fostering children's voluntary reading and positive dispositions towards reading. We argue that, for children, reading celebrations can assist in shifting the focus of reading from decoding to enjoyment, from skill to pleasure. They can also feed forward into wider school RfP provision.

The chapter begins by reiterating the connection between RfP and academic achievement before touching briefly on some of the organisations that support reading celebrations and the possible types of celebration. It explores the idea of reading identity and argues that reading celebrations are a way of reshaping and repositioning reading identities in the classroom. It considers the relevance and importance of being a Reading

DOI: 10.4324/9781003215615-19

Teacher to shape reading celebrations aligned to specific aims, and as supportive to a school's RfP pedagogy. To bring to life what reading celebrations can look like, the ardent voices of two Reading Teachers are heard, their personal and professional commitment to RfP means that reading celebrations are a key part of the reading calendar in their schools.

The why and what of celebrating reading

Primary classrooms have an understandable focus on developing children's decoding and comprehension skills necessary in order to progress with the technical elements of reading. However, this skill-based approach needs to be complemented and augmented with a focus on choice-led reading which develops young children's engagement with texts. Children who develop the habit of reading do better academically (Sullivan and Brown, 2015; Torppa et al., 2020; OECD, 2021) and have better mental health (Clark and Teravainen-Goff, 2018). Thus, schools that develop rich reading cultures in which children choose to read frequently in class and at home, enrich their young readers socially and academically, and positively shape their life chances. With such important gains possible, it is not surprising that RfP is promoted in the English National Curriculum, which highlights the importance to academic progress of 'reading widely and frequently outside as well as in school, for pleasure and information' (DfE, 2014: 41). However, there is still much work to do to nurture volitional reading, as RfP practices in the classroom have been marginalised (Kucirkova and Cremin, 2020). Even research around reading aloud in the classroom, an activity purportedly designed for pleasure, has identified that this time may be dominated by literacy skill-focused talk and include little collaborative book discussion (Moffat, Heydon and Iannacci, 2019). Informal interaction and professional attention to RfP is needed to encourage voluntary reading within and beyond school.

Reading celebrations can contribute to RfP pedagogy by raising its profile and distinguishing it from the teaching of reading. A number of organisations and charities offer support and ideas about celebrating the delights of reading. For instance, well-known in the UK and Ireland, the charity World Book Day (worldbookday.com) encourages schools to get reading. All children receive a book token that allows them to purchase a book from a specially authored set for £1 or €1.50. The charity, working with the Open University, the National Literacy Trust (NLT) and the Centre for Literacy in Primary Education (CLPE), has underpinned their offer with research evidence. Their resources are framed around the RfP pedagogy principles identified by Cremin (2019), that to foster voluntary reading, practice needs to be Learner led, Informal, Social and with Texts that tempt (LIST). The World Book Day website offers resources that schools can used on the day and throughout the year. Recent research by the NLT found that 55% of the 8- to 11-year-olds who responded to the World Book Day survey reported that it had encouraged them to read more, and 30% noted they were more encouraged to do so with parents and carers (Picton, Goodwin and Clark, 2021). Additionally, the Patron of Reading initiative (patronofreading.co.uk) connects specific children's authors, illustrators and poets to schools for sustained periods of time, it aims to inspire young people to read and offers first-hand expert experience of the process of creating children's books.

Another organisation, Empathy Lab (empathylab.uk), seeks to nurture children's kindness, tolerance and understanding through engaging in quality literature that fosters empathy. Running since 2014, it organises an annual celebration on Empathy Day supported by children's authors, illustrators and poets. In addition, a panel of judges selects an empathy book collection and creates book guides each year; the website offers strategies for using these. Such opportunities help children connect to stories, illustrations and poems in subtly different ways and foreground Bishop's (1990) notion of books as windows on others' experiences of the world, real and fictional, with the hope that this understanding might lead to social action. Making personal connections to literature is important and as the Reflecting Realities report (CLPE, 2021) acknowledges there has been an increase in UK children's books featuring a minority ethnic character from 4% in 2017 to 15% in 2020.

Black History month, Pride month and other such celebrations of underrepresented or marginalised groups can be brought into focus for children with quality literature to support children's RfP and importantly expand their understandings of the world.

Reading celebrations do not however have to involve national organisations or whole school communities. Equally important are class or year group events that are simple to organise but offer RfP a higher profile. These might include book-related assemblies for parents, weeks of reading around a theme or even a reading advent calendar with a door to a new book opened each day to read aloud or take home. Also, author visits to school, in person or virtually can be arranged and through careful preparation, wide reading of the author's texts and children's participation on the day, these can make a rich contribution, bringing reading to life and tempting children to read more of the author's work. Thinking creatively about celebrating reading and offering regular events alongside coherent and planned RfP pedagogy can support children's motivation and their perceptions of themselves as readers.

Reader identities

Becoming a 'reader' involves not only skill development but the adoption of a sense of self as a reader, a reader identity (Hall, 2012). Reading celebrations have the potential to help to challenge and reposition children's identities as readers. Identity is a complex mesh of social, cultural, racial, geographical and class-based influences that are difficult if not impossible to tease apart (Scholes, 2019) and one's reader identity is not static, but continues to develop through a lifetime. Early experiences of reading have a powerful influence on how we see ourselves as readers. Our early identities as readers are shaped by the role-models we encounter and are formed in dialogue with home and school reading practices. In homes, play groups and nurseries, board books and picture books are often available to be listened to and enjoyed. However, as children start school, the expected focus of learning to read becomes a reality. Quickly, children learn a different slant on what it means to be a reader, and some may feel the emphasis of reading shifts to letters, to sounds, to notions of progress and their ability. A perception that learning to read is the main goal of participating in reading practices influences children's reader identities, which in turn can become aligned to their assessments of their reading 'competency'. However, reader identities are also shaped by their teachers' conceptualisations of what it means to be a reader, adults' own reader identities and institutional ideas of what it means to be a reader (Cremin, Mottram, Collins, Powell and Safford, 2014; Hall, 2012). Powerful in its influence, children are aware of the 'identity' they have been assigned by the teacher (Hall, 2012). Research in Australia found that enthusiastic boy readers from low socioeconomic communities, who as a group are often assumed to be reluctant readers, hide this 'identity' position in their school environment (Scholes, 2019). For more discussion of boys' engagement in reading, see Chapter 3.

Young children are invited to reading celebrations on an equal basis, freed from any implicit or explicit classroom hierarchies based on levels of fluency, vocabulary, phonic knowledge and comprehension. As Hall points out: 'Creating space for students to rewrite their identities requires students and teachers to shed the typical labels we typically use to understand each other and ourselves as readers' (Hall, 2012: 370). In other words, as reading celebrations do not have set goals in terms of what is usually considered 'reading', participation is open to all on a different, more individual and, potentially, equal basis. What counts as reading is reshaped, and any previously constructed reader identities are rendered less important. Different books and genres are acknowledged, and reading may happen in different places and be influenced by the social nature of the celebration.

This potential can be brought to fruition by Reading Teachers. These are teachers who seek to draw 'on deep knowledge and understanding of the nature of reading developed in part through the experience of being a reader' (Cremin et al., 2014: 67). That is to say, teachers who do far more than teach reading, and whose reader identity and awareness of the social and relational nature of reading influences their pedagogy in order to foster children's RfP (Cremin, 2019).

In the case study that follows, Reading Teacher and English Lead Clare McGreevy, at the time from Lowerplace Primary School, outlines the inspiration behind the six months of planning and the event that became Rochdale's first Children's Literature Festival. Clare, reflecting on her memories of reading as a child, planned the festival in order to offer new opportunities to children. She hoped it would provide a celebration to stimulate RfP in her school and beyond.

The Rochdale Children's Literature Festival

As a Reading Teacher, the Festival had its roots in my belief that reading equals social mobility. Rochdale is an area of high deprivation and, as a result, many of our children are book poor. The level of poverty experienced by many of our families is similar to my own childhood. Two things, however, changed the trajectory of my life: being regularly read to at home by my parents and weekly access to the library. My book-rich background meant that I found a route towards a better future through academia: I wanted to play a part in helping children have the same opportunities that I had.

Inspired by ideas in *The Book Whisperer* (Miller, 2009), I wondered if we could make reading something to shared, enjoyed and celebrated, such that family reading and library visits might seep into the fabric of everyday life. My vision saw children, staff and parents collaborating to inspire a love of reading and develop knowledge of children's literature in school and at home. This vision was cemented by the generous support of Michael Rosen, Frank Cottrell-Boyce and Morag Hood and by the Rochdale community with Madeleine Lindley's Book Shop, and the Central Library actively contributing to and hosting the festival. This backing validated our message: reading is important to Rochdale and is something worth celebrating.

Organisation and planning

The preliminary work within school was key to ensuring the festival was not just a one-off glitzy event. A focused campaign ensured children and families felt involved and invested to build a sense of anticipation. Festival Ambassador Teams, reluctant readers and pupil premium children were empowered to take on significant leadership roles in the planning, this included running RfP assemblies, updating the school community on progress and coordinating festival-related activities. One teacher noted that 'Whilst the Festival was being planned, there was a definite "buzz" in the air from the children and even before the festival, children were already showing a greater interest in reading'.

In school, we launched a range of reading inspired activities including assemblies on the authors attending, reading the authors' books together in class and creating Festival posters. To promote the event, the local media ran a feature on our Festival Ambassadors, a massive boost for the children, which lifted the profile of the Festival enormously. Twitter and Facebook campaigns reached a wide audience and many authors tweeted endorsements of support.

The event

I remember feeling so nervous on festival day. Would everything come together as planned, would people have a good time, would people even show up? I needn't have worried! It was a magical day from start to finish. The children's RfP stalls were brimming over – lists of favourite books, festival bookmarks, posters of Daniel Pennac's (2006) *Rights of the Reader*, tips on how to get everyone reading at home, posters about the Open University Reading for Pleasure (www.ourfp.org) website and so much more! The Festival Ambassadors (previously reluctant readers) explained their love of RfP to visitors and read stories to the youngest guests! There was a buzz in every nook and cranny of the building: the Mayor and Mayoress read on comfy chairs to rapt audiences of children; Richard O'Neill, the author, showcased a range of books on a stall as part of his Diverse Books campaign; massive queues snaked through the library to get their books signed by authors before their performances; an impish granny puppet mingled with the crowds telling jokes and sharing her wisdom; story-stone story-rapping and bookmaking workshops were heaving; families gathered around our wonderful storytellers in the Children's Library; and upstairs on the first floor, our high profile authors wowed packed audiences.

The book-themed funfair-style stalls maximised family fun. We had Willy Wonka's Sweet Shop run by parents, Hook-a-Book, Book Tombola and the like, and one of the schools had a Twitter board for visitors to tweet pictures of themselves at the Festival. All the staff gave up their Saturday and turned up as their favourite book characters, which provided even more magic to the proceedings.

Impact

From 9am until 4pm the whole community as well as visitors from outside the town mingled in tangible vibes of bookish love and celebration. Yet it was not simply an enjoyable event. We know that attitudes towards the library had started to shift, and they even had to call in an extra staff on the day because so many children and families were signing up! 'Holding the Festival in the local library gave the children the opportunity to explore a wide range of genres and excite their imaginations. During the day, lots of children joined the library with many of them eager to revisit to borrow more books' (Nicola Jenkins, class teacher).

The Festival Ambassadors' attitudes and engagement was tracked through pupil and parental questionnaires, and we were delighted that these previously reluctant readers continued to visit the library. Their connection with reading had changed during the preparation for, and the event of the Festival itself, and the influence of library memberships was felt in classrooms. 'I think the Festival was amazing and will inspire more children to read! I think being a Festival Ambassador has helped me and a lot of the children in school and out of school to read books. This shows that having a literary Festival every year will help someone in life with reading' (Soha, aged 11). 'Because the children had expanded their book knowledge, our book talk increased in the classroom. Each week, we spend 10 minutes sharing the books we have recently read – many of which are borrowed from the local library' (Jemma Haynes, class teacher).

The Rochdale Children's Literature Festival was a greater success than I could ever have imagined, it was a catalyst to developing RfP in the school. Observing a step change in the attitudes to reading in the children and the staff has meant that everyone is now involved in promoting and sustaining RfP. It really brought parents on-board too and has strengthened our relationships, our reading community is now more reciprocal and interactive, these are key characteristics of successful reading communities (Cremin et al., 2014). This is a celebration that has been cemented into the Rochdale calendar for years to come!

The celebratory nature of the festival from Clare's case study is evident, but what is important is her insight and foresight as a Reading Teacher not only to inspire the event but to plan one with specific aims, in this case to create real changes in the children's reading behaviours. The festival drew in the community to the extent that the Central Library experienced a 34% increase in children's books issued on the day compared to the previous Saturday. Thus, the festival was able to instigate a shift in children's reader identities to readers who are library members, who listen to published authors, who have fun in book-themed games and whose families read.

After helping with the Festival, my family bought more books for me to enjoy. Now, we have a huge bookshelf that has books squeezed in to fit! Even my parents every time we get a new book take a flick through a few pages. My younger brother and sister have grown up reading loads, which has also brought us closer. (Suraiya, aged 9)

Our children started to see reading as an activity that happens in various contexts – at home, at school, on the playground and in the library. (Ateqa Ali, class teacher)

Social connections through reading resonate strongly in school communities that thrive on interaction within classes, between classes, in peer groups, in the staff room and between children and practitioners. Such schools offer rich social spaces for celebrations. Reading is often seen as an individual pursuit but developing a love of reading is enhanced through book conversations, making recommendations and sharing the experience of reading together. 'Inside-text talk . . . child-initiated and undertaken in informal contexts' (Cremin et al., 2014: 96) can be motivated by celebrations that widen children's access to rich texts a shift in the books and through activities that are designed to encourage talk around texts.

In the second case study, the Reading Teacher Claire Williams, at the time a class teacher and Reading Lead at St. Andrew's C of E Primary School, writes about reading celebrations in her school. The aims of these were to engage readers' networks and build a community of engaged and connected readers by opening opportunities to talk about books and developing children's and teachers' knowledge and enjoyment of non-fiction texts. Framed by World Book Day, the Patron of Reading and Non-fiction November, Claire reflects on how selecting texts to be shared by the whole school ensured that every member of the school community could be part of conversations and celebrations around reading.

Creating social reading communities

As a school, the development of our reading curriculum and pedagogy is underpinned by our commitment to nurturing our children's growth as lifelong readers and to growing as a reciprocal community of engaged readers. Reflecting on my own experiences, habits and practices as a reader, I have moved beyond simply reading and sharing my reading practices in school to exploring the possible classroom consequences of these practices to support children's engagement with reading. Having an appreciation of the social, affective nature of reading and the strong influence of reader-to-reader relationships has been particularly significant in the development of our RfP pedagogy. It has also shaped the ways we plan our involvement in national celebrations to deepen the children's engagement in reading.

World Book Day and the Patron of Reading

There is evidence that reading conversations of an informal nature are crucial to developing engaged reader relationships (Cremin and Swann, 2017; Moses and Kelly, 2018). This mirrors my own experiences as a reader. There was a lack of these types of conversations in our school, so with this in mind creating new opportunities for this kind of social interaction around texts became one of the aims of our World Book Day celebrations. During this we launched our collaboration with writer and illustrator Sarah McIntyre through our involvement with the Patron of Reading initiative. In my school these celebrations take place over a fortnight and are planned to promote sustained impact on our RfP culture rather than being a series of one-off 'feel good' activities. In this case, the celebrations were planned as a starting point to support more spontaneous book talk to flourish over time. Each class across the school chose a book to read aloud and engage with that was written and/or illustrated by Sarah (and her co-author Philip Reeve). These ranged from *Grumpycorn* for the 4- to 5-year-olds to *Oliver and the Seawigs* for the 10- to 11-year-olds.

Reading aloud was an important part of the celebrations and it was key that it wasn't used solely as a conduit for comprehension and related writing activities; rather, it was a relaxed and interactive experience, planned to prompt affective engagement. As a consequence, careful consideration was given to the kind of environments that would distinguish reading aloud of this nature. This included the use of a 'Blanket Basket' in each classroom and a 'Story Tunnel' at Forest School, and teachers engaged in more informal, open-ended discussions about what was being read. At the end of each day, a small group of children from each class visited another class to read aloud from their selected book. By the end of the celebratory fortnight, children and adults across the school had multiple 'books in common'. Informal exchanges about these became widespread;

children from different classes were talking spontaneously about them in the corridors, around their mixed-class tables at lunchtime and on the playground. Two children from different classes, who discovered that they were both reading *Pugs of the Frozen North* by Reeve and McIntyre, even found each other first thing every morning to discuss it. Even on the first day of the Spring term (ten months later), children were walking through the school gates talking about which of Sarah's books Father Christmas had delivered to them! One child reflected, 'I like lots more books. My teacher read my *Pugs of the Frozen North* and I loved it so I asked my Mum if she could buy it for me and she said yes and I read it all day!' The impact of the new opportunities for social interaction around texts that we had planned as part of our World Book Day celebrations far outlived the celebrations themselves.

National Non-Fiction November

A second celebration to address our whole-school development need was National Non-Fiction November. As a teaching staff, we felt less assured in making non-fiction recommendations, and engaged with these texts less frequently in class. Children's surveys highlighted significantly lower levels of engagement with non-fiction, so our participation aimed to ignite curiosity, excitement and pleasure in reading this genre. Each class was gifted a copy of *Shackleton's Journey* by William Grill. Creative ways to share the book encouraged informal conversations, and affective as well as intellectual involvement with the text. Relaxed experiences of reading aloud by candlelight in classrooms that had been transformed into The Endurance were planned, children also engaged in role as the crew members enabling them to immerse themselves in the story.

At the end of the month, we held a whole-school exhibition showcasing our journey for ourselves, our parents and governors. As well as the children's work, at the centre of the exhibition, we created a comfortable, relaxed area with beanbags, cushions and 'book blankets' of non-fiction texts, designed to tempt children and their parents to peruse and prompt further informal book talk beyond the school gates. Comments in the exhibition visitors' book indicated that parents were looking forward to sharing these texts with their children at home, and as teachers we were able to use this to strengthen connections between children's home and school reading worlds. One entry read, 'What an amazing display of the children's work. Well done to the children for all of their hard work and also to the teachers. A fabulous book choice – will be buying a copy!'

There was a real 'book buzz' and evidence of child-initiated, spontaneous book talk throughout November, both within and between classes; children saw their experiences of reading *Shackleton's Journey* as intrinsically worthy of discussion. In the weeks that followed, their views and voices, reflecting their growing pleasure in this genre, shaped the development of new non-fiction collections across the school. In turn, having these new collections enticed further engagement with these more factual texts, supporting children's growth as readers and developing greater breadth and diversity in their reading.

This example reiterates the shaping role of the Reading Teacher in planning this celebration. Claire, as she says herself, 'moved beyond simply reading and sharing my reading practices in school to exploring the possible classroom consequences of these practices'. Her understanding of her own classroom practices and RfP reveals how it is possible to pinpoint particular gaps in children's reading experiences that can be developed through a reading celebration. In this case, Claire's focus was aligned with national initiatives available to schools but was personalised locally. By connecting to her understanding of the fourfold RfP pedagogy (Cremin et al., 2014), Claire was able to complement and strengthen the social nature of reading with a deliberate strategy to grow a set of books and authors in common across the school community. This approach created the conditions to foster RfP through informal conversations about books, building supporting elements of the reading celebration: reading aloud, creating new social reading environments, enabling talk about books and giving additional opportunities to read. The school's whole RfP approach chimes with being Learner led, Informal, Social and supported by Texts that tempt (LIST), as conceived by Cremin (2019).

Maximising the potential of reading celebrations

Drawing together the main threads from two case studies in this chapter, it is clear that Reading Teachers, with their passion and understanding of reading and RfP pedagogy, can maximise celebrations to enhance children's reading identities, their experience of different genres, their understanding of the social aspect of reading, in a range of contexts. In summary, reading celebrations afford young people opportunities to reflect on what it means to be a reader, to read and what counts as reading through the guidance of Reading Teachers. Reading celebrations are, in this way, nested within and support RfP pedagogy as illustrated in Figure 12.1.

Figure 12.1 illustrates the centrality of Reading Teachers in maximising the potential of reading celebrations beyond a one-off event. It foregrounds the potential of a celebration to reposition and enhance young readers' understanding and experience of reading contexts (as in the library in Rochdale), reading genres (as in the excitement of non-fiction texts), the social aspect of reading (illustrated strongly in both case studies in schools, homes and the wider community) and their own reader identity. The case studies demonstrate how celebrations can be designed to focus on one or more of these elements. Yet with the boundaries between them blurred, the positive impact spills over to others. Crucially, it highlights how these ideas about reading celebrations do not compete with RfP pedagogy, but instead can support the key elements underpinning read aloud, social reading environments, independent reading and book talk and recommendations (Cremin et al., 2014).

Reading events come in different shapes and sizes and are best motivated by individual school contexts to make reading special. The Open University Reading for Pleasure site (ourfp.org), outlines a number of Examples of Practice which showcase different RfP initiatives that could form the basis of a reading celebration, including pop up reading picnics, mini-Hay festivals, booknics and reading around the campfire. In addition, practitioners might like to explore other national events, such as the National Poetry Day celebrations in October, Read Aloud Day or focus more locally and connect to events in their area. A number of children's books awards, such as the Blue Peter Book Award or the Carnegie and Kate Greenaway Medal feature quality children's literature that is worth building a celebration around. Finally, awareness events, such as Black History month and World Environment Day, are opportunities to explore children's books with different themes and aims.

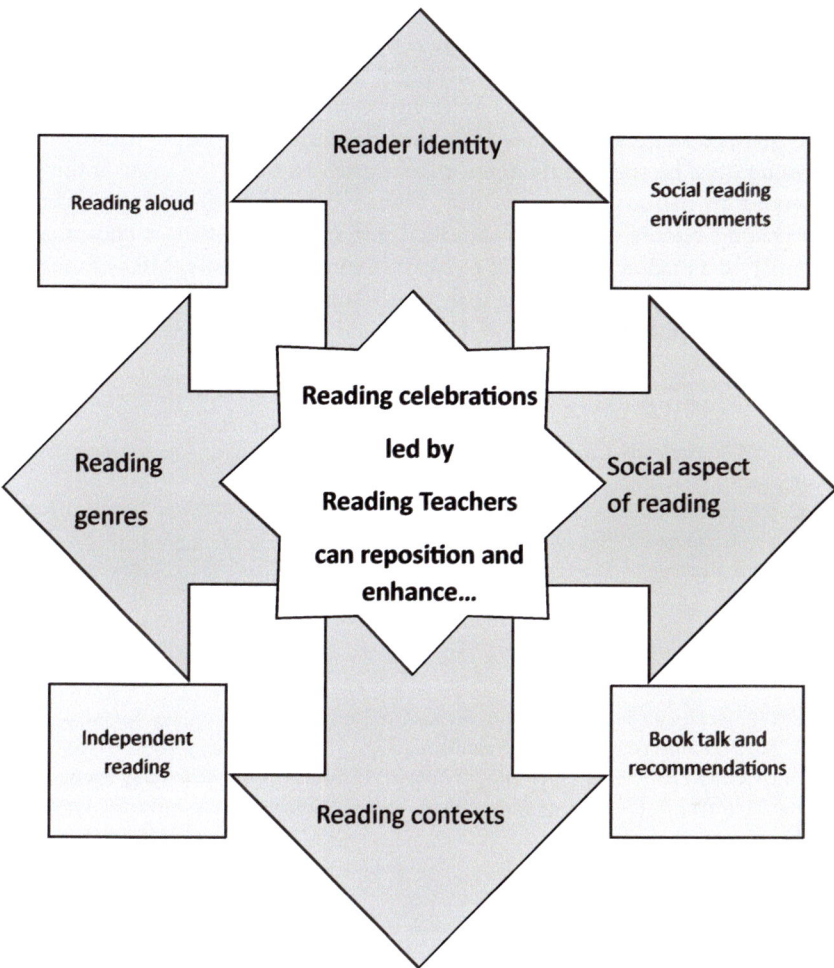

Figure 12.1 Repositioning and enhancing understandings of reading through celebrations within RfP pedagogy

Conclusion

In the eyes of the children and teachers for whom reading as a skill dominates, a celebration can help to reshape understandings of what it means to be a reader and to read. It can strengthen readers' identities by distancing reading from decoding and comprehension. Reading identities during inclusive celebratory events are not linked to levelled and graded readers and reading hierarchies. For children who already choose to read in their free time, celebrations provide further validation for their RfP choices, the excitement of different genres and new titles, the thrill of more of what they love, reading aloud, time to read, to engage in book blether and more. The Reading Teachers' case studies highlight how new contexts can be introduced though a celebration, whether that be library membership, talking about books in the playground or bringing RfP into a home where it was less profiled before. Celebrations therefore have the potential to touch both school-reluctant readers and already avid readers, as well as many others.

It is clear that fostering RfP needs more attention than a cosy book corner and fairy lights; it is more complex and nuanced. Teachers' understanding of the nature of RfP and being a reader must be sufficiently developed in order to make the most of the potential for connecting to national initiatives and creating bespoke events. As this chapter has shown, a reading celebration is far more than just an end of term or end of year treat. The potential for a reading celebration to be sewn into the school's RfP pedagogy so that both teachers and children benefit, is real, and Reading Teachers make reading enticing and ensure that the potential of any celebrations and events are maximised.

Recommended reading

Gamble, N. (2019) *Exploring Children's Literature: Reading for Knowledge, Understanding and Pleasure.* London: Sage Publications.
Miller, D. (2009) *The Book Whisperer, Awakening the Inner Reader in Every Child.* San Francisco: Jossey-Bass.
Open University Reading for Pleasure website www.ourfp.org
Pieper, K. (2016) *Reading for Pleasure: A Passport to Everywhere.* Carmarthen: Independent Thinking Press.

Children's books

Grill, W. (2014) *Shackleton's Journey.* London: Flying Eye Books.
McIntyre, S. (2019) *Grumpycorn.* London: Scholastic.
Reeve, P. and McIntyre, S. (2014) *Oliver and the Seawigs.* Oxford: Oxford University Press.
Reeve, P. and McIntyre, S. (2016) *Pugs of the Frozen North.* Oxford: Oxford University Press.

References

Best, E., Clark, C. and Picton, I. (2020) *Seeing Yourself in What You Read. Diversity and Children and Young People's Reading in 2020.* National Literacy Trust Research Report. Available at: www.literacytrust.org.uk/ (Accessed September 2021).
Bishop, R. S. (1990) Mirrors, windows and sliding glass doors. *Perspectives: Choosing and Using Books for the Classroom*, 6(3).
Centre for Literacy in Primary Education (2021) *Reflecting Realities: Survey of Ethnic Representation in UK Children's Literature 2021.* Available at: https://clpe.org.uk/system/files/2021-11/CLPE%20Reflecting%20Realities%20Report%202021.pdf (Accessed November 2021).
Clark, C. and Teravainen-Goff, A. (2018) *Mental Wellbeing, Reading and Writing. How Children and Young People's Mental Wellbeing is Related to Their Reading and Writing Experiences.* National Literacy Trust Research Report. Available at: https://cdn.literacytrust.org.uk/media/documents/Mental_wellbeing_reading_and_writing_2017-18_-_FINAL2_qTxyxvg.pdf (Accessed September 2021).
Cremin, T. (2019) *Reading Communities: Why, What and How?* Sheffield: NATE.
Cremin, T., Mottram, M., Collins, F. M., Powell, S. and Safford, K. (2014) *Building Communities of Engaged Readers: Reading for Pleasure.* London: Routledge.
Cremin, T. and Swann, J. (2017) School librarians as facilitators of extracurricular reading groups. In J. Pihl, K. Skinstad van der Kooij and T. C. Carlsten (Eds.), *Teacher and Librarian Partnerships in Literacy Education in the 21st Century*, pp. 118–137. Olso: Sense Publishers: New Voices and New Knowledge in Educational Research.

Department for Education (2014) *National Curriculum: Primary Curriculum.* Available at: https://assets.publishing.service.gov.uk/government/uploads/system/uploads/attachment_data/file/425601/PRIMARY_national_curriculum.pdf (Accessed September 2021).

Hall, L A. (2012) Rewriting identities: Creating spaces for students and teachers to challenge the norms of what it means to be a reader in school. *Journal of Adolescent and Adult Literacy*, 55: 368–373.

Kucirkova, N. and Cremin, T. (2020) *Children's Reading for Pleasure in the Digital Age: Mapping Readers' Engagement.* London: Sage.

Miller, D. (2009) *The Book Whisperer, Awakening the Inner Reader in Every Child.* San Francisco: Jossey-Bass.

Moffatt, L., Heydon, R. and Iannacci, L. (2019) Helping out, signing up and sitting down: The cultural production of 'read-alouds' in three kindergarten classrooms. *Journal of Early Childhood Literacy*, 19(2): 147–174.

Moses, L. and Kelly, L. (2018) 'We're a little loud. That's because we like to read!': Developing positive views of reading in a diverse, urban first grade. *Journal of Early Childhood Literacy*, 18(3): 307–337.

OECD (2021) *21st-century Readers: Developing Literacy Skills in a Digital World.* Paris: OECD Publishing. Report available at: https://www.oecd.org/publications/21st-century-readers-a83d84cb-en.htm (Accessed April 2021).

Pennac, D. (2006) *The Rights of the Reader.* London: Walker.

Picton, I., Goodwin, H. and Clark, C. (2021) *Exploring the Impact of World Book Day on the Reading Lives of Children in the UK 2019–2021.* A National Literacy Trust Research Report. Available at: https://cdn.literacytrust.org.uk/media/documents/Exploring_the_impact_of_World_Book_Day_on_childrens_reading_2019-21_final.pdf (Accessed September 2021).

Scholes, L. (2019) Working-class boys' relationships with reading: Contextual systems that support working-class boys' engagement with, and enjoyment of, reading. *Gender and Education*, 31(3): 344–361. https://doi.org/10.1080/09540253.2018.1533921

Sullivan, A. and Brown, M. (2015) Reading for pleasure and progress in vocabulary and mathematics. *British Educational Research Journal*, 41(6): 971–991.

Torppa, M., Niemi, P., Vasalampi, K., Lerkkanen, M., Tolvanen, A. and Poikkeus, A. (2020) Leisure reading (but not any kind) and reading comprehension support each other – a longitudinal study across grades 1 and 9. *Child Development*, 91(3): 876–900.

Reading places

Teresa Cremin

Pondering on what to offer as a tool for thinking about reading, I found myself drawn to the situated nature of reading – to reading and place. My childhood memories of reading are deeply connected to three particular places. My bedroom at home, a Scottish hamlet in the Highlands and the village hall. Each is inextricably linked to my reading history and early sense of myself as a reader. Each still evokes strong emotions, prompting reminiscences and space for reflection.

Place often features in accounts of individual's reading lives, Lucy Mangan (2018) describes the NHS clinics where her mother worked and the reception desk she settled behind at just aged three to read. Margaret Mackey (2016) too, a Canadian professor and librarian captures the power of place in her fascinating auto-bibliography, *One Child Reading*. In this, through pictures and prose, she documents the grounded, individual and local spaces that shaped her early journeys as a reader. Reading places us and in turn we are shaped by the salient places in which we first encountered powerful words and worlds.

DOI: 10.4324/9781003215615-20

My earliest memories of reading are at home, alone in my bedroom. An old, winged armchair with faded blue damask covers was my daytime reading retreat – it held me close, much as my bedcovers did at night. My parents didn't read to us, it didn't appear to have occurred to them, but I was a library member, and was regularly taken to feed my appetite for stories. However, I was never able to stay to read there for long, it was a quick after-school trip to return, renew and borrow at speed. I supplemented the longform narratives I borrowed with magazines, mainly *Jackie* and *Mandy*, which, despite knowing that my mum did not really approve of them, my dad allowed me buy. This no doubt enhanced my interest in and commitment to these texts, on which I spent my pocket money. Having purchased one at the corner shop, I'd fold it carefully into a bag, alongside a Buttersnap bar or Walnut Whip (treats from dad), and eagerly anticipate the moment of opening back in my bedroom.

On our return I'd rush upstairs, shut my door, settle into the armchair and devour the magazine and the sweets – furtively stuffing the evidence under the bed afterwards out of mum's sight. In particular I delighted in the black and white photo-stories which, after weeks of tension and discord, often ended in that longed for teenage kiss. The comfort of that chair, with its moon shaped tea stain, loose threads and purple nylon cushion holds part of me in its arms, even now. Envisaging it, I feel a bodily intensity, a sense of safety and a sadness at days long gone. The view from the window, and the peace and the privacy allowed me to just be – to find my rhythm and place in the imaginary worlds of fiction which I adored. At school, whilst I swapped these 'illicit' magazines with friends and we shared our predictions and hopes for the characters, I don't recall ever discussing my book reading. At home, as my sister and brother didn't much care for reading; we rarely talked about it.

My pleasure in reading was also sustained by our family holidays in western Scotland. My dad took my brother fishing, my mum and sister would bird watch or go on long walks to find wildflowers. Personally, I read. Alone in the bracken, on a windy beach, beside a loch, or on a rocky outcrop, I'd go on adventures far more exciting to me than my siblings' literal realities. Characters from Eleanor Brent Dyer, Alan Garner, Susan Cooper, Enid Blyton, the *Readers' Digest* real-life stories and many more became my constant companions, alongside the seabirds whose calls still takes me right back to that rugged landscape. I was often left with a meat pie, a sandwich, or a sausage roll and a Tunnocks' caramel wafer, and would once again settle down to the seriously engaging business of reading. The scenery varied, but the secluded time and space to read was what I valued, and although the ground was sometimes rough or damp, I didn't care. On our days out to other places, if it rained, I was left in the car or at a bothy at my own request, happy to read and imagine. I deeply valued the peace and privacy of those reading journeys, which appear regularly to have involved eating! Ullapool, the nearest town, was an hour away on a single-track road and there was no library, so whilst I took new books with me each vacation, I was obliged to reread the books in the croft. I drew comfort from the steadfastness of these texts, the predictability and consistency of the cast of characters to whom I returned year after year. Place played a key role in these early encounters; my reading was always situated – both at home (always alone in my bedroom) and on holiday (always alone and frequently outdoors).

At the village hall however, the opposite was true. This was also the local meeting space for young and old in our community – a place of shared reading. Here I participated in Brownies, Guides, Rangers, the amateur drama and church youth clubs and it was here that I encountered reading as a more collegial and social practice. Perched on a stool in the wings of the stage, I sat through many rehearsals and performances as the junior drama society prompt. I sometimes trod the boards and valued the opportunity to discuss with fellow actors what the playwright might have meant and how we could convey it. I also took part in myriad gang shows, pantomimes, magic shows and nativities, reading and discussing the various scripts and bible passages, and repeatedly singing chants, hymns and songs with others. The hall echoed with laughter, conversation and activity around these shared texts, but there were quiet times too when rehearsals were in full flow and we simply listened, prepped our lines or read our own books.

These reading places – my bedroom, the Scottish highlands and the village hall were not merely contexts in which I read, but secure affinity spaces for me as a young reader. Spaces in which I experienced reading as personal, social and affective, and always deeply embodied. Whilst I read by myself in my bedroom and the bracken, I was in the company of fictional characters whose words and worlds beguiled me. In the village hall, I was enriched as a reader by the physical company of others, the togetherness of scripts and singing and a strong sense of belonging from participating in shared endeavours.

Context counts in our early and later reading encounters and shapes our experience of being a reader. Looking back, I wonder if any particular places come to mind for you as a young reader? If so, then you might ask yourself:

- Why were these places so memorable?
- Does their memory surface any feelings or emotions?
- Can you recall any related smells, sounds or practices?
- Were there any people around you and were they involved?
- Did these places involve talk about texts in any way?

Of course, reading in school is quite different from reading at home or in the community. School expectations, routines and timetables shape the day. When I was at school, reading for pleasure was viewed as a home focused hobby, there was a library which we could visit at lunchtime but as this meant I lost time with friends, I rarely did. We received comprehension lessons, studied literary classics and wrote our required responses. We were never encouraged to engage in recreational reading, nor do I recall a teacher ever recommending a single book. Now with RfP mandated in England and its wider impact on children's lives recognised, more schools are seeking to create reading spaces to invite and entice children and in which they can become engrossed in texts, sharing these with each other informally and conversationally. This is not an additional extra; it should be seen as part of every reader's right.

There is a real danger however that buying buses, tents, tree houses and caravans to deck out as libraries, and funding sheds, boats, baths and sofas to enrich classroom reading areas, merely becomes an act of institutional window dressing. These physical spaces overtly indicate to parents, governors, Ofsted inspectors and the children that the school values reading. But it is not enough.

In developing book nooks or outdoor reading crannies, we need to attend to their use and the way in which our RfP pedagogy nurtures children's desire to read in them and, significantly, to read at home. Whilst the aesthetics of the space matter, the presence of cushions, bean bags, toys or blankets cannot on their own engage young readers. The texts themselves and the children's access to them matter far more. In our research, we found classroom reading corners were mainly used for time out for bad behaviour, or as extra workspaces, and very rarely for voluntary reading (Hempel-Jorgensen, Cremin, Harris and Chamberlain, 2018).

With a wider number of places to read around schools being created, thoughtful monitoring of their use is essential. If they are offered simply for optional lunchtime reading for example, then it is likely they will just be inhabited by keen readers. Attention needs to be paid to their inclusivity, especially after the novelty of the new book nook has worn off. Timetabling access to both the school library and these mini reading spaces can help, as can the support of adults or older children who can model, chat and share their passion, as well as respect children's right to read alone.

Involving the children is also key, enabling them to own and shape the creation of reading places and ensuring these are informal and comfortable on their terms. Exploring the notion of favourite places to read with children is also an option when sharing your own. Some children may not have experienced the comfort and pleasure of reading, eating and relaxing at home or out of doors, so establishing a monthly reading and hot chocolate session with biscuits and blankets or offering outdoor booknics can model this and make reading time – indoors or out – special. Some schools also send home book bags with related soft toys, the book and a hot chocolate sachet, and others invite their children to create home-based reading dens and share visuals of these.

There is no right way to proceed, but as a Reading Teacher considering your past or present reading places, their accompanying associations and texts is a valuable starting point. For me, looking back, I now realise that the old winged armchair, the Scottish highlands and the Peter Aubertin Hall are not only part of my reading history – of who I was – but have also shaped who I have become as a reader. They moulded my feelings, attitudes and perceptions towards reading and reveal much about its personal, social, situated and embodied nature.

References

Hempel-Jorgensen, A., Cremin, T., Harris, D. and Chamberlain, L. (2018) Pedagogy for reading for pleasure in low socio-economic primary schools: Beyond 'pedagogy of poverty'? *Literacy*, 52(2): 86–94.

Mackey, M. (2016) *One Child Reading: My Auto-bibliography*. Edmonton: The University of Alberta Press.

Mangan, L. (2018) *BookWorm: A Memoir of Childhood Reading*. London: Square Peg.

Conclusion

Reading Teachers of tomorrow

Teresa Cremin, Helen Hendry, Lucy Rodriguez Leon and Natalia Kucirkova

It is every child's right to read for pleasure. The International Literacy Association (ILA, 2018) defines this right as the opportunity to read freely, voluntarily and with delight – and to read any kind of text. Many teachers recognise this right, and, alongside teaching phonics, language development and comprehension, give time and space to nurturing volitional reading in the young.

Reading Teachers however go further. These highly reflective professionals hold up a mirror to their own reading lives and seek to learn about reading and being a reader to enable them to enhance their reading for pleasure provision. Additionally, and significantly, Reading Teachers spend time getting to know children as readers, they find out about their attitudes, behaviours and identities in order to tailor their pedagogy in responsive ways. Combining an understanding of reading with knowledge of their young readers, Reading Teachers can make the experience of reading both more authentic and more relevant. Through this process they more effectively encourage children to choose to read in their own time – to read for pleasure.

The key characteristics of Reading Teachers include a desire and openness to learn about reading, a commitment to developing a rich knowledge of children's texts and of

DOI: 10.4324/9781003215615-21

individual readers, and a rigorously planned and evaluated RfP pedagogy. Being a Reading Teacher is not a fixed state, it is an ongoing journey. It involves personal and professional noticing – documenting – reflecting and – acting upon ever evolving and nuanced understandings about reading. As knowledgeable professionals and reading role models, Reading Teachers reflect upon the potential synergies between being a reader in their personal lives and being a teacher of reading in their professional lives. They use their understandings to adapt their provision, involve children in reshaping the reading curriculum and track the consequences on the young people's volitional reading (Cremin, Mottram, Powell, Collins and Safford 2014; Cremin, 2021a; Gennrich and Janks, 2013).

Through this process of continual reflection Reading Teachers often begin to question the extent to which a 'schooled' version of reading holds sway in their classroom. Have school expectations and reading formulas come to dominate their practice? What kinds of agency and rights are children really offered? Is their volitional reading still tethered to reading outcomes? Research indicates that when teachers hold limited or 'schooled' conceptions of literacy and reading, their practice can limit students' identities as readers, reducing the likelihood that they will choose to read (Hall, 2012; Hempel-Jorgensen, Cremin, Harris and Chamberlain, 2018). So, it is important to understand reading through the unofficial lens of children's everyday home reading lives and practices as well as the official lens which frames their experience of reading in school. In order to develop as a Reading Teacher of tomorrow and positively impact on children's engagement in reading, you may wish to consider these questions and reflect on yourself as a reader. You could start by looking back at your own reading history and reflecting upon your experiences of choice-led reading as a child.

Looking back to learn

Reading histories represent rich resources to learn about the nature of reading. Thinking about your own memories of reading and the influence of people, texts and contexts on your reading and life journey may lead you to remember particular moments or texts with emotion, or even recall the physical sensation associated with reading a particular text (Cremin, 2021b). Remembering may even trigger a desire to read texts from your childhood again and connect with the child you once were. As Waller argues such texts create strong 'affective traces' that 'act like threads that resonate as they are first spun or as they are touched again in remembering or re-reading' (2019: 89–90). Perhaps you recall swapping comics with friends at school, enjoying bedtime stories, or reading in the dark under the covers? Perhaps you didn't enjoy reading in school as a child, though you may have had treasured texts at home. Engaging in this reflective process may cause you to ponder on the influence of your family's social and cultural practices, such as attending a faith centre, the library, sports club or other community venues and the significance of others in your early reading life. The networks that you experienced and the ways they influenced your development as a reader are worth your attention.

Capturing your reading history visually may help you reflect and consider the extent to which children in your class view themselves as readers, and whether a focus on their reading memories might support each individual's growing sense of self as a reader. If you noticed the importance of your reading networks, then why not look more closely at the children's reading relationships. Who talks to whom about reading? Which children swap books? Which children rarely initiate reader conversations with you and appear not to be connected to others as readers? Building on your observations, you could offer more reader-to-reader activities, create new mini book groups or reading buddies to support less-engaged youngsters for instance, helping them develop a stronger social support system around reading.

As this book has highlighted there are many ways to share your reading life. You could share the visual of your reading history and invite children to make their own, perhaps by selecting their top five texts to date. Or you could borrow a box of books from a younger class, enabling the rereading of texts from yesteryear as children become re-acquainted with old favourites. Alternatively, you could make a class reading history or display of your 'books in common' – those you have shared and read together. As the novelist EE Nesbit (1911) wrote 'There is no bond like the bond of having read and liked the same book'. Reading bonds are socially motivating for all readers and make reading a more shared, relaxed and sociable experience in school. As fellow readers, Reading Teachers will also participate in this construction of reading as a social practice – part of the ethos and culture of the classroom.

What is critical however, is not the activities that might be triggered by your reflections, (e.g. reading buddies or re-visiting once loved books), but noticing the impact of these opportunities on the young readers. So, for example, as children reread books from yesteryear, you will be engaged as a Reading Teacher in professional noticing and closely observing their engagement. This will help you to discern, for instance, which books less-engaged readers gravitated towards, and which friends they chose to share these with. You can build on these formative observations to offer finely tuned personalised next steps for young readers. As well as revisiting your reading history to learn about reading, you may also want to consider your own and the children's contemporary reading practices.

Learning from your current reading life

Teachers, in tune with the rest of the population, read widely, for example engaging with newspapers, magazines, emails, articles and social media posts (Duncan and Freeman, 2020). In addition, as education professionals, teachers read research reports and policy documents alongside a plethora of other materials, with and on screens as well as on paper. Many will also regularly read more longform texts, such as reference texts, fiction and non-fiction, adults' and/or children's books, where their engagement may be more sustained. Much of this reading, whether short or longform, for whatever personal or professional purpose can be described as reading for pleasure, since it is volitional in nature and as we have stressed before whilst the experience of 'pleasure' is not always involved, agency always is. Reflecting on the range of texts you choose to read can be enlightening, as through noticing, documenting and reflecting upon the diverse range of texts you read across 24 hours for instance, you may come to widen your understanding of reading. The visibility of your online reading, the amount of everyday incidental print you encounter, your range of reasons and motivations for reading may all become more evident. This is likely to prompt you to consider what the children in your class view as 'reading'. Are their conceptions tied to their assigned 'reading book' or as Thompson (2019) found to their guiding reading book and related notions of proficiency and progress? If reading is tethered to school skills in children's minds, this may have negative consequences, prompting some to remain disengaged (Hempel-Jorgensen et al., 2018).

After sharing your everyday reading with the class, you might invite them to notice and document their reading lives beyond the school gate as well. They could undertake a 24-hour read, create a reading river (collages which depict your reading over a longer period of time (see Cliff-Hodges, 2018), or participate in a reading treasure hunt (see Williams, 2021). In this way you will get to know more about each reader's wider engagement which is particularly important for 'RfP disadvantaged' readers. You may find that some children who rarely choose to read school sanctioned texts, may be avid readers of other text types outside of school. There is a tendency for some text types to be reified over others in schools, but as the EU Expert Panel on Literacy states:

> There should not be a hierarchical ranking of reading material. Books, comic books, newspapers, magazines and online reading materials are equally valid and important entry points to reading for children and adults alike. . . . Books and other printed texts are important. But in recognition of the digital opportunities, people should be encouraged to read what they enjoy reading, in whatever format is most pleasurable and convenient for them.
>
> (European Commission, 2012: 42)

As a Reading Teacher you will no doubt recognise this and seek to make available a wider range of texts in school, encouraging children to draw on their out-of-school interests and preferences. Taking a more encompassing view of reading, and offering new forms of participation and engagement, can enable children to begin to appreciate that reading in the real-world counts. They will come to see that they are already meaning makers, reading for multiple personal and social purposes, this can help children develop a more positive sense of themselves as readers. By exploring contemporary reading, you can also help parents come to re-view reading.

Looking forwards: a call to action

As the Reading Teachers and their co-authors in this book have shown, there is no one size fits all, no set of strategies which will enable you to become a Reading Teacher in the 21st century. Being a Reading Teacher involves so much more than new ideas for classroom practice; it involves an interest in and commitment to noticing your reading habits, behaviours and preferences and becoming more aware of the complex and shifting influence of text and context on your identity as a reader. By learning about the children as readers too, you will want to introduce subtle pedagogical shifts and new opportunities that are shaped to support their reading for pleasure.

We believe it is a professional, social and moral responsibility to foster the habit of reading in childhood. Understanding more about the personal, social and relational nature of reading is invaluable subject knowledge for all teachers – for those who seek to nurture children's RfP it is essential knowledge. A broader understanding of reading as placed and embodied will also help you to build and sustain communities of engaged readers which stretch well beyond the school gate. Such inclusive communities are characterised by interaction and reciprocity. They embody a culture which values everyone's reading, regardless of their text preferences, their reading practices or the languages they choose to read in. At the heart of these communities are Reading Teachers who are prepared to challenge long-held views around the status of different text types, and who boldly re-imagine ability-based views of children as readers.

So, we close with a call to action. We invite you to reflect upon the lived experience of reading and being a reader, and, informed by research and practice, make the experience of reading more authentic, more relevant and more engaging for all the young readers you work with. Reading for pleasure has the potential to change children's lives and life chances. As a Reading Teacher of tomorrow you can maximise this potential. The choice is yours.

References

Cliff-Hodges, G. (2018) Rivers of reading: A research method to explore young adults' personal reading histories. In A. Arizpe and G. Cliff-Hodges (Eds.), *Young People Reading: Empirical Research Across International Contexts*, pp. 55–70. London: Routledge.

Cremin, T. (2021a) The red thread of reading for pleasure: Reading Teachers. *Books for Keeps.* Available at: The Red Thread of Reading for Pleasure: Reading Teachers – Books For Keeps.

Cremin, T. (2021b) My journey from childhood reader to reading researcher. In S. M. Morris, L. Rai and K. Littleton (Eds.), *Voices of Practice: Narrative Scholarship from the Margins*. London: OUP.

Cremin, T., Mottram, M., Powell, S., Collins, R. and Safford, K. (2014) *Building Communities of Engaged Readers: Reading for Pleasure*. London and New York: Routledge.

Duncan, S. and Freeman, M. (2020) Adults reading aloud: A survey of contemporary practices in Britain. *British Journal of Educational Studies*, 68(1): 97–123. https://doi.org/10.1080/00071005.2019.1610555

European Commission (2012) *EU High Level Group of Experts on Literacy: Final Report*. Luxembourg: Publications Office of the European Union.

Gennrich, T. and Janks, H. (2013) Teachers' literate identities. In K. Hall, T. Cremin, B. Comber and L. Moll (Eds.), *The Wiley Blackwell International Research Handbook of Children's Literacy, Learning and Culture*, pp. 456–468. Oxford: Wiley Blackwell.

Hall, L. A. (2012) Rewriting identities: Creating spaces for students and teachers to challenge the norms of what it means to be a reader in school. *Journal of Adolescent & Adult Literacy*, 55(5): 68–373.

Hempel-Jorgensen, A., Cremin, T., Harris, D. and Chamberlain, L. (2018) Pedagogy for reading for pleasure in low socio-economic primary schools: Beyond 'pedagogy of poverty'? *Literacy*, 52(2): 86–94.

International Literacy Association (2018) *The Case for Children's Rights to Read*. Available at: https://literacyworldwide.org/docs/default-source/resource-documents/the-case-for-childrens-rights-to-read.pdf (Accessed 27 July 2021).

Nesbit, E. (1911) *The Wonderful Garden*, Republished 1935. New York: Coward-McCann.

Thompson, B. (2019) *Hidden Messages about Reading: What Do We Communicate to Children about Reading for Pleasure*. Available at: https://ourfp.org/eop/hidden-messages-about-reading/ (Accessed December 2021).

Waller, A. (2019) *Rereading Childhood Books: A Poetics: Perspectives on Children's Literature*. London: Bloomsbury.

Williams, C. (2021) *Reading Together Treasure Hunt*. Available at: https://ourfp.org/supporting-rah/reading-together-treasure-hunt-eop/ (Accessed December 2021).

Index

Note: page numbers in *italics* indicate a figure and page numbers in **bold** indicate a table on the corresponding page.

academic texts 68; *see also* children's books/literature/texts
action research projects 6
Adeola, Dapo 80
affective benefits 74, 81
affective consequence of reading aloud 76
affective engagement 50
agency, children's 4, 8, 40, 59, 61, 71, 76–77, 90, 105–106, 117, 122, 127, 141, 145, 147, 151, 194–195
agents of learning 40
Alexander, Kwame 109
Animal Ark series (Daniels) 73
Antrobus, Raymond 24
Apple, commercial interest of 41–42
assessments 36, 63, 78, 88, 108, 152, 156, 176, 178
Astro Girl (Wilson-Max) 80
attention, children's 4–5, 9, 21–22, 36, 65, 77, 80–81, 83, 122, 128, 194
audio books 76
auditing: book talk 96; knowledge of children's texts 22–23, 32
authentic texts 25–27
autonomy 58–59, 61–62, 83, 108–109, 154–155

background knowledge 3, 129, 146
Balen, Katya 31
Bartram, Simon 80
Bedtime Story in a Bag activity 171
behavioural consequence of reading aloud 76
Bell, Clare 117–118, 122
Blake, Quentin 127
book: blankets 48; choices 47–49; clubs 87; discussions 39, 72, 111, 177; displays 97; events 98; as mirrors 79; related quizzes 39; selection 71
Book Café 167, *168*

book club community *see* online reading communities
Book of Hopes, The (Rundell) 22
bookshelf recording sheet *110*
bookshelves 61, 65, 94, 97, 122, 140, 152, 181
Book Swaps 166–167
book talk 52, 72, 87–98, 117; around self-chosen texts 109; based on non-fiction topics 49; child-led 88–90, 92–93, 95; classroom culture of 95–96; conceptualisation of 88; forms of 88; and inter-thinking 91–93; motivational power of 88; peer 95; points to be considered for auditing 96; in practice 92–93, 96; pupil-led 87; *vs.* recall 90; and recommendations 92; reflexive and responsive approach to 96; significance of 87–89; social and emotional aspects of 90; strategies for promoting 95, 97–98; *vs.* teacher-led classroom talk 88–89, 95–96; and text comprehension 91
Book with No Pictures, The (Novak) 77
Boy at the Back of the Class, The (Rauf) 22
boys' engagement with reading: enhanced RfP pedagogy 52; lower level of 46–47, 51; reading will and skill 45, 47–48, 50–52, 62; social class and income impact on 52–53; stereotypical 51; two stranded approach to 51–52; *see also* engagement with reading
Breakfast Club 169–170
Bryon, Nathan 80
budgets 122, 138–139, 158–159

Can Bears Ski? (Antrobus and Dunbar) 24, 26, *26*
Carter, Carol 151–154
Catchpole, James 30
celebrating reading 176–178
'celebrity' authors 21–22
Centre for Literacy in Primary Education 5, 22, 24, 80, 157, 177–178

characters 22, 24–25, 27, 29–30, 48–49, 77, 81–82, 88, 90, 93–94, 109, 178, 180, 189–190, 191
childhood reading 21, 22
child-led book talk 88–90, 92–93, 95
children's books/literature/texts 17–18, 21–23, 25, 31–32, 50, 92, 115, 117, 135, 147, 169, 193; accessibility 30; awards 97; *Can Bears Ski?* (Antrobus and Dunbar) 26, 26; *Book of Hopes, The* (Rundell) 22; *Boy at the Back of the Class, The* (Rauf) 22; diversities of 25; *Emmanuel's Dream: The True Story of Emmanuel Ofosu Yeboah* (Thompson and Qualls) 30; graphic novels 28–29; *Here We Are: Notes for Living on Planet Earth* (Jeffers) 22; *Mayhem Mission* (Islam and Khandaker) 31; National Literacy Trust's survey of 24–25; *October, October* (Balen and Harding) 31; 'Own Voices' texts 25–27; *Perseverance, The* (Antrobus) 26; picture books 30; published in UK 24; reasons for choosing 24; representation issue 25; triggering empathy 27–28; *What Happened to You?* (Catchpole and George) 30; *When Stars Are Scattered* (Mohamed and Jamieson) 27, 30–31; *see also* digital books; knowledge of children's texts
Children's Digital Book Award 42
choice-led reading 2, 4, 74, 77, 109, 121–122, 131, 142, 177, 194
class book clubs 97
classroom 4–7, 17, 23–25, 36–38, 42, 45–46, 48–49, 56–59, 69, 75–76, 79, 81, 83, 88, 92, 95–98, 103, 106, 108, 114–117, 119–120, 122–123, 129–130, 138–141, 143, 145, 147, 151–154, 159, 172, 181–183, 194–195; culture of book talk 95–96; first-grade 71; nursery 89, 127; practice 3, 6, 9, 104, 115, 122, 142, 183, 196; primary 48, 177
Click Clack Moo, Cows that Type (Cronin) 77
CLPE *see* Centre for Literacy in Primary Education
cognitive engagement 50
collaboration 156, 182
'comfy reading' style 48; *see also* independent reading
comics 2, 22, 69, 129, 145, 157, 167, 170
commitment 81, 121, 127, 137–138, 141, 145, 182, 189, 193, 196
communities of readers 2–3, 6, 25, 41, 57, 71, 81–85, 117–118, 131, 136, 138, 142, 146, 167, 171–176, 180, 190–191, 196; building 30–31, 38; fostering sense of 59; local 155–156, 163–164, 166, 172; during online schooling 155; reading aloud and 83; reciprocal 159, 182; social atmosphere of 71; whole-school strategies to build 154–155; working with families to build 155–156

community involvement 163; empowering families 171–172; engaging with families and communities 164–167; engaging with wider community 172–173; implications of 173; listening to families 167–170; reading in children's homes 170–171; recommendations for 173–174; for subject knowledge development 24
competency 58–59, 178
competition 36, 57
comprehension 3–5, 17, 39, 74, 76, 78, 80, 82–83, 88, 90, 101, 104, 140, 179, 182, 185, 193; activities 137; lessons 78, 191; problems 28; questions 142; reading aloud impact on 76; strategies 87; tests 50, 76
confidence, children's 3, 41, 77, 106, 139, 144, 146, 153, 166, 172
connections 14, 29–31, 41, 50, 59, 73, 76–80, 96, 116–117, 123, 128, 138, 155–156, 172–173, 176, 181; definition of 79; emotional 147; intertextual 80; during reading aloud 79–80; text-to-self 79; text-to-text 79–80, 93; text-to-world 79
contextualised text talk 75
conversations 3, 23, 26, 37, 40–41, 48–50, 60–61, 65, 75, 78, 80–81, 83, 88, 90, 92, 94, 115, 117–118, 122–123, 144, 153, 157, 181–182, 191; affective 81; casual 2; free-flowing 95
Covid-19 pandemic and digital reading 36–37, 97, 104, 144
critical engagement 29
Cronin, Doreen 77
crowdsourcing feedback 41
curiosity, children's 14, 46, 50, 57, 104, 122, 151–152, 157, 159

Dahl, Roald 22, 80
Daily Independent Reading Time 105
Daniels, Lucy 73
DEAR *see* Drop Everything and Read
decontextualised language, reading aloud impact on 75
digital books 31, 35, 43; 3Cs framework of 37; benefits of 36–37; design of 36, 41, 42; enhancements 36; to expand reading communities 38–40; future directions of 42; improving educational quality of 41–42; to motivate reluctant readers 37; pedagogical implications of 38; *vs.* print books 36; teachers' role with 41
digital reading 18, 37
digital RfP 36
digital teaching 36
DIRT *see* Daily Independent Reading Time
disability 25–30
disengaged readers, graphic novels for 29

diversity 5, 7–9, 22, 25, 49, 123, 183
Drop Everything and Read 105
Dunbar, Polly 24
Duyvis, Corinne 25
dyslexia, responses of children with 30

Early Years Foundation Stage Framework 5
e-books or electronic books *see* digital books
Education Endowment Foundation 5
Emmanuel's Dream: The True Story of Emmanuel OfosuYeboah (Thompson and Qualls) 30
Empathy Lab 177–178
empathy, texts triggering 27–28
engagement with reading 2–6, 30–32, 37–39, 40, 41, 45–48, 46, 50–55, 57, 71, 73, 74, 77–79, 81, 88, 90, 95–96, 102, 105, 109, 115–116, 123, 127–128, 135, 140, 145, 158, 164, 166–167, 172, 177–178, 181–183, 194–196
entertainment companies 42
enthusiasm 38, 42, 95, 106, 123–124, 144
ethnicity 5, 23, 25, 47
Everybody Reading in Class (ERICs) 105
excitement 143–144, 156, 183–185
expert reviews, in selecting e-books 42
exploratory talk 91–92
extratextual talk 75

families 3, 5, 9, 13, 26, 31, 36–37, 50, 53, 65, 79, 166–175, 179–181, 194; and communities, engaging with 164–167; empowering 171–172; and home reading practices 163–164; listening to 167–170; reach out to 155–156; and social justice 143–146
fantasy genre texts 25
favourites 23, 167; all-time 102; old 68–69, 103, 195; share and discuss 69
feedback 41, 153, 159, 164, 168–169, 173
fiction texts 3, 5, 13–15, 41, 45–50, 68, 80, 104, 157, 189, 195
Fireside Reads activity 171–172
fluency tree 61
freedom 15, 47, 105–106, 139, 141, 159
'free reading' 3
'free voluntary independent reading' *see* reading for pleasure
free voluntary reading 74
friendships 59, 62, 93, 96

gender 18, 46, 51, 53
gender differences, in RfP 2, 52; boys' lower engagement 46–47, 51; experienced by girls 45–46; girls' engagement with non-fiction 48–50; importance of 45; motivation to read 46; reading attainment 2; reasons of 45, 46; school reading curricula 46; stereotypes 46; *see also* boys' engagement with reading; girls' choice of text

general motivation theory 57
generosity 15
gingerbread-reading figures 104
girls' choice of text 47; fiction books 48; non-fiction books 48–50; school context for 47
Google, commercial interest of 41–42
graphic novels 22–23, 25, 31, 47, 97, 167; benefits for disengaged readers 29; in digital format 37–38; to motivate reluctant readers 37; slow reading of 28–29; triggering empathy 27–28

Harding, Angela 31
head teachers 24, 47, 118, 121–122, 135–141, 143, 145–147
Here We Are: Notes for Living on Planet Earth (Jeffers) 22, 106
home environment 162
home reading practices and families 163–164
Hulme-Cross, Benjamin 63

identities as readers 4–9, 13–15, 18, 47, 50, 53, 57, 59, 76, 90, 92, 94, 103, 130, 151, 163, 178–179, 185, 193–194, 196
ideological model of literacy 163
income impact, boys' engagement with reading 52–53
independent reading 5, 72; challenges 102, 108–109; children's autonomy 109; children's responsibility for 108–109; definition of 102; for developing fluency 101; experience as readers and 102–104; making time for 106, 108; perseverance and stamina 109–111; as planned pedagogic routine 101–102, 104; planning for 106–108; setting time aside in school for 104–106; silent 118; space for 105, 106; timetable 106, **107**; time to choose 105–106; tinkering with 104
informed reading 22
in-person reading aloud 76
instructional leadership 136–138, 141–142, 147
interactions 40, 46–47, 61, 77–78, 96, 102, 105, 143, 154, 181, 196
interests, children's 15, 19, 23, 29, 37, 50, 78, 80, 97, 116–117, 121–122, 147
International Collective of Children's Digital Books 41
inter-textual connections 80
inter-thinking, and book talk 91–93
intrinsic motivation 58; classroom conditions cultivating 59; *vs.* extrinsic motivation 56, 57
Islam, Burhana 31
It's a No-Money Day (Milner) 79

Jalongo, Renck 116
Jamieson, Victoria 29
Jeffers, Oliver 22, 106

joyful reading 71
Julian at the Wedding (Love) 79

keen readers, benefits of being 2–4
Khandaker, Farrah 31
King Arthur (Hulme-Cross) 63
knowledge 2–3, 7, 21–24, 47, 49–51, 75, 81–83, 91, 95, 106, 115, 123, 129, 138–140, 142, 153, 156, 158, 164, 179, 181–182, 193, 196
knowledge-based curriculum 101
knowledge of children's texts 17–18, 21–22, 47, 72, 103, 115, 125, 135, 143, 147, 156, 179, 193; audit of 22–23, 32; community approach to developing 24, 32; diagram of *23*; importance of 50; strategies for improving 31–32; *see also* children's books/literature/texts

language 19, 27, 37, 76, 79, 81, 91–92, 95, 157, 171, 196; comprehension 58; development 89, 91, 163, 193
leadership 136, 141, 158
Learner led, Informal, Social and with Texts that tempt 177
learner-led reading aloud 78
librarians 150–155, 157–161, 172, 188
library 13, 47, 62, 76–77, 114, 116, 119, 122, 140, 142, 147, 150–159, 172, 179–181, 184, 190–191, 194
library café initiative 156
Library Live sessions 155
LIST *see* Learner led, Informal, Social and with Texts that tempt
listening 58, 61–62, 73, 76–77, 144, 147, 167–168
literacy 5, 17, 19, 35, 37, 39, 41, 96, 106–107, 135, 162, 163, 177, 194; skills 52, 167, 171; theory 57
literate identities 39
literature, children's 21, 23–25, 27, 29, 31, 47, 88, 103, 143–144, 156, 167, 179
lobbying, for e-book quality improvement 41
lockdown 14, 24, 80, 169, 171–172
Look Up! (Bryon and Adeola) 80
lower socio-economic status (SES) schools, performative pedagogy in 72

Man on the Moon (Bartram) 80
'Matthew effect' 4, 58
Max the Champion (Strick and Stockdale) 79
Mayflower Community Academy, parental and community involvement at 162–163; empowering families 171–172; engaging with families and communities 164–166; engaging with wider community 172–173; implications of 173; listening to families 168–169; reading calendar 164–166, *165*; reading challenges *170*; reading in children's homes 170–171; recommendations for 173–174
Mayhem Mission (Islam and Khandaker) 31
Meek, Margaret 60
memes 68
Milner, Kate 79
mobile reading culture 40
Morpurgo, Michael 22
motivated readers, support needed by 3–4
motivating children to read 2, 4–5, 18, 21, 38, 58
motivating young readers 56
motivation for reading 5, 39, 46, 53, 56–58, 60, 62, 65–66, 89, 95, 103, 121–122, 136, 138, 146, 162–163, 173, 195; extrinsic 56–57; intrinsic 50, 57–59, 121–122; social 57–58, **59**
Motivations for Reading Questionnaire (MRQ) 57
multicultural picture books 25
multiple narratives, reading simultaneously 13–14

narrative role play 97
National Curriculum in England 17, 22
National Literacy Trust 24, 177; on school library 150; survey of children's books 24–25
National Non-Fiction November 183–184
Naylor-Ballesteros, Chris 79
NLT *see* National Literacy Trust
non-fiction books 2, 15, 25, 37, 41, 45–47, 48–50, 52, 74, 79–80, 144, 157, 167, 182–184, 183, 195
Norwegian classrooms, digital books in 42
Novak, BJ 77

October, October (Balen and Harding) 31
OECD *see* Organisation for Economic Cooperation and Development
old favourites, rereading 69
online book clubs *see* online reading communities
online content 22
online library 39
online reading 36
online reading communities 40, 155; book-focused dialogue 39; children's engagement in 39–40; dialogue possibilities in 40; need for 38; pedagogical principles 40; reading choices 38–39; structure for 38; teachers' role in 40–41; weekly sessions 39
online schooling, communities of readers during 155
on-screen media 69
Open University 22, 177
Organisation for Economic Cooperation and Development 2, 45, 50, 104, 177
Our Story app 41
OU/UKLA Teachers' Reading Group 31
Own Voices texts 25–27, 30–31

parental involvement 162–163; empowering families 171–172; engaging with families and communities 164–167; engaging with wider community 172–173; implications of 173; listening to families 167–170; reading in children's homes 170–171; recommendations for 173–174
partnerships 41, 141, 163–164, 169–170, 173–175
Patron of Reading initiative 177, 182–183
peer-based professional networks 24
peer book talk 95, 96
peer-to-peer recommendations 49
Pennac, Daniel 127–130
perceptions 6, 40, 46, 61, 81–83, **82**, 116, 143, 163, 178
performative pedagogy 72
perseverance 26, 108–109
Perseverance, The (Antrobus) 26
personal connections 30, 93–94, 178
personal experience to text 26–27
physically engaging environment 115–117
picture books 22, 28, 30, 64–65
PIRLS *see* Progress in International Reading Literacy study
PISA *see* Programme for Student Assessment
poetry 2, 14–15, 22–24, 68, 74, 80, 83, 144, 157, 167
positive attitudes 41
positive reading effects 41
preferences, children's 2, 6, 8, 23–24, 50, 53, 77, 88, 90, 92, 96, 104, 116, 121, 146, 196
primary schools 45–46, 136, 151, 164, 181
print books 36, 38
privacy 189–190
professional development 22, 41, 146, 159
Programme for Student Assessment 2, 5, 19
Progress in International Reading Literacy study 1–2, 5
psychological needs: innate and basic 58; intuitive care for 62
pupil-led book talk 87
pupil recommendation shelf 97

quiet reading 76

random choice, notion of 116
RAPS *see* Responsibility, Autonomy, Perseverance and Stamina
Rauf, Onjali Q 22
reader-reader relationships 3
reader recommendations 49, 72, 87; points to be considered for auditing 96; in practice 93–95; significance of 92; strategies for promoting 97–98; teachers and peers 92
readers 130, 178–180, 182, 184–188, 196; becoming conscious as 6–7; engagement 105; experience as 102–104

reading: achievement 57, 62, 65, 135, 136, 152, 176; activities 61–62, 123, 156, 164, 166, 168, 173; behaviours 40, 46, 48–49, 51, 105, 108–109, 181; café 156; characterisation of 2; choices 2, 4, 18, 36, 38–39, 40, 47–50, 48, 52, 59, 61–62, 64, 69, 77, 80, 92, 102, 105–106, 108–109, 108–111, 115–116, 117, 118, 121–123, 123–125, 127, 139, 144, 152, 154–155, 157, 168, 170, 183; comprehension 39, 52, 76, 88, 90; conferences 60; confidence 39; culture 25, 36, 40, 59, 65, 79, 92, 95, 110, 136, 140, 142, 144, 146, 151, 155, 158, 172, 195–196; enjoyment 3, 5–6, 13, 27, 31, 46, 50, 52, 57, 62, 69, 71, 89, 92, 106, 121, 143, 145, 164, 167, 169–171, 173, 176, 182; experiences 2, 4, 13, 37–38, 58, 65, 76, 104, 116, 121, 142, 181, 183, 193–194; factors influencing identification of content of 38; fluency assessments 51; habits 74, 92, 104, 106, 116, 119, 121, 141, 153, 156, 177, 196; identities 6, 13–15, 61, 69, 92, 94, 97, 103, 106, 115, 145, 167–168, 176, 178–179, 181, 184; immersion 38; motivation 19, 57–58; networks 57; preferences 17, 65, 94, 97, 115, 117, 119, 121, 123, 131; for proficiency agenda 74; relationships 57, 65, 135, 151, 153–154, 156, 194; as social and relational act 58, 62, 64–65; spaces 52, 114–115, 121, 123, 139, 191; two sides of 56; *see also* engagement with reading
reading aloud 71, 73–84, 90; benefits of 74–76; children make connections during 79–80; children's interaction in 77–78; children's involvement and agency in 77; children's perceptions of 81–83, **82**; choice of texts for 80–81; and community 83; factors influencing impact of 74, **75**; high quality 74; in-person 76; learner-led 78; during library visits 76; misappropriation of 78; popular authors for 80; purposes of 74; quiet reading after 76; shared repertoire of 'books in common' through 76; teacher-led 74, 79, 89; in UK homes 74; voicing texts 80–81
reading attainment 2–3, 50–51, 135, 150
'reading buddies' 97, 105
reading celebrations 176, 186; contribution to RfP pedagogy 177; maximising potential of 184–185, *185*; organisations and charities 177–178; and reader identities 178–179; Rochdale Children's Literature Festival 179–182; social reading communities 182–185
reading communities 3, 25, 31, 38, 40, 65, 76–77, 81, 83, 115–116, 131–132, 135, 137, 154–156, 181
reading environments 15, 72, 114–119, 114–125, 121–125, 139, 143, 151, 184–185
Reading Framework, The 5, 132

Reading Head Teachers 118, 135, 147; cultural change to embed RfP 139–140; empowering staff 142–143; families and social justice 143–146; gathering a team 140; instructional leadership of 136–137, 141, 142; leadership models of 136–137; of primary schools 136; prioritising RfP pedagogy 137–141; as role models 136, 141–142; role of 135–136
reading journey 102–103; noticing 61–64; reading as social and relational act 62, 64–65; social influences 60–61, 63
Reading Librarians *see* school librarians
reading materials 18, 22
reading places 188; beach *189*, 190; chair *188*, 189; village hall *190*, 190–192
reading poetry 14
reading shed *124*, 130
reading skills 45, 50–51, 53, 60–61, 65, 106, 167; developing 78; technical 136, 142
Reading Teachers 8, 10, 15, 18, 193; children's engagement with RfP and 47–48; concept of 2, 5–7; continuum of additive practices to represent 7; definition of 135; key characteristics of 193–194; *see also* book talk; digital books; gender differences, in RfP; knowledge of children's texts; motivation for reading; reader recommendations; reading aloud; Reading Head Teachers; RfP pedagogy; social reading environments; time to read
reading time 61, 64, 69, 97, 102, 104–107, 109; cosy 105; dedicated 77; independent 64, 95, 102, 104, 109–110, 115, 121; protected 103
reading will and skill, link between 45, 47–48, 50–52, 62
recall 73, 96, 127–128, 189, 191; *vs.* book talk 90; literal 89
recommendations 7, 15, 23–24, 49–50, 62–66, 87–89, 91–93, 95–99, 106, 108–109, 115–119, 121, 124, 139, 154, 159, 169, 172–173, 184
'reconnect' time 24
'recreational reading' *see* reading for pleasure
reflexive and responsive approach to book talk 96
relational pedagogy 59
relational support 65
relationships and book talk 90
relaxed reading time 97
Responsibility, Autonomy, Perseverance and Stamina 111
RfP *see* reading for pleasure
'RfP disadvantaged' readers 4
RfP pedagogy 9, 52, 63, 71–72, 105, 128–129, 136, 138–141, 146, 177, 182, 184–185; book talk 72, 87–98; developing 72; independent reading 72, 101–111; integrated nature of 105; reader recommendations 72, 87, 92–98; reading aloud 71, 73–84, 90; social reading environments 72, 114–125

RfP pedagogy and Reading HTs 136; budget planning 138–139; challenges to embedding 139–140; changing systems of 142; children's outcomes and life chances of 143–144, 144–145, **145**; empowering staff 142–143; gathering a team for 140–141; identifying priorities of 141; leadership models of 136–137; monitoring and maintaining 146–147; prioritising 137–139; role model for 141; school development plan 138–139; school environment at 142; SSP teaching 138
rights as readers, children's 2; mediating 129; right not to read 127–128; right to be quiet 128; right to read for pleasure 193; right to re-read 129–130
Rights of the Reader (Pennac) 127, 180
Rivers of Reading 116
Rochdale Children's Literature Festival: event of 180; impact of 180–182; organisation and planning of 179–180
role models 2, 6–7, 50, 91, 136, 141–142
Rowling, JK 22
Rundell, Katherine 22
Russian classics 14

scaffolded silent reading 101, 106
school community 17, 137–138, 144–145, 147, 156, 158–159, 166, 178, 180–182, 184
school contexts 47, 136–137, 163, 173
school development 135–137, 143–144
school environment 51, 118–119, 141–143, 146, 178
school librarians 150–151, 158; building communities of readers 154–156; characteristics of 151; curating resources and making recommendations 157–158; good practice with teachers 158; library café initiative 156; positive pastoral role of 151; reach out to families 156; recommendations for practice of 159–160; support from school to 158–159; time and expertise to build relationships 153–154; whole-school level strategies 154–155
school libraries 49, 119, 139, 141, 157, 160; environment conducive to relationship building 151–153; impact on attainment 150; importance of 150; physical space of 151, 155; positive pastoral role of 151; reach out to families 155–156; separation from classroom 152
school reading curricula 46
Seddon, Alex 115–117
See-Think-Wonder routines 29
self-determination theory 61
self-determined motivation 62
self-efficacy 6, 57–61, 58, 65, 90
self-motivated volitional reading 51–52

Shadow children's book awards 31
shared reading practices 163
Shark in the Dark (Sharratt) 89
Sharratt, Nick 89
shy reader, confidence of 41
skill and reading will, link between 45, 47–48, 50–52, 62
skim reading strategies 36
slow reading approaches 28–29
Smith, Conradi 80
Sneinton C of E Primary School 164; engaging with families and communities 166–167; engaging with wider community 172–173; listening to families 169–170; reading in children's homes 170–171
social activities, preferred use of time for 24
social and emotional aspects of book talk 90
social class 5, 47, 52–53
social connections 3, 31, 49, 76, 155, 181
social determination theory 58–59
social influences, on reading 60–61, 63–64
social interactions 60, 63, 64–66, 78, 91, 131, 182–183
social justice 143, 145
social media 68
social motivation for reading 56–59, 57–58, **58**, 61, 63, 65, 71
social nature of reading 87, 117, 184
social networks 48, 49
social persuasion 61
social practices 49, 57–58, 116, 163, 173, 190, 195
social reading communities 24, 182–184
social reading environments 72, 114–125, 139, 143, 151, 184–185; across schools 122–124, *124*; children's interest, choice and motivation 121–122; children's space and place 119–121, **120**; choice-led 117; head teacher's perspective 118; importance of 114; physically engaging reading environment 115–117; principles of 115; socially engaging reading environment 117–118; and social reading practices 118–119; traditional book corner 119; transforming 118
socio-cultural theories of reading 57, 91
socio-economic backgrounds and e-books 36
Space Boy for Planet Omar: Accidental Trouble Magnet 64
stereotypes 46
St Joseph's Primary School, RfP pedagogy at 136; challenges to embedding 140; changing systems of 142; children's outcomes and life chances of 144–145, **145**; empowering staff 142–143; gathering a team for 140–141; identifying priorities of 141; leadership models of 136–137; monitoring and maintaining 146–147; prioritising 137–139; role model for 141; SSP teaching 138

St Matthew's C.E. Primary Teaching and Research School, RfP pedagogy at 136; budget planning 138–139; challenges to embedding 139–140; changing systems of 142; children's outcomes and life chances of 143–144; empowering staff 142–143; gathering a team for 140–141; identifying priorities of 141; leadership models of 136–137; monitoring and maintaining 146–147; role model for 141; school development plan 138–139; school environment at 142
Stockdale, Sean 79
story frames 35
story-sharing experience 13
Strick, Alexandra 79
subject knowledge 9, 22, 23, 24, 142
Suitcase, The (Naylor-Ballesteros) 79
systematic, synthetic phonics (SSP) teaching 138

teacher-facilitated small groups 97
teacher knowledge 17, 18; *see also* knowledge of children's texts
teacher-led classroom talk 88–89, 95–96
teacher-led reading aloud 74, 79, 89
teachers: digital books and 41; online reading community and 40; reader identities and pedagogy 5–6
Teachers as Readers (TaRs) research 5–7, 21, 58, 87, 88, 96, 101, 103, 115, 119, 132, 137, 139, 142, 158
teachers' perceptions 46–47
technology enabled reader recommendations 97–98
Tell Me approach 29
text: choice for reading aloud 80–81; comprehension and book talk 91; representation 18; types 8, 23, 46–47, 49, 52–53, 92, 157, 196
text-to-self connections 79
text-to-text connections 80, 93–94
text-to-world connections 79
thinking and book talk, relationship between 91
time to read in school 101, 102–103; approaches to protect 105; making 106, 108; obstacle for making 104; *see also* reading time
transformational leadership 138
trust 38, 62, 64, 83, 93, 122, 159
Twitter 24–25, 108, 166

UKLA *see* United Kingdom Literacy Association
Undefeated, The (Alexander) 109
underachievement, vicious cycle of 51
Uninterrupted Sustained, Silent Reading 105
United Kingdom Literacy Association 102, 116
USSR *see* Uninterrupted Sustained, Silent Reading

Visible Thinking approach 29
vision 31, 47, 88, 136–137, 140, 145, 179
visual activities, preferred use of time for 24
visual reminder 23
vocabulary 5, 74, 104, 135, 179; acquisition 3; learning 36; reading aloud impact on 75
voices 22–23, 25, 31, 76, 79–80, 82, 92, 94, 128, 183
voicing texts 80–81
volitional reading 5–6, 17, 51, 56, 58, 75, 81, 101, 132, 151, 157–159, 194–195
volition and social interaction 72
voluntary reading 78
Vygotsky, Lev 91

Walliams, David 22
#WatchMeBecomeaReader, participating in 169
Weekly pupil-led book reviews 97
well-being 45, 59, 62, 82, 146, 152
What Happened to You? (Catchpole and George) 30
What Is That iBook for children 41
When Stars Are Scattered (Mohamed and Jamieson) 27, 30–31
whole school RfP culture 151
will to read 4
Wilson-Max, Ken 80
World Book Day website 177, 182–183
writing identity 15
writing skills 3